LIVING WITH THE WIND AT YOUR BACK

Seven Arts to Positively Transform Your Life

Dr. David E. Shaner

Living With the Wind at Your Back
Seven Arts to Positively Transform Your Life

Written by Dr. David E. Shaner

Foreword by Robert E. Carter, Professor Emeritus, Trent University

Connect, LLC
Greenville, SC

Copyright © 2014 by Dr. David E. Shaner

All rights reserved. No part of this publication may be reproduced or transmitted in any form or by any means, electronic or mechanical, including photocopying, recording, or any information storage and retrieval system, without permission in writing from the author.

Connect, LLC website: davidshaner.com

First edition
Printed in the United States of America

Library of Congress Catalog Card Number: *forthcoming*

ISBN (print, softcover): 978-0-9960938-0-4

Dedication

With love and gratitude, this book is dedicated to all my teachers. The Universe Itself is the true inspirational teacher...*Kaiden*.

Contents

Dedication		3
Contents		5
Foreword by Robert E. Carter		7
How to Read and Use This Book		13
Author's Note		15
Detailed Contents - A List of Questions		17
Introduction		35
Chapter 1	The Art of Preparation	47
	Daily Exercises	67
Chapter 2	The Art of Compassion	79
	Daily Exercises	111
Chapter 3	The Art of Responsibility	117
	Daily Exercises	152
Chapter 4	The Art of Relaxation	161
	Daily Exercises	209
Chapter 5	The Art of Conscious Action	223
	Daily Exercises	263
Chapter 6	The Art of Living Naturally	269
	Daily Exercises	316
Chapter 7	The Art of Service	329
	Daily Exercises	379
Glossary		381
Exercises Summary		387
Seven Arts Testimonials		401
Acknowledgements		407
About the Author		409
Index		413

Foreword

The Japanese philosopher Keiji Nishitani (1900-1990), warned that thinking of ourselves as separated from other people, and from things generally, is to make us "forever separated from ourselves"[1] as well. Our natural state is one of connection, not separation, of being in relationship, and not in isolation.

The sense of isolation, so evident in modern times, is an inevitable outcome of our belief in individualism. An individual ought to be dependent on no one and, carried to an extreme, stands separate and alienated from family, friends, society, and even nature. Sharply distinguishing self from "other," rather than seeking out common bonds, has led to the modern problems of depression, addiction, meaninglessness, and a profound severing of any real connection with the earth.

Is there a way to heal the modern heart and mind, a path that leads to interconnection, shared values, and the integration of the person? Can we learn to act as harmonious body-minds, seeking to create a better social and natural environment? This book charts a pathway through such difficulties. Professor David Shaner describes how to remain centered and focused; he edges the reader closer and closer to a life of joy, fulfillment, growth and social contribution. This is an important book for our times, for it seeks to help you connect with something larger than yourself.

---

[1] Keiji Nishitani, *Religion and Nothingness*, Translated with an Introduction by Jan Van Bragt. Foreword by Winston L. King. Berkeley/Los Angeles/London: University of California Press, 1982, p. 10.

Life today has become a hectic schedule of work and obligations disconnecting us from ourselves, each other and the world. What Professor Shaner presents is a method that taps into "the wealth of possibilities for your life". It is a method designed to enhance meaning and growth, and to eliminate fear, anxiety, and depression. Anyone who follows the simple exercises even part way will experience personal transformation and growth in the midst of living an otherwise ordinary life. Whether one is Christian, Muslim, Jewish, Buddhist, Hindu, or atheist is of no concern; the method of *The Seven Arts* will only enhance and refine what is already present. It may appear to be magical but, in fact, the insights which Shaner has drawn upon are both contemporary and ancient, both Eastern and Western and, hence, have long since been tested by countless men and women who have used them successfully before. Rather than being magical, these insights and principles are natural.

The theory is simple: each individual already has incredible powers which have not yet been recognized. Rather than offering rigorous training to develop what was not present before, the wisdom presented here conceives of training as a releasing of powers and abilities that have been there all along. The trick is to get out of the way, to eliminate certain attitudes, beliefs, and emotions which block becoming who it is that you already are.

Perhaps I may be allowed to provide my own personal experience here. Professor Shaner arranged for me to attend the World Camp of *Aikido* in Tochigi, Japan. Because I was researching a book on the Japanese arts and ethics, I was quickly given examples of the incredible power, or energy (*ki*) available to us all. "Hold your arm out, almost straight, and try to resist." I tensed my muscles, trying to resist my partner's attempt to bend my arm, but my arm was easily bent. I had used the skills that I had been using all of my life:

employing tension and muscle-power to achieve my ends. Then, I was instructed to focus my mind on a spot (the "one point") about three inches below my navel, and to relax completely, no longer engaging in a muscle contest. The flow of *ki*-energy coursing through my arm made it impossible for even the strongest martial artist to bend my arm. Superhuman strength is, in fact, just human strength with the entire universe behind it, but we are generally unaware of the flow and availability of such energy altogether, let alone the means to tap into this energy.

Living with The Wind at Your Back: Seven Arts to Positively Transform Your Life engages the reader with the author's personal experiences: as a downhill ski racer with the Olympic Valley U.S.A. Ski Team in Squaw Valley, California; a Sheriff's Deputy in Aspen, Colorado; as one of a handful of *Aikido* practitioners to have risen to the seventh degree black belt level; and as a student taught (for more than forty years) by Master Tohei, whom many say is the most skilled *Aikido* artist since the original founder, Morehei Ueshiba (O-Sensei), developed the art. As a Sheriff's Deputy, for example, he was called upon to train the local police in the compassionate art of "arrest control." The challenge was to convince senior officers that force was not the only, or the best, way to subdue lawbreakers. A compassionate approach required that anger and threat be dissipated, rather than confronted head-on with yet more anger and greater force. We are drawn closer to the author through examples such as this one, as he opens his life to our scrutiny in attempting to show what is possible, and to chart the pathway to such success, joy, happiness and personal fulfillment.

As with most profound matters, the facts are actually quite straightforward and simple. The path to self-transformation begins with (1) the recognition that your own life is itself the actual training ground of practice. A positive outlook, together with an honesty about who one is, is the first step forward. The second step (2), the art of compassion, is something of a spiritual one: you are not a flawed human being in your depths, but you are as perfect as this magnificent universe. In fact, you are the universe. It is not that we are "in" the universe, like being in a building which is separate from us; rather, we are a living cell of the universe, an integral part of the universal whole. The universe is not separate from us but, instead, we need to understand that each of us is the universe, and that the universe expresses itself as each and every thing that is. Such wisdom is the source of compassion, for one is no longer capable of injuring, or hating, or destroying that of which one is an inextricable part. Just as one does not desire to cut off a part of one's body, neither would one wish to do injury to the incredible whole which is oneself. The remaining steps along the path are: (3) taking full responsibility for your thoughts and actions; (4) learning how to truly relax, to receive and experience rather than to impose; (5) to become fully conscious in choosing how to act; (6) learning how to become natural and effortlessly spontaneous in the way you live and act; and then (7) putting into practice the lessons learned through your contributions to others, and to society at large. This is the pathway, complete with exercises that will bring about the required shifts in perspective through daily practice. And it works!

Shaner is skilled in encouraging the reader to develop his/her abilities, to take responsibility for what one does and thinks, and to reach beyond one's isolated ego to a sense of self that genuinely embraces others, all the way to the distant edges of the universe. It is to learn that the universe, or God, is the **"Wind at Your Back"** if you allow it to be. There is power enough to change your consciousness, and even to begin to change your world. Being led by the force (*ki* energy) of the universe itself results in a selfless humility, for the small ego-centric you has been transformed and is now a large cosmic you. Service to others, compassion, and the ability to enter into the joys and sorrows of others is now natural to you; it has become your nature.

Through keeping a journal of your practice, and by moving through one practice after another, the journey from a troubled and all-too-often humdrum existence gives way to an expanded sense of joy and happiness, purpose and meaning, until your embrace now genuinely includes those you love, your environment, and the source of all that exists. Ironically, it is this expanded sense of love and compassion which will make every one of us lovable for the very first time, for love requires selflessness. To be full of yourself is to block love, but to be open is to focus on the other; it is to be open and empty, capable of letting love in while, at the same time, being able to love without one's ego getting in the way. This is true self-cultivation and self-transformation.

All of this is actually within your grasp, and The Seven Arts process is your own personal guide. This is an opportunity to practice living life to its fullest, day by day, moment by moment, in the ever-unfolding presentness of "now."

Robert E. Carter, Professor Emeritus, Trent University

Author of **Encounter with Enlightenment**, **The Nothingness Beyond God**, **Becoming Bamboo**, **Dimensions of Moral Education**, and **The Japanese Arts and Self-Cultivation**.

How to Read and Use This Book

This book is about asking questions and discovering answers for yourself.

I have tried to pose common questions throughout each chapter. These are questions I have asked myself at one time or another. **Living with The Wind at Your Back: Seven Arts to Positively Transform Your Life** was written by simply reflecting upon my own life experience in response to asking questions.

Even more important is the fact that you have your life and experiences, too! The stories in this book simply reflect my own journey asking questions and trying to live in ways that would help me to answer them for myself. What about your experience? What are your life questions and how are you attempting to answer them in your life?

While the stories contained herein are my own, you will be able to create your own experiences relevant to the Seven Arts process by simply trying the exercises at the end of each chapter. Even a little bit helps. If you spend five minutes each day trying some of the exercises, then you will receive five minutes of benefit seeing yourself, and events that come your way, in a new light. Since I believe we all share the same or similar questions, I am offering very simple exercises that will help you to connect your daily life experience to your own "Journey of Positive Personal Development."

My experiences and stories have taught me much but, after all, it is only *my* experience. However, for the past thirty years I have had the pleasure of developing the Seven Arts and teaching them to others in a variety of contexts...

academia, business, athletics, personal development as well as spiritual development. I can say that, if you follow the personal development exercises at the end of each chapter, then you will be creating your own track record of life experiences that will help you to *understand for yourself* the positive transformation that can take place for you and your loved ones.

We all have different "life stories," but we all have similar needs! Therefore, I hope my own stories will at least make you think what might be possible for your own life. My experiences are not extraordinary. Anyone can create similar experiences for themselves just for the asking! In other words, the exercises will help you to discover for yourself the lessons I have learned simply by asking questions and pursuing answers consciously in a variety of fields, disciplines, and contexts.

I hope you will read the stories and find them fun, interesting, provocative and maybe even disturbing. When I lived the stories, they certainly had all these effects on me (and many more). Most importantly, however, I hope the stories may inspire you and give you confidence that you too can fulfill your dreams just by applying yourself in very simple ways outlined in the exercises at the conclusion of each chapter.

I wish you well on your Journey of Positive Self Transformation.

Author's Note

My teacher, Koichi Tohei Sensei, passed away on May 19, 2011, at the age of 91. Since he enthusiastically reviewed the initial draft of this work in the fall of 2004 long before his passing and, more importantly, due to the personal sense of our close relationship and his continuing presence in my life, I have chosen to retain the present tense of the original text when referring to him.

The tone and depth of this book vary. For example, there are sections that are narrative and straightforward accounts of events, and others that contain humorous stories where the events seemed to twist and turn, due perhaps to my own lack of preparation and/or simple ignorance to perform otherwise. There are other sections where the voice is more philosophical and scholarly due to my career in academia. I elected to retain all these "voices" in the main text in order to portray my experiences naturally; after all, Tohei Sensei always taught me to "Be Natural" (Jp. *Shizen ni*).

This book is simply my sharing what I have learned thus far in a life filled with abundance. Accordingly, I am filled with gratitude to all my teachers. I invite you to slowly and carefully read through what may seem like the more difficult sections precisely because the content may be distant from your own life experience. Let the words and descriptions wash through your awareness for it is these same sections that may become the seeds for future insight as you apply the Seven Arts exercises to your own life.

Detailed Contents
A List of Questions

Throughout the book are questions that readers can ask themselves and thereby participate more fully in the material. Below is the listing of these questions and the section headings that follow.

Introduction

Have you ever wondered where you came from?   35

My Father, the Disciplinarian:
You Must Be Productive to Gain Approval

Have you ever wondered about the lasting effects of your upbringing?   38

My Mother, the Theologian:
What if I Want to be A Buddhist, Mom?

Have you ever wondered what your life might be like had you not met a particular person?   39

My Third Parent, Master Koichi Tohei

Have you ever wondered if what you think you know is really true?   41

The Seven Arts Have Been Discovered, Developed, and Put to the Test

Have you ever wondered why you have to learn everything the hard way?   44

The Seven Arts Will Transform Your Life (or)
I Wish I Knew Then What I Know Now!

Chapter 1 The Art of Preparation

Have you ever wondered if you were really applying yourself as best you can?   47

Practice versus Cultivation

Have you ever wondered if you are really a spiritual person?   48

Your Life Itself is Your Monastery

Have you ever wondered if you are deceiving yourself; not being honest with your inner voice?   49

Start with Personal Honesty: YOU ARE HERE

Have you ever wondered if what you are learning in school is relevant to your real interests?   51

Direct Experience and the Academy

Have you ever wondered what wise people really know?   53

Enlightenment is a Verb

Have you ever wondered why you are here?   54

Who or What Are You, Really?

Have you ever wondered what it would be like to meet the leader of a nation?   58

Mrs. Gandhi:
Preparing for Individual and Cultural Change

DETAILED CONTENTS

Have you ever wondered if different people representing different sides of an argument are really talking about the same thing?   60

Self or No-Self (Selflessness):
Daya Krishna and David Kalupahana

Have you ever wondered why deep truths seem so simple?   64

The Golden Rule and Selflessness:
Preparing for the Art of Compassion

Daily Exercises To Facilitate The Art of Preparation

Have you ever wondered if real progress is just undoing prior mistakes?   67

Daily Training is Like Peeling an Onion

Have you ever wondered if you are really clear about what you want and think is most important?   70

Exercise 1:
Positive Self-Talk
Personal Development Affirmation (PDA)

Have you ever wondered why quiet seems so much better than noise?   73

Exercise 2: Make Silence Your Friend

Have you ever wondered if you can really be honest with yourself?   75

Exercise 3: Practice Self Honesty

Chapter 2 The Art of Compassion

*Have you ever wondered how to accomplish
what you know you should do?*   80

The Challenge is not Knowing What to Do,
It's is Knowing HOW to Do It

*Have you ever wondered if you are isolated, alone,
and not understood?*   82

Experiencing connection with the Dynamic Universe

*Have you ever wondered what you would do
if you were attacked?*   85

Compassion and Conflict in Action

*Have you ever wondered what it would be like
to participate in a grand, real life experiment?*   88

Dick Kienast, Aspen and a Great Experiment
in Social Justice: Trust is a Social Good

*Have you ever wondered if what you were doing
might attract national attention?*   91

CBS: Sixty Minutes

*Have you ever wondered what it would be like
to be a policeman or policewoman?*   92

Compassion, Aikido, and Law Enforcement

*Have you ever wondered if you could pass
a difficult test even though some people may
not want you to succeed?*   97

DETAILED CONTENTS

Passing "The Test":
Deep Calmness and Conflict Resolution

*Have you ever wondered what it would be like
to be threatened with a gun?*   101

The Power of Compassion:
Weapons, Hostages, and Violent Tempers

*Have you ever wondered what it would be like to
feel deeply connected to everything around you?*   107

You Are the Universe, and the Universe Is You

Daily Exercises To Facilitate The Art of Compassion

*Have you ever wondered what it would be like
to communicate without words?*   111

Exercise 4:
Can You Feel the Energy of the Universe?

*Have you ever wondered what it would be like
to give people your undivided attention?*   115

Exercise 5:
Practice Compassion Through Mindful Attention

Chapter 3 The Art of Responsibility

*Have you ever wondered about the long term
effects of actions taken today?*   118

Free Will and Causation:
What You Sow, So Shall You Reap

*Have you ever wondered if you can ever
really change?*   123

You Are Free: You Can Change Your Subconscious
and Unconscious Mind

Have you ever wondered why you "get what you need"?   124

The Seven Stages of Spiritual Development
are Sequential and Need Based

*Have you ever wondered if you are parenting
well and preparing your children for life's
most difficult challenges?*   127

Eggaberth, the Mountain Goat: Patience and Discipline

*Have you ever wondered if you can ever
really be selfless?*   130

Otomo Training:
The Art of Awareness and Selflessness

*Have you ever wondered why you seem to be late
when it matters most?*   132

Be an Invisible Mirror:
Move Quickly on the Letter "N" of the Word "Now"

*Have you ever wondered if you can change things
at your core?*   136

Deep Down...
You Know the Things You Need to Change:
Redirection, Not Suppression

*Have you ever wondered if you can really know
your subconscious mind?*   139

You Can Choose to Live Mindfully:
Take Responsibility for all Levels of Your Consciousness

DETAILED CONTENTS

Have you ever wondered if you can stick to a plan over the long haul?   142

Seven Arts Mean Twenty-One Phases of Personal Development: Make Patience, Discipline, and Awareness Your Silent Friends

Have you ever wondered if you can let go of the things making you stuck?   146

Renouncing the Fruit of Your Labor

Have you ever wondered what would happen if everyone changed with you?   147

Choose for Yourself, Choose for the World

Daily Exercises To Facilitate The Art of Responsibility

Have you ever wondered if you could be more patient, tolerant, and "bite your tongue"?   152

Exercise 6: Take a Deep Breath: Introspect Before You Act

Have you ever wondered if you could serve your loved ones better?   157

Exercise 7: Be an Otomo: Empty Yourself and Serve Others Selflessly

Chapter 4 The Art of Relaxation

Have you ever wondered if you could learn to relax?   161

Transforming Stress into Relaxation

Have you ever wondered if it were possible to truly see things differently?   164

Rediscover Your Original Self:
Relative Thinking and Absolute Thinking

Have you ever wondered if you are going through life with your emergency brake on?   166

Release Your Life-Brake:
Crafting Your New Life-in-the-Making

Have you ever wondered if there is something more, something beyond you, yet you keep getting in your own way?   167

It's Not Your Power: Throw Away Your Separate Self

Have you ever wondered what it would be like to be one of those people skiing fast and crashing on the "Wide World of Sports"?   170

Applying Deep Relaxation in Daily Life:
The Case of Downhill Racing

Have you ever wondered what it would be like to do scary things and overcome your fear?   173

Let's Do Scary Stuff! Rock Climbing, Jumping Out of Airplanes, and Speed Skiing

Have you ever wondered "why me," "why now"?   180

Prepare for the Unexpected: Argentina, the Army, a Misplaced Gate, and a Whole Lotta Trouble!

Have you ever wondered if you are really stronger relaxed?   187

DETAILED CONTENTS

The Power of Relaxation

Have you ever wondered how consciousness works?   189

Intentional Consciousness Explained:
Three Orders of Awareness

Have you ever wondered why your thoughts are always "of something"?   192

Third Order Awareness

Have you ever wondered if you could truly focus your mind?   193

Second Order Awareness

Have you ever wondered if you could really empty your mind?   195

First Order Awareness

Have you ever wondered if you could calm yourself through meditation or prayer?   197

A Pathway for Genuine Transformation

Have you ever wondered why meditation seems so strange?   200

Mantras, Mudras and Mandalas

Have you ever wondered if you could change mental and emotional habits?   202

The Process of Transformation

Daily Exercises To Facilitate The Art of Relaxation

Have you ever wondered if you could calm yourself quickly in the midst of a stressful day?   209

Exercise 8: Dynamic Breathing

Have you ever wondered how to meditate and whether it would truly make a difference?   214

Exercise 9: Dynamic Meditation

Chapter 5 The Art of Conscious Action ─────────

Have you ever wondered what it would be like to "Live with Wind at Your Back"?   225

Selflessness, the Universal Mind, and the Way of the Universe

Have you ever wondered if the past and future really exist because you can't actually go there?   227

Reconsider Time: Present Memories, Present Dreams, and Present "Conscious" Action

Have you ever wondered if you are wasting your time?   229

This May Not Be a Rehearsal:
Applying Conscious Action in Daily Life

Have you ever wondered if you could act without thinking "what will everyone else think"?   231

Begin with Small Steps: A Seventh Grade Confirmation Class Dropout Leaves High School Early

Have you ever wondered what it would be like to face your fears with greater confidence?   236

DETAILED CONTENTS

When Facing Adversity or a New Challenge,
Return to Deep Calmness in the Present Moment:
The Hand On My Shoulder

*Have you ever wondered what it would be like
to represent your country?*   237

Representing My Teacher in Japan

*Have you ever wondered what it would be like
to represent something important all over the world?*   240

Representing My Teacher in Russia

*Have you ever wondered if you are being watched
and helped by a friend or silent partner?*   243

Representing My Father

*Have you ever wondered if you could
live your dreams?*   251

The Wellspring of the Universal Mind: Trust,
Get Out of Your Own Way, and Ride Like the Wind

*Have you ever wondered what you could achieve
if only you were clear and focused?*   252

Clarity, Visibility, Focus and Alignment:
Applying Conscious Action in the World of Business

*Have you ever wondered what would happen
if you and everyone around you improved every day?*   255

Executing the Business Plan Means
Collective Conscious Action

LIVING WITH THE WIND AT YOUR BACK

Have you ever wondered why people do not always do what they say they will do?   258

Execution: Take Responsibility and Do What You Say

Have you ever wondered what it would be like to be on a successful team?   261

Seven Arts Business Success Stories

Daily Exercises To Facilitate The Art of Conscious Action

Have you ever wondered if you could be more calm and relaxed all the time?   262

Exercise 10: Return and Presence the World Around You

Have you ever wondered if you could exceed your wildest expectations?   263

Exercise 11: Apply Conscious Action in Your Daily Life

Chapter 6 The Art of Living Naturally ─────────

Have you ever wondered if life is really a process of learning?   270

Living as a Causal Process of Awakening

Have you ever wondered who you can believe and why?   274

Two Philosophical Camps: Science and Ethics

Have you ever wondered why lessons learned take time and why maturity and wisdom go hand in hand?   276

DETAILED CONTENTS

Personal Transformation is a Causal Process

Have you ever wondered why you are doing what you are doing?   278

Harvard University: My Interdisciplinary Research and Its Causal Consequences

Have you ever wondered if you are a product of nature or nurture or both?   280

Sociobiology Debates: Professors Stephen Jay Gould and Edward O. Wilson

Have you ever wondered what it would be like to spend a day with royalty?   289

An Audience with the Emperor of Japan, His Majesty Emperor Akihito

Have you ever wondered how dreams come true?   293

The Place of Peace: Ecocentricism, Sustainability, and Bodymind Education at Furman University

Have you ever wondered what it would be like to make an important discovery?   298

Pure Experience and Rare Book Libraries: A Cross-Cultural Insight

Have you ever wondered why you feel spiritual in nature?   302

Biophilia as Intimacy with Nature

*Have you ever wondered why you keep
getting in your own way again and again
in the same way?*   301

Attachment and Dis-connection

*Have you ever wondered why you think you
know what someone else is thinking or will say?*   305

Two Attachments: What Happens When You Know
What Others Will Think and Your 'Stuff' Goes Up in Smoke

*Have you ever wondered,
"How the hell did that happen"?*   314

A Treat From the Universe: Be Positive and Grateful

Daily Exercises To Facilitate The Art of Living Naturally

*Have you ever wondered if you could feel your heart
beat, your skin breathe, or the earth rotate?*   316

Exercise 12: Be In and With Nature

*Have you ever wondered if something deep inside
you is causing you to act in self-destructive ways?*   317

Exercise 13: Be In and With All Your Emotions

*Have you ever wondered if there is something hidden
inside you causing you to be very sad but you just
don't know exactly what it might be?*   321

Are You Sad?

*Have you ever wondered if there is something hidden
inside you causing you to be really angry
but you cannot put your finger on it?*   322

Are You Angry?

*Have you ever wondered if there is something hidden
inside you causing you to hold back, or have fear,
or be insecure, but you cannot understand
why these feelings sometimes arise?*   324

Are You Afraid?

*Have you ever wondered if there is something hidden
inside you causing you to remain blocked,
causing you to repeat the same mistakes,
and causing you to be unable or unwilling to move
beyond past errors and correct your moral compass?*   325

Do You Only Feel Shame and Guilt?
Or, Can You Feel Sorry?

*Have you ever wondered if there is something hidden
inside you causing you to not be truly happy?*   327

Are You Happy?

Chapter 7 The Art of Service

*Have you ever wondered if you could practice
what you preach?*   329

Know Thyself Deeply... Your Whole Self
and then Love Thy Neighbor As Thyself

*Have you ever wondered if you are truly accountable
in this life or beyond?*   332

The Universe has No Secrets:
Doing Good in Secret 24 Hours a Day

*Have you ever wondered if you could teach people
well what you know how to do well?*   335

Individual Exercises (*Hitori Waza*),
Two Person Exercises (*Kumi Waza*), and
Continuation Exercises for Daily Life (*Tsuzuki Waza*)

*Have you ever wondered if you could truly be
in control of yourself?*   337

Taigi Arts: First Control Yourself, and Then You Can
Lead Others Well in Daily Life

*Have you ever wondered, "Oh, now I get it."
Why did that take so long?*   339

Ki ga Tsuku:
You Must Experience and Realize Deeply for Yourself

*Have you ever wondered if you could get away with
something?*   341

The Monastic Bond of Mutual Protection:
Why Can't We Get Away With Anything?

*Have you ever wondered what it would be like to be
vindicated?*   346

You Are All Too Slow!... Well, Not Really

*Have you ever wondered if the people you are
talking to actually get it?*   351

Are They Learning and Discovering For Themselves?

*Have you ever wondered why you always have to take
one step at a time?*   356

DETAILED CONTENTS

Kaizen: Improvement is a Continuous Process
in All Spheres of Development - Personal, Spiritual,
and Business

*Have you ever wondered what it would be like to focus
all your energy when you need it most?*   357

Managing Life's Obstacles in the Improvement Process

*Have you ever wondered if you could be a gracious
host when your guest is acting like a jerk?*   364

Security and the "Art of Service" at Caesar's Palace
and the Mirage Casino

*Have you ever wondered how some people learn things
so quickly?*   363

Master, When Do You Practice?

*Have you ever wondered why the learning sticks when
you "do it"?*   365

Engaged Learning and Service Learning

*Have you ever wondered when you will start applying
yourself as you know you can?*   370

How Will You Apply The Seven Arts?

Have you ever wondered about starting "now"?   372

Considerations about Time and
Personal Development

*Have you ever wondered if you could
make a difference in this world?*   376

Follow Your Dreams – Enjoy!

Daily Exercises To Facilitate The Art of Service

Have you ever wondered...?   379

Exercise 14: Serve Others in Daily Life

Glossary   379

Seven Arts Testimonials   385

Acknowledgements   391

About the Author   393

Introduction

I have written this book to help you experience the wealth and depth of possibility for your life. Through daily practice of the Seven Arts—Preparation, Compassion, Responsibility, Relaxation, Conscious Action, Living Naturally, and Service —I will show you concrete ways to serve others, realize your dreams and experience your true potential. In short, no matter what your "need" for personal improvement may be ... I will show you how it is possible to "Positively Transform Your Life."

I have been abundantly blessed with the inquisitiveness, opportunities, drive, and ability to undertake and successfully accomplish a wide variety of things in my life. I have been helped greatly along the way by many, to all of whom I am deeply grateful, but the three who were the primary architects of my life and are the most responsible for my successes are my father, my mother, and my teacher, Koichi Tohei Sensei. Why was their impetus so significant? Well, let's see ...

Have you ever wondered where you came from?

My Father, the Disciplinarian:
You Must Be Productive to Gain Approval

My father used to tell me to do my "work before play," or sometimes he would say "You may get hit by a bus tomorrow!" ... meaning do what is important now! The work ethic he taught me was reinforced when I became a young athlete growing up in the sixties in Chicago. This was the era of the Bears versus the Green Bay Packers in the "Black and Blue" Central Division of the National Football League. I also got my fill of Green Bay Packer Head Coach Vince Lombardi's philosophy, captured by his saying, "When the going gets tough, the tough get going." These early lessons gave me a strong desire to succeed, which provided the impetus for me to undertake significant endeavors in a wide variety of pursuits.

Some accomplishments

>I have earned a doctorate in Comparative Philosophy from the University of Hawaii. I have enjoyed the experience of teaching at Harvard University and currently serve as the Herring Chair Emeritus of Philosophy and Asian Studies at Furman University. I have received Fulbright Awards, National Endowment for the Humanities and National Science Foundation grants, written books, founded and edited a book series with thirty-seven volumes, traveled the world many times over, and produced all the publications expected by academia. I have been a deputy sheriff, and for years trained the security staff at Caesar's Palace and the Mirage Casino Resort Hotels. For over thirty years, I have been a successful business consultant to many large, publicly traded, multi-national companies like Frito-Lay, Duracell, Gillette, and Owens Corning Composites, as well as privately held companies including Milliken (textiles), Umbro (Sporting Goods), Ryobi, (Motor Products), Synthetic Industries (Synthetic Textiles), and J.W. Aluminum (Rolled Aluminum). I have served as a television commentator for CNN and NBC on Japanese culture, politics, and business. I have received awards from, and been granted an audience with, the Emperor of Japan, His Majesty Akihito. I have competed against and later trained world champions in a variety of sports

and have mentored musicians and opera singers at the Metropolitan Opera House. I also have seriously studied the martial arts of Shinshin Toitsudo and Shinshin Toitsu Aikido for over forty years and trained two Aikido taigi world champions.

People have asked, "How have you done all this in your brief life?" Sometimes my answer to this question is, "This life may not be a rehearsal." Or, I might say, "This life IS nothing more than a series of precious present moments and I am just trying to make the most of them!" And sometimes when I am asked this question, I fondly remember the days of my youth growing up on our small farm and hearing I my father's voice saying. "Do your chores today because you might get hit by a bus tomorrow!" It took me years to figure out what he meant, but now I realize that he was just trying to instill a sense of urgency and responsibility in my daily life. The point is that I have been an active person trying to experience deeply the wealth and depth of possibility for my own life. I have written this very personal book to share with you "the lessons" I have discovered along the way. I organize them into the Seven Arts.

Now to get us off to an open and honest start, **you can throw out all the credential-speak in the two paragraphs above.** Really. If you are operating out of the need for approval by accomplishing a long list of things, or a need to "show" or perform for others, then it is a formula for disaster in your life. You might learn to set goals and objectives. You might learn to have a strong drive for achieving results. You might even learn about toughness and discipline. However, if you are operating in this way driven by the need for approval, then you are creating for yourself a belief system where your inner voice will always tell you "I'm not good enough" and every success will further validate this deep misunderstanding. This is a true formula for suffering and disaster.

My parents in 1984—Dr. Charles H. Shaner and Janis D. Shaner.

I would like you to know that you are "good enough" right where you are. It is your gift to "be" right where you are as this is the healthy starting point for your journey. More than just the healthy starting point, it is the ONLY place you can begin, right where you are. My Dad taught me a lot of wonderful things, but life is much more than pursuing accomplishments in order to get someone else's approval.

Have you ever wondered about the lasting effects of your upbringing?

My Mother, the Theologian:
"What if I Want to be a Buddhist, Mom?"

A strong work ethic and a healthy sense of urgency in fulfilling tasks were key ingredients in my early home education. Even then I felt that something more was involved than putting the accomplishments of one's life in place and

INTRODUCTION

then suddenly becoming a genuinely happy person. My mother helped me fill in part of this picture. Whereas my father was the disciplinarian, the "you must be productive to gain approval" sort of a person, my mother was the philosopher and theologian. I was a very curious child and young adult. To illustrate, when I was in the seventh grade, I was expected to join the family Methodist church by going through summer "confirmation" school. I protested to my mother after only one class. I came home and declared that my "choice" (to officially join the church as a so called "adult" member) was vacuous; in my mind it just wasn't a "real" choice! How could I exercise a free choice when I did not know what other possible choices were available? I asked my mother, "What if I want to be a Hindu, a Buddhist, or Jewish, or practice Islam or whatever?" Joining the church was not a real choice until I learned about other educated possibilities. To my amazement, my mother bought my argument as a sincere wish. Instead of forcing me to go to Methodist summer confirmation school, and instead of thinking I was just trying to opt out (*albeit* creatively) of summertime religious study, she agreed to conduct "home" summer study under her guidance. During that summer, we studied the major religions of the world. This sense of open curiosity and diligent investigation affected me deeply. I became, in part, the product of a disciplined drill sergeant (my father) and a theologian (my mother). What kind of influence did your parents or guardians have in helping to shape the person that you are today?

Have you ever wondered what your life might be like had you not met a particular person?

My Third Parent, Master Koichi Tohei

Finally, a third debt should be shared as background because his influence upon my thinking is as deep as the influence of my parents. Today, after forty plus years, the teachings of Master Koichi Tohei (Sensei) continue to serve as my teacher and mentor. He is the perfect combination of my parents. He is both a philosopher and a man of intense discipline, focus, and action. Master Tohei's teachings are woven throughout this book. His influence upon me has had the force and impact of a third parent, and he continues to serve as my teacher. (*See Author's Note)

Author and Master Koichi Tohei in Hawaii. About 1993.

To me, Master Tohei is truly a person who knows the Way of the Universe, who has genuine wisdom about life and how to meet the challenges, changes, and opportunities it offers with calmness, power, and joy. More importantly, he has the singular ability to teach this wisdom to others in ways that are understandable and compelling. He has tirelessly dedicated himself to sharing his teachings with others in Japan and all over the world. He has never been afraid, during public martial arts demonstrations or in regular aikido classes, to put his teachings to the test. And he has always encouraged his students to do the same. **If a teaching or principle is true and universal, then you should always be able to put it to the test.**

Being with him over the years instilled in me this willingness to test what I know in the *dojo* (training facility), in business, and in daily living. Only by this honest and sincere testing have I been able to develop deep confidence in the principles, and grown to know them intimately. Have you ever put to the test your most heartfelt beliefs, values, principles, and opinions? How might you do this?

Have you ever wondered if what you think you know is true?

The Seven Arts Have Been Discovered, Developed, and Put to the Test

The Seven Arts explained in this book are the result of having successfully "put to the test" all that I have learned thus far in my life. The Seven Arts were developed through my active seeking; they represent a combination of my own real-world experience with the education and training that I have sought out my entire life. The Seven Arts represent the keys to personal transformation that I have practiced and taught to others over the last thirty years. I have shared personal stories in each chapter only to illustrate the powerful impact of the success of these Seven Arts. If you apply these principles to your own life, you will experience the profound transformation that the Universe "gifts" to you in every waking moment.

I have learned that working out of "accomplishment" or working to win the "approval" of a parent, spouse, co-workers, an employer or anyone outside of yourself is ultimately a formula for personal disaster. You are not loved or lovable, nor can you receive love deeply, simply because of your accomplishments, your titles, or your résumé. Happiness and success will forever evade you if you are acting out of something other than a direct awareness of your deepest, inner divine Self. It is for this reason that the Socratic maxim *"Know thyself"* is critically important. Knowledge alone, however, is not enough. Not only must you know yourself deeply, but also you must *"know how to act"* deeply; that is, you must first learn to walk the path of life with self-restraint where action is in service to others; and second, you must continue to learn more deeply on this same path where action is still in service to others but self-restraint is no longer necessary. When this second level of development happens, there is no separate self to restrain.

In other words, Knowledge and Action must become One. Knowing deeply and knowing how to act deeply (what I call "Conscious Action") are at the heart of the Seven Arts transformation process. Action, work, or deeds performed in your daily life always arise out of some knowledge base and emotional motive. "Wisdom" in many traditions refers to an awareness or self-knowledge of the "connection" between our motives, our actions, and the consequences that inevitably occur in daily life. Action (Sk. *karma*) is emphasized in the classic Indian text, *The Bhagavad Gita*, as follows: "Yoga is Wisdom in Work" (2:50) or an alternative translation, "Yoga is Skill in Action" (2:50). Later it is said, "Action is superior to inaction" (3:8) or "Action is greater than inaction" (3:8). "Yoga" here refers to a specific kind of "activity"; that is, the lifelong transformational process of "yoking." In this process, you "yoke" (as in union, bond, join, or connect) your deep, true, divine Self to the Universe by cultivating an experience of immediate *unity* with the Universe. Alternatively, it is interesting to consider that YOU (your deep, true, divine Self) are the yolk (of an egg) and the Universe is the WHOLE egg. Yoga then can be interpreted as this process of UNION between not only Self and Universe, but also between knowledge and action yielding wisdom.

The Sanskrit root *yuj* is likely the shared term that gives us this sense of "connection" as in Middle English (M.E.) *yok* for yoke and *yolke* for yolk. In this interpretation, "Knowing thyself" deeply and "actively working" with deep insight means to live in harmony with the Universe. This is Conscious Action. This process of personal self-discovery will lead you to the supreme ecstasy of "Being One with the Universe."

Accordingly, as we begin this journey together, I encourage you to begin reflecting deeply upon the relationship between your thoughts, your feelings, and your actions in daily life. By intimately experiencing the interrelationships between thoughts (intellect), feelings (emotions), and actions (behaviors), you come to "know yourself" deeply. This is something that everyone can learn to do. Learning to become keenly aware of the interrelationship between mind, body, and emotion will serve to clarify the process of harmonizing all three in your daily life. It may sound complicated at first but, trust me—everyone can do this! When you learn how to harmonize your mind, body, and emotions, you will discover your true gifts. You will learn how to become the person you wish to be. You will find yourself at the helm of a stable life as though you have a deep keel assisting your ability to stabilize a course when your environment becomes turbulent. Even in a storm you will feel as though the "wind is at your back." In short, you will discover that you do have the ability to "make your dreams a reality."

Have you ever wondered why you have to learn everything the hard way?

The Seven Arts Will Transform Your Life (or)
I Wish I Knew Then, What I Know Now!

These Seven Arts form the basis of a clear means for anyone to transform their life into a more positive and fulfilling one. These lessons or Arts are so powerful, once they are cultivated and practiced in daily life, because they put you into accord with the Universe Itself. The Universe IS life itself and it has a rhythm just like your own life has a tempo and a rhythm. The power of these Seven Arts will enable you to live your life moving from victim to leader, from helpless to empowered, from groundless to firmly rooted, from powerless to powerful, and from spiritually lost and isolated to spiritually complete, connected, and fulfilled.

All of these transformations apply equally to the spiritual realm, to the world of personal relationships, and even to the material world of work and business. By focusing on your inner development first and foremost, your relationships will transform for the better. The prosperity you experience will be a direct reflection of the gifts you are willing to offer to every human being you encounter.

Ultimately, you are responsible for your spirit and, therefore, your spiritual development. As you develop an awareness of your deep, inner self in this Seven Arts process, you will come to the realization that you are also responsible for your conscious mind, your subconscious mind, and even your unconscious mind. And, since all three "levels" of your mind inevitably serve as the root cause of your daily life actions (behaviors), you will simultaneously realize that you are responsible for **all** your actions and their causal effects in the Universe. By cultivating the Seven Arts in your life, you will actually **experience** the power of this responsibility (something that is far more enlivening than just reading this narrative description).

When you are in a harmonious relationship with God, or Spirit, or the Universe (I use these interchangeably), you will experience the ecstasy of fulfilling your dreams simply because they are in accord with God's purpose for you. Or, put another way, **you will be thinking and acting in accord with the Principles and Laws of the Universe.** This means that you are no longer driven by the selfish desire to fulfill only your personal wants, wishes, and desires. Instead, you will be acting in accord with a higher purpose in service to others. The whole of the Universe is but One Spirit and One Energy (Jp. *Ki*). Accordingly, all things, all distinctions, all thoughts and all actions are ultimately rooted in your original connectedness with the Universe.

The Seven Arts are one way to clarify and reveal your actual oneness with the Universe. You will come to experience directly this oneness and know for yourself your fundamental divinity and that you are loved beyond measure for the person you are right now. The truth is that you are not separate, not alone, and could not possibly sustain your life and your existence apart from the *Ki* of the Universe.

Since we normally think of ourselves as individuals who are separate from others and separate from nature and the Universe, it will be important for us to explore this perspective in detail as it represents the way in which the world appears to us in our everyday life. As we move through the Seven Arts process, I will refer to this worldview as the "Relative World." This is our view of the world characterized by habitually interpreting ourselves as separate from, and perhaps in a conflict with, others. This manner of viewing the world is one that arises due to our habit of viewing things (and ourselves) as separate. And, the root cause of this way of interpreting our experience is ultimately occasioned by our habit of viewing the world through the lens (and filter) of our limited perspective and personal history.

Possessing a relative worldview contrasts sharply with the "Absolute World" in which we can experience an original, natural connection with others and the Universe. Let's begin to understand the Universe as it appears to us in the "Relative World" of our daily existence versus the "Absolute World" that we can know and experience directly through our connected consciousness that is always present.

Let's start with the Art of Preparation.

1

The Art of Preparation

*"At fifteen, I set my heart upon learning...
At seventy, I followed my heart's desire
without overstepping the line."*

Confucius
The Analects, **Book II, Verse 4**

---

*Have you ever wondered if you were really
applying yourself as best you can?*

Practice Versus Cultivation

In Japanese, there are two terms that may help me explain the type of "Preparation" I am suggesting. The two terms are *keiko* and *shugyō*. *Keiko* refers simply to "practicing" as in going to a soccer practice session with teammates or sitting at the piano for daily practice. *Shugyō,* however, refers to a type of practice that entails a *twenty-four hour a day commitment to training and personal development*, a practice that would be better translated as "cultivation." When you are engaged in the prospect of knowing and acting in accord with your deepest spiritual Self, then you must commit yourself to a form of awareness where everything in your world counts. Nothing can remain undone or unimportant. The commitment appropriate to *shugyō* means attending to every detail of your conscious life, waking and sleeping. Successful personal transformation must be approached and prepared for in a manner consistent with *shugyō* "cultivation" and not merely *keiko* "practice."

Have you ever wondered if you are really a spiritual person?

Your Life Itself is Your Monastery

The Art of Preparation is a form of *shugyō*. Just as going on a weekend retreat (or actually experiencing true monastic life) allows you to share experience with a community of like-minded "seekers," your life itself (seen as one whole) can be turned into a learning retreat twenty-four hours a day. *Your life itself is your monastery.* Your relationships, your work, your daily commute, your family, shopping, household chores, reading, vacations, etc., combine to create your monastic life. By learning to become truly awake and aware of how you are relating to, and indeed creating, your personal monastery, you will be able to start the process of deep personal transformation. This daily *awareness* of your "inner" conscious states and "projected" conscious states, is the key to personal discovery.

Have you ever wondered if you are deceiving yourself, not being honest with your inner voice?

Start With Personal Honesty: YOU ARE HERE
The Art of Preparation starts with valuing the practice, and even the habit, of deep personal honesty. You must be willing to be honest with yourself. This includes honesty regarding your perceptions, opinions, judgments, and inner conscious states. Living a life of daily introspection, reflection, and personal honesty is so important because your own mental states exert a powerful influence on everything in your life. Accordingly, your journey to transformation must start with your own mental states. To go anywhere, you must first know where you are. When referring to a map or when you go to a shopping mall, we all must start with "YOU ARE HERE." If you are not honest with yourself at the onset of your journey through personal transformation, then you will never get to your chosen destination. This destination is leading a life that is completely fulfilling at every moment because you know, and can directly experience, that you are deeply fulfilled in your CONNECTION with the Universe that sustains your every breath.

Preparation is the art of knowing truly and honestly WHERE YOU ARE at every single moment. Cutting through the layers of your conscious "baggage", your personal history, and your pains and anxieties is possible only if you begin to understand how YOU have been responsible for your entire life experience. This life experience includes your opinions, values, and beliefs. It includes your perception of yourself, your relationships, and your work. In fact, it makes up your entire worldview. Ultimately, this life experience underlies your connection (or lack thereof) with your highest consciousness. This highest, original, and most pure consciousness lies beneath the layers of your personal thoughts and emotional history that you have accumulated over your entire lifetime.

Let's return to the shopping mall directory. It says, "You are here." But where is "here" really? *"Where* are you NOW?" *"Who* are you RIGHT NOW?" *"What* is the true nature of your existence NOW?" There is a field of philosophy that asks these critical questions called "Ontology." Ontology is the study of "being" or "existence." The word ontology comes from the Greek *"ontos"* which means "being" or "existence" combined with the word *"logos"* which means "the study of."

Of course, you can study a myriad of ontological theories from both the Eastern and Western philosophical traditions about the nature of the Universe and the nature of individual human beings. However, since this book is not intended as an academic treatise, I will simply outline for you an ontology that is based upon my own personal experience and the experience of my many teachers.

Ultimately, what you are is the same as the Universe Itself. You and the Universe are pure energy. The Universe is One and YOU are a part of this single inter-connected Universe. Philosophers and theologians refer to this as "monism." This can also be referred to as Spirit. The word for this unitive universal energy or spirit in Japanese is *"Ki"*, in Chinese *"Chi"* or *"Qi"*, and in Sanskrit *"Brahman"* or sometimes *"Prana."* However, the term you use is not what is critical for your journey – believe me! What is critical is that you understand and experience for yourself the fundamental unity between you and the Universe. You and the Universe are already one, connected and unified. The inseparable linkage between your thoughts, feelings, actions, and their consequences in your daily life already evidence the fact that you and the Universe are not separate—you are already One with the Universe. The process of positive personal transformation is thus a process of bringing this reality to your conscious awareness.

Have you ever wondered if what you are learning in school is relevant to your real interests?

Direct Experience and the Academy

My own participation in academic philosophy has clearly shown me that there is a world of difference between learning about something that is a field of study (even from highly qualified experts) and directly experiencing it. I received my doctorate thirty-four years ago in the field of Comparative Philosophy from the University of Hawaii. I had both the honor and privilege to study under the most gifted and productive scholars in the field. The Philosophy Department at the University of Hawaii has been recognized since its inception as the world's most prestigious school for graduate study in the field of Comparative Philosophy. My dissertation committee included Professor Eliot Deutsch, the successor to Charles A. Moore who was the founder and original editor of the premier peer review academic journal in the field of Comparative Philosophy—*Philosophy East and West*. Also supervising my work was Professor Roger Ames, a specialist in Chinese Philosophy and current editor of *Philosophy East and West*. Another doctoral committee member was Professor David Kalupahana who also supervised my master's degree work specializing in Causation (Dependent Origination) and Early Buddhist Philosophy. Professor Kalupahana is the world's leading authority on the earliest of all Buddhist texts – the Pali *Nikayas* and Chinese *Agamas*.

Professor Winfield Nagley, a scholar of nineteenth-century western philosophy, served as my practical guide advising me how to effectively manage the hurdles of graduate study in a most competitive department.

Finally, Thomas Patrick Kasulis served as my doctoral dissertation chairperson in the area of Japanese Buddhist Philosophy. The title of my dissertation was the *The Bodymind Experience in Japanese Buddhism: A Phenomenological Study of Kukai and Dogen*. Even back in graduate school (starting thirty-eight years ago), the actual "Bodymind Experience" that I discussed was the direct result of my training with *Ki-Aikido* Master Koichi Tohei. While the aforementioned group of scholars at the University of Hawaii taught me and mentored me as an academic, I had already been training for years in the teachings of *Ki* and *Aikido* through Master Koichi Tohei and his instructors. Under his guidance, I discovered that the real *experiential* understanding of *Bodymind Awareness* must be cultivated (*shugyō*) through your own daily practice of breathing, meditation, and personal study.

I now understand that my interest in studying Comparative Philosophy at the prestigious East-West Center and at the University of Hawaii was merely the logical extension (that is, pursuing the terminal Ph.D. degree) of my seventh grade "World Religions" home study course taught under the direction of "Professor" Janis M. Shaner, my mother (see Introduction). Preparation "to study *about* consciousness" has helped me to converse in the vocabulary of professional philosophy and to teach my university students *about* consciousness. But teaching, studying, and learning about consciousness does not necessarily lead one to the *direct experience* of consciousness that the Art of Preparation aims to cultivate. So, you can be relieved to know that it is not at all necessary for you to engage in academic study in order for you to *experience directly* who you really are. But what kind of wisdom does this direct experience lay bare?

Have you ever wondered what wise people really know?

Enlightenment is a Verb

In many ways, and for many reasons, the world of intellectualizing *about* enlightenment, or consciousness, or self-actualization is an impediment to your *personal* journey. Enlightenment is an *action* verb, not a noun. You as an originally enlightened being are energy in action. You are an energetic process that is in a state of constant flux and impermanence. Enlightened consciousness is not something someone "has" or "possesses." To intellectualize it, hold it, covet it, or celebrate it is to lose it. Enlightened life and consciousness is a way of living that never ends; you are conscious energy in perpetual creation. In short, my point is that if all you have done is learned *about* enlightenment through academic reading only, and if your study is not based upon or does not "connect with" your personal life experience, then you should *"throw it all away"* (Jp. *kanzen ni nuku*)! Your life should not be lived because of what you have read, nor should you believe in the personal testimony of others – including mine contained in this book. Your life should be lived in the light of your own experience. At the conclusion of each chapter, I will share with you ways for you to *discover for yourself and validate for yourself* (using your own experience), the Seven Arts and truths of personal development for positive self-transformation. Your journey is a process, an on-going activity, and must be yours alone. And, your journey must also *connect* to your own on-going life experience, including especially your experience of *connection* with your true, divine Self. My testimony or the testimony of others must surrender ultimately to the greater validity of your own spiritual knowledge and experience.

Have you ever wondered why you are here?

Who or What Are You, Really?

Let's put book learning and the personal testimony of others aside and return to the first question that lies at the foundation of the first of the Seven Arts, the Art of Preparation – "WHO OR WHAT ARE YOU, REALLY?" Consult your own experience, your own life. How do you *feel* (not just think) at this very moment? Do you feel separate? Are you a discrete individual distinct from your immediate surroundings? Can you feel your heartbeat? Can you feel your breathing? Can you feel your skin breathing? I believe that many people live in the illusion of being a *separate self;* that is, you may think that you are a person defined by your mental states interpreted as *distinct* and *separate* from your own body, your energy, your environment, your God, and your divine Self. The "illusion" is that you are a separate, independent self that *thinks, acts,* and *feels emotions.*

    In contrast to this illusion, I would like to suggest to you that you are pure energy, Divine Energy. You are One with the *Ki* (life force) of the Universe that creates and sustains you at every moment of your existence. You are One with the whole of creation. In your original and natural state, you are the energy that is the life force of all living things. Your mind, body, and spirit are divine and represent the same energy that makes you *not separate* from the world that sustains you. You can learn to *feel* and *directly experience* your innate *connection* with this life force by deeply calming yourself in sincere, relaxed, and present meditation.

The key point arising from your experience and direct awareness of your connection with the Universe is that the "reality" you had believed heretofore to be the case (the "illusion") was actually the mere product of your own intentions. If this connection is not a part of your direct experience, it is because your conscious mind, subconscious mind, and unconscious mind are artificially "covering over" (Sk. *samvrti*) the pure, base reality that is, in fact, the same as your original and natural state of being. Your acquired, systematic, and habitual way of seeing yourself as *separate* from the world around you is reinforced by the vocabulary of your daily life experience. "Subject/Object," "good/bad," "right/wrong," "here/there," and "up/down," etc., are all merely words expressing polar opposites that reflect our created, man-made (not God-made or Universal) point of view.

From the standpoint of your divine consciousness, these are all *"relative"* truisms; they are not *"Absolute"* Universal Truths. Our essential nature is fundamentally different from the relative worldview imposed by your daily life experience that oftentimes fuels the aforementioned "illusion." The relative worldview is occasioned by an illusion of sorts that has its seeds in the habituated mind-set that "sees" and "interprets" the world through the conceptual filters called separation and dualism. The concepts of separation and dualism are caused by, and systematically reinforced by, our use of language as well as the daily habit of simply seeing, viewing, or thinking about ourselves as *separate selves*.

Viewing the world from this relative worldview naturally leads to confused motivations underlying our daily life action. A person with a belief system based on separation is motivated to act by external influences. For many people, their conscious mode of operation is fundamentally *"fear based."* That is, many of us tend to view the world out of a perceived (or unconscious) *need for approval.* We seek to "fit in," to "gain approval," and satisfy *someone else's definition* of how you should be. If you believe that you are separate from others, naturally you operate from a view of the world defined by external influences instead of leading your conscious life from a vantage point of *connectedness* with your deeper divine Self. The *desire to please* these external influences is fundamentally driven by a deep sense of separation or insecurity. Ultimately then, the desire to please is driven by the *fear* of not being accepted or connected, or perhaps the *fear* of not conforming to someone else's (separate) view of reality.

However, it is possible to view reality *as it really is* rather than viewing it based upon insecurity, fear, anxiety, and tension. A host of mental, physical and emotional problems arise from this illusionary, fictitious view of the world. Conversely, when we are connected to our deepest, truest, divine Self, we can reflect (like a mirror) all things, all events, and all affairs clearly and thus operate from a position of deep calmness, awareness, and silence. This kind of awareness occasions the necessary clarity for our consciousness to act as One with the Universe. When this happens, all suffering, pain, and trauma fall away naturally and effortlessly. Preparing ourselves to live in this manner (*Living with the Wind at Your Back*) is at the heart of the Art of Preparation.

How do we go about realizing these truths that allow us to meet each day like a mild spring breeze? The first thing we must do is "cut through" the ideological obstacles that *cause* you to remain attached to a relative view of the world. For example, there has been a great debate in theology and philosophy about whether or not persons are endowed with an immortal soul. In the orthodox Hindu tradition, for example, this permanent, eternal soul is called *ātman*. For the Greek philosopher Plato, it was called *psyché*. Christianity, Judaism, and Islam, refer to an immortal soul that lives on after our bodies die.

One of the heterodox schools of Indian thought is the tradition of Buddhism founded by Siddhartha Gautama (the historical Buddha). Siddhartha is the historical "Buddha", so called because "Buddha" means the "honored one" or "one who is *awake*." The Buddha argued against the orthodox Hindu view of *atman* (the belief in the existence of a separate, unchanging, permanent, eternal soul). Instead, the Buddha stated that we have no independent, permanent, eternal soul that can be verified in our daily life experience. Therefore, he called his view the philosophy of no-self, no-ego or *anātman* (the opposite of *ātman*).

It is important to understand that the Buddha is not denying the existence of a universal/connected self; he is denying the existence of an independent, ontologically separate Self that becomes habitually conceptualized as an eternal soul. The true Self, the Buddha countered, is an interconnected Self. The true Self is indeed a divine Self that is connected to, and One with, the Universe. The true Self is empty of a separate existence. The word *selflessness* captures the meaning of a truly connected Self. It is a Self without borders. In the same way, the term *selfishness* captures the meaning of a truly independent, separate self. Selfishness is characterized by excessive craving, covetous, and dogmatic desires. The causal seeds of this kind of activity are occasioned ultimately by the intrusion of an illusion (relative thinking). The illusion is carried with us from cradle to grave...it is equivalent to living with an incorrect view of change (in particular) and the way of the Universe (in general). The illusion is caused by our false sense of independence and separation. This basic concept is rooted in the notion of ego.

We will return to this important observation about selflessness after another brief story.

Have you ever wondered what it would be like to meet the leader of a nation?

Mrs. Gandhi:
Preparing for Individual and Cultural Change

Over thirty years ago, during the summer of 1982, I was fortunate to experience the mental and emotional "attachments" that many people possess in relation to the Self/no-self debate, including how these attachments may stand in the way of individual and cultural transformation. I was in India conducting research as part of a Fulbright Fellowship. Prime Minister Indira Gandhi was preparing for her first meeting with President Ronald Reagan (then in his first term). He had just made negative public comments about communist and socialist regimes as "being the axis of evil" as part of his famous "Evil Empire" speech delivered before the House of Commons (United Kingdom) on June 8, 1982. While these famous phrases were directed at the Soviet Union during the Cold War, Mrs. Gandhi was rightfully concerned as she sought the assistance of President Reagan to help modernize her country. Her concern about President Reagan's impression of India was due to the fact that while India was the largest democracy in the world, the Socialist Party (of which she was the head) was freely and democratically elected into power. Her administration was

THE ART OF PREPARATION

"Prime Minister Indira Gandhi was preparing for her first meeting with President Ronald Reagan..."

Photo taken by author at the meeting with
Fulbright Fellowship's members. New Delhi, 1982.

eager to "change the culture" and seek American support (and resources) to help modernize India. My part of the project was to conduct a study on the affects of certain indigenous village belief systems upon peoples' willingness (or lack thereof) to accept change and modernize various aspects of their life patterns. Some changes included family planning, the use of birth control, the use of chemical additives to increase crop yields, and various new sanitation and health-related (disease prevention) practices.

The question was, would villagers with ninety-nine percent illiteracy consider some of the recommended changes as actions that might be interpreted as going against certain religious beliefs and practices? For example, what if lifestyle changes (family planning, sanitation, disease prevention practices) were considered to create negative karmic consequences that might befall someone engaging in these new activities? What if something like family planning and the use of modern birth control methods were considered to be something that would adversely affect one's eternal soul (*ātman*)?

For Prime Minister Gandhi to succeed in her efforts to modernize, she needed to understand how to *prepare* her citizens for change – for *personal and village life transformation*. Without adequate preparation and understanding of each village culture, Prime Minister Gandhi would likely fail in her efforts to transform peoples' individual welfare, village life, and the life of her nation. Without *education first* to enable changing peoples' consciousness, then lasting *follow-through action* and behavioral *change* (no matter how well intended) would never take root and lead to significant changes in the welfare of villagers that make up most of the population of India.

Have you ever wondered if different people representing different sides of an argument are really talking about the same thing?

Self or No-Self (Selflessness):
Daya Krishna and David Kalupahana

Shortly after visiting with Prime Minister Gandhi at her residence in New Delhi with Fulbright Scholars, I became gravely ill. Soon I was scheduled to visit the University of Rajasthan where fortunately I had a friend – Professor Daya Krishna. Professor Krishna was arguably the most famous living Indian philosopher and I had come to know of him since he was previously a Visiting Professor at the University of Hawaii. Given his eminent stature, he was asked (in 1982) to serve as the interim President of the University of Rajasthan. Administrative work was not at all his interest, but he performed his duty (*dharma*) by carrying out his temporary assignment in order to serve his university.

My 103 F° fever was as high as the nighttime temperature in India during the months of June and July. Professor Krishna and his lovely wife took me into the Presidential Palace, which was their temporary home during his interim Presidency. Mrs. Krishna gave me fluids continuously as I battled dehydration. Professor Krishna preferred to stay at home with a fellow philosopher and keep me company rather than performing the administrative duties that he so disliked. His passion for "give and take" philosophical argument was intense. Much to his wife's chagrin, he delighted in debating me every day, being somewhat blind to my very ill condition.

Professor Krishna was aware that, at the University of Hawaii, I had been a student of Professor David Kalupahana, the world's leading expert in the field of Early Buddhism. Early Buddhism is the most influential school of heterodox Indian philosophy. Professor Kalupahana was the student of and heir to his teacher, K. N. Jayatillike, who was the leading expert in the early Buddhist texts. Both scholars (Jayatillike and Kalupahana) were from Sri Lanka. Naturally, Professor Krishna, who was a Hindu, assumed that, as a direct student of Professor Kalupahana, I was a card carrying Early Buddhist and proponent of the heterodox Buddhist doctrine of no-self or *anatman* (which is the denial of the orthodox Hindu doctrine of the immortal soul or Self called *atman*). Professor Krishna, in direct contrast with Professor Kalupahana, was THE eminent Indian sage of orthodox Hindu philosophy that includes the six orthodox schools of *Advaita Vedanta, Nyaya, Vaiseshika, Yoga, Samkhya,* and *Mimamsa*. Each of these schools was considered to be an orthodox school in so far as each system adhered to the doctrine of *atman* which (again) is the belief in a permanent, eternal soul/Self.

Professor Krishna's passionate concern for the *historical significance* of this ideological debate between Self and no-self (selflessness) was so great that even though the Hindu/Buddhist debate has continued for over 2,400 years, he chose to sit at my bedside and debate *me* in my delirious state. Needless to say, his charming wife was unsuccessful at rescuing me. He would say, "You believe in some kind of reincarnation or transmigration, right?" "Yes," I said. "Then without believing in a permanent eternal soul (*atman*), exactly what is it that carries over from one life to the next?"

Of course, he knew the Buddha's answer (and Professor Kalupahana's and my own); namely, that "*sankharas*" or "*dispositions*" (conscious and unconscious) are the karmic residue that carries over from one life to the next. But these "dispositions" (Sk. *sankharas*) are not fixed, eternal, and unchanging. Rather, karma and karmic dispositions are things that can be altered. *Spiritual development and the spiritual path you choose have much to do with eliminating the adverse affects of karmic dispositions residing deep within our consciousness.* What Professor Krishna lacked was the experiential element that for me reconciled the apparent inconsistency between belief in reincarnation and rejection of an eternal soul. Suffice it to say, that without direct experience and training, the philosophical debate becomes groundless and suffers from the conscious, linguistic, and theoretical "attachments" that characterize the defense of ideological dogma. The only way to truly know about such matters is through direct personal experience and this requires that you train yourself. Real committed training (*shugyō*) begins with the Art of Preparation.

I eventually returned to health and thanked Professor Krishna and his wife for their concern and willingness to restore my bodily fluids at considerable cost. Over the course of my stay, all of my discretionary research money had been depleted simply purchasing bottled water. In parts of India in the summer, it can easily reach over 110 degrees in the day and remain near 100 degrees even at night. Without air conditioning, one must replace fluids all day and night while not contracting illnesses due to drinking contaminated water. My previous work in the villages had taken its toll and I was grateful to Professor Krishna for bearing the cost of my illness. I was especially grateful for the lesson made clear to me concerning the relationship between an intellectual life and a life focused upon direct experiential training.

The academic confusion surrounding this debate is simply focused upon the distinction between your **ego-based self** and your true, divine Self. The ego-based self is the false self created by *sankharas* (karmic dispositions) that are acquired as a result of *personal cravings, attachments to things and events,* and *judgments of people and their behavior.* Your **true divine Self** is the true Self, which is the same as *no-self* characterized by *selflessness.* The ego-based self creates your "relative" view of the world. Accordingly, as a result of ego-based thinking that craves fulfillment from outside itself, you *separate* yourself from the world around you. In contrast, by developing the heterodox doctrine of no-self (*anātman*), the Buddha was telling us of the ultimate illusion and false view of the "relative," "separate," "self-created," "ego-based" self that actually "covers over" *(samvrti)* our deeper, true Self (*no-self*) which is *not separate* from the Universe. In short, selflessness and the doctrine of *no-self* (*anatman*) are one and the same; there is no separate Self that exists independent of the Universe that sustains all of us.

When you operate from your ego, you operate out of *separation, fear,* and the *need for approval.* Your notion of "success" is based upon the ability of your ego to satisfy your personal cravings. Your deeper, true Self, on the other hand, is really a *no-self* in the sense that it has no *independent* existence. This true Self is thus merged in union with God, Spirit, or the *Ki* (energy) of the Universe. The unity you experience with the Universe gives you the *direct experience of connection,* not separation. From this vantage point of supreme connection, you have no independent, separate existence. You experience unity, connection, and mutual interpenetration, not isolation. This is an experience that is joyful, blissful, and enables you to witness your original nature that is one with (not separate from) the Universe.

Have you ever wondered why deep truths seem so simple?

The Golden Rule and Selflessness: Preparing for the Art of Compassion

The joy and bliss associated with this direct experience of connection with the Universe may be characterized further as a love for all living things. The Golden Rule becomes an easy doctrine to practice because you ARE the "other" person. *"Do unto others as you would have them do unto you."* You have no intention to harm because it is akin to harming yourself. The spirit of divine connection is original and is manifested *naturally* in this mode of being. In this state of awareness, compassion emanates from your divine Self (no-self). Compassion is thus original, sincere, genuine, and natural in the sense that it is not *manufactured,* it is not *legislated,* it is not *commanded,* and it is not even *intended.* This is the same as having no ego and no independent attachments that cause you to feel separate and dis-connected from the needs of those around you. The spirit of *loving all creation* is thus consistent both with the view that we have a soul and with the view that we do not.

Soul or no soul, Self or no-self, we all have the ability to directly experience our original connection with the divine, the Universe. By *preparing yourself* to experience directly this unitive life force, you will be cultivating fertile ground in order to experience the second of the Seven Arts –the Art of Compassion. *The experience of your universal soul and your divine Self IS the same as the experience of no-self and selflessness.* You have no independent self when you view the world from more clear (less dispositions - *sankharas*) states of spiritual consciousness. No independent Self means to be without Self; in other words, the condition of *selflessness*. From the standpoint of relative thinking, the doctrine of no-Self and the doctrine of an Eternal Soul (that is related to God, the Universe, or Spirit) are two separate theological/philosophical doctrines. From the standpoint of Absolute Thinking, however, they are actually One and the same.

The following daily exercises will help you to *prepare yourself* to become deeply familiar with your consciousness, your environment, your relationships, and "the monastery" of your entire daily life world. By following these exercises mindfully, and on a daily basis, you will begin to *prepare yourself* to experience a deeper, truer view of who you really are. When the layers of mental and emotional baggage are stripped from your consciousness, you will begin to taste the depths of your true and original connectedness with the Universe. Once this happens, a world of infinite creativity and possibility will be available to you *experientially.* You will not need to count upon the "words," "testimony," "approval," or "expertise" of other so-called "spiritual experts" or texts.

You will begin to sample your true core being. This true Self, when harmonized with the energy of the entire Universe, will enable you to transform your spiritual life, interpersonal relationships, and overall well-being. When faced with conflict or scarcity, you will be able to tap the source of all creation and you will be able to *trust* that your path will lead you to fulfill your true mission with a healthy, positive outlook toward life. Others will sense your sincerity, trust you, and serve the same ends that you pursue because your *Conscious Action* (see Chapter 5) *in service to others* will be based upon your highest consciousness—loving and protecting all creation. When your personal intentions and motivation come from a place of universal thinking, not selfish thinking, then the Universe "naturally" (that is, "causally") provides for you a vehicle for positive personal transformation. When we "let go" of relative thinking, then Absolute Thinking and a Universal Mind are born. When this happens, you will be living and acting in accord with the principles of the Universe. This is the meaning of selflessness; thus, we are prepared to discuss the second art—The Art of Compassion.

**Daily Exercises
To Facilitate The Art of Preparation**

*Have you ever wondered if real progress
is just undoing prior mistakes?*

Daily Training is Like Peeling an Onion

The most important point in applying the lessons and positive benefits described in each of the Seven Arts is to establish a *pattern and a habit of daily training*. At first you should start with very conservative goals and on a daily basis practice positive development habits that do not take a lot of time. Gradually you will be more comfortable and able to dedicate more time for daily breathing, meditation, and the other recommended exercises. The exercises should first be pleasurable because if they are too severe or too difficult, then your motivation and enthusiasm for change will diminish. Although these exercises will require a commitment of time, please remember the difference between real cultivation (*shugyō*) commitment, and mere practice (*keiko*) as described in this chapter. The critical difference between practice and cultivation is in the level of commitment and sincerity that you bring to your project – the creative change process for positive personal transformation. When you combine easy techniques (breathing, meditation, journaling, etc.) with a sincere commitment to lasting change, you will transform yourself gradually, and almost imperceptibly, on a *daily* basis.

    I compare this *daily* training process to the daily process of learning a foreign language, which has always been frustratingly difficult for me. Each day you attend class, take quizzes, learn new vocabulary, sentence structure, and so on, and each day you feel overwhelmed. You are not yet fluent in, for example, Chapter One vocabulary of your Japanese 101 course. You continue to study and now you are in Chapter Fourteen. You feel just as challenged (and behind) in Chapter Fourteen as the day you felt challenged (and behind) in Chapter One for the very first time. However, upon reviewing and looking back, and at sometime without you ever realizing it, you somehow became fluent in Japanese Chapter One material! While Chapter Fourteen is still difficult, Chapter One material became a breeze without your *conscious* knowledge.

Developing your awareness and accessing your deeper Self on a daily basis can follow a similar pattern of learning and personal development. Please take small training steps or bites each day and develop the pattern or habit of consistent training time focused upon developing your awareness of the MONASTERY, which is YOUR LIFE. Remember, your aim is to access your highest consciousness and to do that you need to work through an entire lifetime of thoughts, ideas, and judgments that have "covered over" your Original Self. *Daily training is like peeling an onion.* The process of consciousness training is one of discovery and uncovering the habits of your mind and the history of your emotions that prohibit you from accessing your deepest spiritual gifts and original connectedness to God, Spirit, and the Universe Itself defined as ONE.

Preamble to the Exercises

While some books are read for entertainment, this book is not meant for only reading. While the concepts discussed might be interesting (hopefully), they cannot be understood completely by approaching them purely from an intellectual viewpoint. These Arts come to life only through your direct experience. In order to fully experience the Seven Arts, a commitment must be made to *execute* the exercises at the end of each chapter. In fact, what I mean by the term "Arts" is that YOUR LIFE IS A WORK OF *"ART"* THAT YOU CREATE. The Arts represent the *artistry* of your life-in-the-making. Your twenty-four hour a day "cultivation" (not just a few hours of "practice") reflects the quality of your artistry of being-in-the-world.

There are two basic ways that you can approach reading and completing the exercises in this book. The first is to read through the book completely, and then go back, read the summaries and work on the exercises in their respective order in a step-by-step sequence. The other is to read one chapter, perform the exercises to the point that they become second nature (and that you are not attached to them), and then move on to the next chapter and new exercises that build successively upon the preceding chapter and exercises. In both approaches, your commitment to continued training over a long period of time (*shugyō*) is the most important thing. There is nothing simple or easy about deep personal transformation.

I recommend the former approach because I want you to be excited and committed to the Seven Arts in their entirety. Hence, doing each exercise, with the theoretical knowledge of how the Seven Arts relate to each other will help you achieve proficiency in each of the exercises throughout your journey.

Beginning to chart a course of study in which you implement the Seven Arts in your daily life requires a great deal of reflection and honest self-evaluation. *In order to accomplish this, it is important to record and analyze these self-reflections in a journal.* If you already write in a journal, then I would ask that you devote a portion of your journaling to Seven Arts cultivation. If you are not currently journaling, I urge you to start a Seven Arts Journal in order to chart your growth journey. Many of the exercises require you to observe different situations. Externalizing your observations through journaling will help you to clarify what you are experiencing (mentally, physically, emotionally, and spiritually) and will help you to unlock the hidden meaning of your new experience in different situations.

Have you ever wondered if you are really clear about what you want and think is most important?

Exercise 1:
Positive Self-Talk
Personal Development Affirmation (PDA)

This is setting the foundation for intentional living and the transformation process; it serves as the beacon, the compass, the true north as you progress. At this first stage you are defining the goals and purpose of your life.

From the time that you are a young child, others are pulling your mindshare in multiple directions, e.g., parents, teachers, friends, relatives, and even corporations through mass media and advertising. For example, it is probably hard to find a 4-year old in America who does not know what the golden arches represent. This, in and of itself, is not a bad thing unless you have no direction for yourself. Developing a positive personal development affirmation is like putting a stake in the ground for yourself and your direction in life. This statement constitutes the foundation from which all Seven Arts are built. It is imperative that you determine who you are, where you are, and what direction you want to go. The PDA is not a to-do list or a tactical strategy. It is a statement about your very essence...your true being. This exercise should not be taken lightly and you should not proceed to any other exercise until this first exercise is

THE ART OF PREPARATION

complete. Take at least one day or one week or one month to consider your PDA. It is worth at least eight hours of introspection if you desire to chart a meaningful course for your journey through the Seven Arts.

In developing your PDA, you should ask yourself the following questions:

1. When all is said and done, what will be my *legacy* in this world?

2. When I am at the end of my life, what kind of person will I have been?

3. How do I wish to treat others?

4. How should I treat myself differently than I am currently treating myself?

5. What quality do I admire most in others?

6. What quality do I admire most in myself?

7. What meaning and purpose do I wish to fulfill and bring to this world?

Creating a PDA requires preparation and thought. The PDA is a work in progress. As you go through the **Seven Arts** journey, you may gain new insights that may require you to modify your PDA. Here is an example of a simple, yet thorough, PDA.

"I will dedicate myself to accessing my true gifts in service to others. I will use silence to listen to myself and to others more deeply. I will not judge, not criticize, and not blame. I know that I am truly the only one responsible for my consciousness and my actions. I know deeply that, through my choices, I am

continually creating my consciousness, my relationships, and my world at every moment. From this moment forward, I choose to take responsibility for my life. From this moment forward, I choose to forgive myself and others, love myself and others, and serve myself and others to the very best of my ability."

Each night before you fall asleep and when you first awake in the morning recite for yourself a personal development affirmation. The Art of Preparation is about developing positive habits that start the positive change process. The words you use each day have a powerful effect upon your overall outlook toward the entire transformation process.

You can write your own positive affirmation message and keep it with you each day to repeat as often as you can. If you are struggling with a specific spiritual anxiety or relationship anxiety at home or at work, then you can modify your affirmation in order to coach yourself into positive daily habits of speech and action. During the day when you feel yourself falling into self-criticism and judgment, pull out your positive affirmation "mission statement" and recite it to yourself. The more you approach your change process with deep commitment and sincerity, the more you will be setting yourself up for success. To be receptive to change, you must remind yourself of your affirmation and commitment to the change process many times each day. Remember you are breaking habituated patterns of consciousness that have grown and developed throughout your entire life. The Art of Preparation sets the stage for personal change and positive development with sincerity and true commitment. A solid foundation established with the practice of Exercise 1 will help you access the many treasures and infinite possibilities that are yours to behold.

*Have you ever wondered why quiet
seems so much better than noise?*

Exercise 2:
Make Silence Your Friend

This is the most basic daily exercise. Here you simply practice reducing the "noise" of your busy mind. Let your critical, judging mind take a rest. Your aim is to learn how to be calm and still even for just a short time.

Recognize that the voice of God, Spirit, and the Universe Itself is silence; it is quiet calmness. Begin to make serenity and silence your source of strength. Take five minutes three times a day to just sit quietly. Of course, this is just *preparation* for Dynamic Meditation and Dynamic Breathing to be described in later chapters. For now, gift yourself five minutes of calmness immediately after you recite your positive affirmation (described above in Exercise 1). Just do nothing and think about nothing in particular for five minutes at least three times a day. Hear your own internal voice and allow it to be calm and clear as you sit quietly. As thoughts and ideas arise, let them melt away softly. Practice the art of non-attachment by letting go of your own internal "self talk." Let go of the voice in your inner consciousness that analyzes, that judges, that blames, and that criticizes and is defensive. Just sit, be still, and be present.

After your early morning quiet "sitting," find another five minutes during the day to just sit in silence and learn to make peace with the stillness of your calm, serene, and silent mind. At night, immediately after you once again recite your positive affirmation, begin your last quiet meditation for five more minutes. Preferably do this just before you go to bed. You will find that if you do so, your sleep will be deep and you will awake in the morning more rested, more calm, and more at peace with yourself. After each quiet time, record in your Seven Arts Journal your specific observations and physiological responses to this practice. In short, record the positive effects that doing these activities has had upon you throughout the day.

"This daily practice of silence, non-judgment, and non-attachment will soon come as 'second nature' for you."

This daily practice of silence, non-judgment, and non-attachment will soon come as "second nature" for you. The more you access your true Self, the more that silence, non-judgment, and non-attachment become your allies. By beginning in this simple manner, through a combination of these first two simple exercises, you will *prepare yourself* for deeper training in the future, and you will be building the necessary solid foundation to know your true Self and to live in harmony with the Universe Itself.

> *Have you ever wondered if you can really be honest with yourself?*

Exercise 3:
Practice Self Honesty

Now you move to the next stage, focusing upon "awareness of self." This exercise is setting a most basic foundation piece for cultivating self-honesty down the road. Think of it as a college course entitled "Self-Honesty 101."

The previous two exercises have now prepared you for Exercise 3—the Practice of Self Honesty. Your PDA is pointing you toward true north and your silent meditation is clearing your mind of countless other distractions. You may already see glimpses of your true Self coming forward.

This exercise is an experiential one. Throughout each day you can turn your life into a contemplative monastic environment just by the power of your own mental and emotional self-discipline and overall awareness. As often as you can, *think deeply before you speak.*

When I was a Sheriff's Deputy in Aspen, Colorado, I learned an important lesson. When responding to an emergency with lights flashing and sirens blaring, we were taught to think first and take time to make a plan, and then ask for help using our radio. Unfortunately, police officers themselves DO get caught up in emergencies. The statistics show that too often innocent bystanders are struck and killed by fast driving, too aggressive law enforcement and emergency "first responders." Often, officers arrive quickly, and hopefully safely, only to *start* their thought process of what to do next. Just as the phrase *"think before you speak"* applies in daily life, "think before you act" and "think before you drive too fast" were the lessons emphasized for all officers in Aspen, Colorado. We were taught to drive safely, safely enough to think, safely enough to assess the situation, and safely enough to make an "action plan" so that when we did arrive at the scene, we could act "consciously." With Conscious Action, we could follow through and successfully execute the plan we made while driving safely.

In the same way that thoughtful action is essential to emergency police response, thoughtful speech is essential in daily life. Nothing is so important and so urgent that you should just "blurt it out", speaking before you think and feel where others are on the issue at hand. When faced with conflict and interpersonal struggle at home or at work, we tend to just react and often make matters worse by unconsciously antagonizing those around us. If you are in a boat and your boat is taking on water, do you want to react by going below and cutting a hole in the hull of the boat? The answer is "of course not"; however, this is exactly how some of us react to our struggles! It may seem simple but *practicing sincerely and deeply the Art of just taking a breath and reflecting before you speak* can make an enormous difference in your daily life. In this exercise, simplicity yields great power. Through this practice, you will find yourself creating opportunities for many short meditations throughout the day.

By reflecting wisely, your words will gradually have new meaning, new sincerity, new credibility, and new power, thus positively affecting and connecting with those around you. Others will see and feel your mindfulness. And it is no gimmick. By practicing mindful listening and reflecting honestly on your own "agenda" before you speak, you will gradually (in a drop-by-drop fashion) be learning to "know thyself" in the true context of your lived experience with others. You cannot calm the waves of your mind, or your self-criticisms, or your criticism of others unless you first become *aware* of them.

In combination, these three simple exercises (1. Practicing *Daily* Positive Self-Talk, 2. Practicing *Daily* Silence, and 3. Practicing *Daily* Honest Introspection) are the bases of the Art of Preparation. If you perform them routinely, they will enable you to build a foundation for knowing your true Self and for living in harmony with the Universe. True Self understanding is occasioned only by honest introspection and reflection about your own internal states of mind, your emotions, and your lived experience (being) with others. You cannot "calm," "peel," "erase," or "let go" of that which you have not brought into your conscious awareness. Once you are *aware,* you can *understand.* And, once you understand, you can begin the transformation process required to embrace true spiritual development, true interpersonal relationships development, and true personal development in service to others. These three daily practices prepare you for changes in your life that will lead to serenity and abundance, thus enhancing the lives of all of those around you.

After practicing daily honest introspection during your conversations, record in your Seven Arts Journal the observations you make. Did you receive different reactions from people you ordinarily encounter? Did you learn anything different about yourself or others? Did the ultimate purpose of your conversation come to fruition? Did you feel rooted in your PDA?

Let's proceed to the second art—The Art of Compassion.

2

The Art of Compassion

*"Staying in touch with
the reality of suffering
keeps us sane and nourishes
the wellsprings of understanding (prajña)
and compassion (karuna) in us."*

Thich Nhat Hanh
Interbeing

Remembering the Golden Rule might be an easy way to get to the essence of The Art of Compassion: *"Do unto others as you would have them do unto you"* (Matthew 7:12). Confucius emphasizes compassion for others with the "Silver Rule" from his book, **The Analects.** In passage XV.24, Tzu-kung asked, "Is there one word which may serve as a rule of practice for all one's life?" Confucius answered, "Is not reciprocity such a word? Never do to others what you would not like them to do to you." My teacher, Master Koichi Tohei, includes a similar guideline in his teaching called the "Five Principles to Lead Others." He expresses this guideline in the fourth principle which says, *"Put Yourself in the Place of Your Partner."* Practicing this principle is critically important when performing all *Aikido* arts used for self-defense. *Aikido* is really nothing other than practicing the Golden Rule, the Silver Rule, compassion, and non-dissension put *in motion.*

Have you ever wondered how to accomplish what you know you should do?

The Challenge is Not Knowing What to Do; It's Knowing HOW to Do It

So, if all this is so obvious, what is the problem? What is the challenge of actually *practicing* these ideals and making them an integral part of our daily life? People either do not know *how* to put the Golden Rule into action in their daily life or they find themselves *unable* or *unwilling* (consciously or subconsciously) to actually practice the Golden Rule in spite of the clarity and universality of its message.

Compassion and sympathy for others are natural consequences of feeling deeply connected to God, your divine Self, the Universe Itself. When you ARE the world around you in a fundamental sense, you naturally (Jp. *shizen ni*) express love and kindness as an extension of your conscious connection to the Universe Itself. *Shizen ni*, translated as "naturally," also serves as the inspiration behind the sixth Art of Living Naturally. "*Shizen ni*" is one of my teacher's favorite expressions. "Do everything 'naturally,'" he always says. The key to experiencing directly this kind of connection is the process of understanding and feeling deeply that the Universe is not static. Things, events, and people do not exist in isolation. The Universe is energy which is constantly in motion. This life force that sustains and creates all things is constantly in flux.

This belief that we are fundamentally connected to the constantly changing life energy of the Universe is the basis of Chinese Daoist philosophy and cosmology. The Chinese concept of "*fu*" or "returning" represents an exchange of *yin* and *yang* energetic dimensions of a singular, universal force referred to as the *Dao*. The *Dao* generates, sustains, and supports all of creation in a constant exchange of *active,* expressive energy (*yang*) with the *restorative*, creative, life renewing energy (*yin*). All people (male and female) have both energetic qualities. At night when you rest, the *yin* energy becomes dominant restoring and renewing yourself. And, during the day, the active and expressive *yang* energy is dominant as you are engaged in your daily activities. Regardless of the name or cultural context in which you describe it, the life energy of the Universe is sustaining your existence at every moment. The activity of your heart and lungs, the movement of your blood, the activity of food digestion, and even the cell decay and regeneration at work in your body are all functioning due to this unitive, universal energy. Fortunately, all of this activity occurs at every moment without your conscious intention. It is simply the Way of the Universe. Personal health and well-being are functions of the proper *balance* between these two dynamic components of a singular energy. Putting the Art of Compassion into practice and acting in accord with the Art of Compassion are occasioned when you first recognize and experience deeply your fundamental connectedness to all living things.

Have you ever wondered if you are isolated, alone, and not understood?

Experiencing CONNECTION with the Dynamic Universe

The motto of the organization *(Ki no Kenkyukai)* founded by my teacher, Master Koichi Tohei, is as follows: *"Let us have a universal spirit that loves and protects all creation and helps all things grow and develop. To experience the unity of mind and body and become One with the Universe is the ultimate purpose of our study."* People are surprised to hear this kind of thinking from the person responsible for bringing the martial art of *aikido* outside of Japan for the very first time in 1953. Master Tohei understands deeply that the *Ki* (life energy) of the Universe is *the* single unifying force. Aikido means literally, "the Way (*do*) to Union (*ai*) with the life force (*Ki*) of the Universe." When you see and experience the Universe as a single entity of which you are a part then, at that very moment, you break through the confines of what we called in Chapter One "Relative Thinking." When we engage our consciousness in "Absolute Thinking," we see and experience the Universe as One and we understand deeply the illusion of independent existence and personal isolation. This is an illusion that may have guided our previous ways of seeing, thinking, and being in the world. To borrow an analogy from the Greek philosopher Plato, the awakening is like coming out of a cave. The consciousness of Relative Thinking is seen as an illusion when you free yourself to experience the reality of being connected intimately with the Universe. Relative Thinking (like life "in the cave") is seen as illusory because you now understand new possibilities...you can truly come out of the cave and free yourself from such confined feeling and thinking. Now the world of Absolute Thinking (life "outside the cave") is at your doorstep.

"Master Tohei understands deeply that the Ki (life energy) of the Universe is the single unifying force."
Koichi Tohei.
About 1962.

To begin to awaken to the reality of living in an intimately connected Universe, consider how your mere entrance into a room changes everything. Imagine that you simply walk into a room and serve as a distraction, or an interruption, to whomever is in the room and whatever is going on there. You might enter a meeting at work, or enter a room at home where your spouse is on the phone, or walk in on your children engaged in their own activity. You do not need to say anything. Your mere presence observed by others changes their consciousness, their words, and their actions. Your colleagues invite you to join the meeting, your spouse looks up and smiles, your children ask you to hand them a toy. This is more than the result of mere interruption. The interruptions cannot be helped because energy is constantly being exchanged in this dynamic, ever-changing Universe. Furthermore, the whole character of your presence affects the consciousness of those in the room.

I illustrate this point quite easily with my college students. I walk into the classroom with an armload of graded term papers. The students know that it is time to receive their grades as well as my handwritten "feedback" comments. For this classroom exercise, I purposefully look kind of grumpy just to make the point about energy exchange. Of course, my grumpy professor act is still a secret to my unsuspecting students. I say nothing and just stand at the front of the room behind my lectern. I look into their terrified eyes and drop the entire stack of papers, seven inches thick, onto the table beside me. Crash! Then I look at them sternly and utter the words, "I have graded all your term papers and made very (pause), very (longer pause for dramatic effect) extensive comments." All the pre-class social chatter is transformed into dead silence; you can hear a pin drop.

Then I smile and say, "Fortunately for you this brief classroom exercise this morning has been a small demonstration. You can all relax now... I am not returning your term papers today." The energy of the room immediately changes to calm again and I tell the students that today's lecture is about the classical Chinese Daoist understanding of life, energy, and the interconnectedness of all things. "The energy of the Universe is not just physical energy," I tell them. "This energy includes mind, emotion, and spirit. I believe that all of you just experienced this phenomenon. You could all feel the energy of the entire classroom change. Moreover, you experienced your personal energy change during today's illustrative activity. Energy is constantly being exchanged in all realms of the Universe. Indeed, this fact is inescapable."

Let's see how this experience of connection with the dynamic Universe can influence our everyday life.

*Have you ever wondered what you
would do if you were attacked?*

Compassion and Conflict in Action

Apart from classroom theatrics, I can now illustrate the power of compassion and energy *(Ki)* in resolving conflicts. You may be struggling with a spiritual conflict, a relationship conflict, and/or a work-related conflict. The Seven Arts that I am describing in this book can be used to turn your personal conflicts into positive, creative energy where new opportunities and solutions are manifested simply because your consciousness has changed. Conflict can be the best opportunity for you to change your state of being. All that is necessary is for someone to guide you and give you the tools. As illustrated by my classroom exercise, energy is always being *exchanged* both within you as well as between you and others. This energy can be tapped and has the potential to completely transform your life for the better. Let's begin!

I have a friend I have known for years who is a kindred spirit in the work of turning conflict into magical opportunity. He is author and educator Tom Crum. Tom has written three powerful and influential books – **The Magic of Conflict, Journey to Center** and **Three Deep Breaths**. Each book describes the process of transforming conflict into opportunity. Tom also uses the art of *Aikido* as a vehicle for his work teaching others to manage stress and conflict. Tom's students learn to create new possibilities that can, in his words, transform *"A life of work into a work of art."*

I first met Tom in the late 1970s when he invited me to teach *Aikido* at the Aspen Snowmass Academy of Martial

Arts. It was a pleasure to stay with Tom at his home in Aspen, drink *miso* soup from mugs for breakfast, and commute with him up to the large training facility tents located in the high elevations above the town of Snowmass, Colorado. Tom and his partners had created a series of open-air *dojos* (training halls) using very large and tall tent structures amidst the glorious setting of the upper elevations of the Rocky Mountains. Tom invited only the top experts from many martial disciplines and so there was a great opportunity to share and learn from each other. There were Marshall Ho (*T'ai Chi Ch'uan*), Danny Inasanto (who was Bruce Lee's successor – *Jeet Kune Do*, *Wing Chun*, and Filipino *Kali*), Bob Duggan (*Huangdo*), as well as *Aikido* (taught by Tom and me) and other martial arts and martial artists.

I had just returned from training as an *uchi deshi* (live-in student) with Master Tohei at the old Ki Society headquarters in Haramachi, a part of the Shinjuku section in the city of Tokyo. I was familiar with the mountains of Aspen and the wonderful culture of fine ski resort communities from my years as a competitive ski racer. For me, this move to Aspen right after my *uchi deshi* training and the completion of my graduate studies was a heartfelt relief. After concluding my 1) graduate school comprehensive examinations at the University of Hawaii, 2) doctoral research at the Eastern Institute in Tokyo with Professor NAKAMURA Hajime, 3) *uchi deshi* training with Master Tohei at the Ki Society in Tokyo, and 4) move to Cambridge to write my doctoral dissertation at Harvard University under the direction of Professor Thomas Patrick Kasulis, I openly welcomed a return to the mountains. Little did I know how my life was about to change.

One of my *Aikido* students at the Aspen-Snowmass Academy of Martial Arts was Sheriff Richard "Dick" Kienast. Dick was an intellectual and a most introspective and socially conscious man who was educated in the "Great Books" tradition at Notre Dame. He had been teaching at St. Mary's College in the San Francisco Bay Area when he decided to take his family to Aspen for his sabbatical leave. He would "pound nails" as a carpenter to support his family, commune with nature, read, write, and restore himself before his return to college teaching. So how did Dick, the college educator on sabbatical, become the Sheriff of Pitkin County, Colorado?

The famous writer Hunter Thompson, author of **Fear and Loathing in Las Vegas**, was living in Aspen at the time and decided (in 1970) that he would run for sheriff on an ultra-leftist platform. For example, in addition to his rather unusual and unconventional ideas about law enforcement, Hunter wanted to work with the Aspen City Council in order to get rid of the streets in downtown Aspen and plant grass instead! In Hunter's way of thinking, this would ensure the absence of automobile pollution as well as the protection of local pedestrians who might otherwise be struck by out-of-control rental cars driven by tourists traveling the icy streets of Aspen. Well, if you were familiar with the "locals" in Aspen in the 1970s, then you would not be surprised to learn that it looked like Hunter had a slight chance of being elected Sheriff of Pitkin County running on this kind of ultra-environmental protection/safety platform.

Hunter lost the election in 1970 but, had he won, he was planning on having Dick serve as his Undersheriff. In 1976, there was an off year election since the elected Sheriff was forced to resign mid-term. Dick was one of five new candidates and he embraced some of Hunter's feelings about the role of public servants and their obligations to the citizenry. The concepts caught on with the electorate and Dick was elected Sheriff in the 1976 off year election. Dick ran again in 1978 (the regular election period for a new term) and it was at this time that Dick read Sissela Bok's newly released book entitled **Lying: Moral Choice in Public and Private Life**. From this inspired work, Dick found his philosophical focus as well as his public voice citing Shakespeare's **Othello** in his inaugural address.

Have you ever wondered what it would be like to participate in a grand, real life experiment?

Dick Kienast, Aspen and A Great Experiment in Social Justice: "Trust is a Social Good"

Dick pondered the idea and thought that this would be a great opportunity to put into action some of the ideas and social justice practices that he admired and believed in as a result of both his academic study and his college teaching experience in the 'Great Books' humanistic tradition. Dick's favorite book was Plato's **Republic** in which the philosopher describes a just society. Hunter's original invitation to Dick (that is, to serve with him in the Office of Sheriff) was an occasion to actually conduct a sort of grand experiment in Social Justice that Plato merely talks about in the **Republic**. This opportunity, Dick concluded, was the perfect occasion to put his learning and values into action. And so, Dick responded to Hunter's invitation and found his calling, his true "mission" culminating in his 1976 election and 1978 re-election to serve as Sheriff of Pitkin County! Dick Kienast, the socially conscious, card-carrying humanist was now literally "the new Sheriff in town"!

Dick had ideas about who should be in law enforcement. He hired all kinds of interesting people who were highly educated and shared his vision about social service and social trust. I still have his election poster framed and hanging in my office. The 1978 campaign slogan is a quotation from

Sissela Bok's book **Lying: Moral Choice in Public and Private Life** – *"Trust is a social good to be protected just as much as the air we breathe or the water we drink."* Dick recruited, hired, and trained law enforcement officers who shared this vision. For Dick, this quotation captured his belief that *law enforcement was about compassion; it meant building real trust within the community; it meant serving others and giving back to society.*

Dick convinced me that, since I had recently completed my doctorate in Comparative Philosophy, and since I loved to ski – well... maybe I would be willing to return to the Aspen ski resort community and join his group of socially conscious merry men and women and serve alongside them as a Deputy Sheriff law enforcement officer. I had met some of the other deputies while teaching *Aikido* at Tom Crum's Aspen-Snowmass Academy of Martial Arts. Each Sheriff's Deputy that I met was well educated and had an interesting story to tell about *how* they joined up with Dick and *why* they worked to promote social trust. Dick also told me that he had a secret wish – that *all* his deputies achieve the proficiency of first-degree black belt *(Shodan)* in the Art of *Shinshin Toitsu Aikido* founded by my teacher, Master Koichi Tohei.

Dick's specific offer was, "You can ski (which you love), you can live in the mountains (which you love), and you can join in a profound social experiment applying humanist principles to law enforcement (which he knew the philosopher in me would also love)." At Furman University where I would later teach, we might call this kind of a massive experiment "engaged learning" where theory is put into practice. For Dick, key decisions that he made as Sheriff were frequently guided by first consulting the works of Plato, Aristotle, Aquinas, and Augustine. Dick's offer to join the social justice experiment appealed to me and so I began to seriously consider becoming a full time law enforcement officer.

I was ready to participate in Dick's vision by training all of his deputies in *Aikido*, but there was one hitch to joining his experiment. Since the department's training budget was not enough to hire me simply as a full-time *Aikido* instructor, I would have to become a full-fledged, sworn Deputy Sheriff. Finally, I said "Why not!" I would be joining some interesting and talented deputies who were as enthusiastic as I was in making Dick's vision ("Trust as a Social Good") a reality. While serving as Sheriff's deputies, many people discovered a passion for public service that changed not only their lives but also the lives of countless other citizens with whom these officers interacted on a daily basis. This group of deputies included Billy Belfrey who was said to be the youngest U. S. Army Captain and decorated pilot who served in Vietnam; Bob Braudis, who after serving two terms under Dick's leadership was later elected as Dick's replacement as Sheriff of Pitkin County where he has since served its citizens continuously for five consecutive four year terms; Tom Stevenson, who later became the Chief of Police in Aspen; Art Smythe, who later became the Chief of Police (the Marshal) in Snowmass Village, Colorado; Keith Ikeda, who became the Chief of Police in Basalt, Colorado; and Fred Gannett, who is now a judge in Eagle County in Vail, Colorado. Judge Gannett's name maybe familiar because he presided over the highly publicized Kobe Bryant (Los Angeles Lakers) sexual assault case.

The social trust "experiment" worked because each of these former Pitkin County Deputies understood the legacy of compassion and trust. By working together, we built a real world social contract between "the people" of Pitkin County and "the deputies" who served as government officials. The passion for public service (that formed the work of these

Sheriff's Deputies) has been recognized clearly by a citizenry that has over the years been treated fairly, compassionately, and honorably. All of this was due to Dick's original vision that *"TRUST IS A SOCIAL GOOD."* The phenomenal success of his tenure as Sheriff and the later success of his Deputies show that compassion and trust are social virtues that deserve to be practiced and protected.

Have you ever wondered if what you were doing might attract national attention?

CBS: Sixty Minutes

Not everyone was happy, however. Building trust and showing compassion for the citizenry meant that Dick did not believe, on moral grounds (**Lying: Moral Choice in Public and Private Life**), that public servants should perform undercover work as part of law enforcement. To go "undercover" was to live a lie; it was a premeditated breach of "social trust" which Dick believed violated the social trust "contract" that he had made with the people of Pitkin County during his election campaign. To make a long story short, the CBS program "Sixty Minutes" described the conflicts that occurred when the federal government (the Drug Enforcement Agency and the FBI) conducted their own undercover investigations within the jurisdiction of Pitkin County, Colorado. The main conflict was that the use of armed force by Federal agents put local law enforcement officers at risk because we were unaware that the "good guys" (the Federal agents) were the ones doing the shooting. When guns are involved in getting the "bad guys," it is good to cooperate with the locals, or at least let the local "cops" know what's going on, especially when things get nasty. One time Sheriff's deputies and Aspen City police officers received a call from dispatch regarding serious violence and yet the locals did not realize (we were never told) that the gunfire was actually the activity of fellow law enforcement officers, *albeit* "undercover" Federal DEA agents, engaged in a "buy bust" set up to arrest drug dealers in our area.

This situation made for rather dangerous crossfire conditions for all parties involved. The source of this conflict between the undercover methods used by the Federal officers and the non-lying/trust philosophical approach of the Pitkin County Deputies (who would later be trained in *Aikido*) became the focus of "Sixty Minutes" broadcasts.

This dilemma relates directly to the Art of Compassion— let me explain.

Have you ever wondered what it would be like to be a policeman or policewoman?

Compassion, Aikido, and Law Enforcement

Aikido is a most Compassionate Art. The idea behind this martial art is to defend yourself, disarm your opponent if necessary, and then pin or lock up the "bad guy" in such a manner that they are immobilized *without* breaking bones or using excessive force. Like the exchange of universal energy described earlier, you simply take what the "bad guy" gives you, a strike, punch, kick, or whatever, and neutralize the attack peacefully. This emphasis on handling a violent situation peacefully and compassionately is why Dick wanted all his deputies to achieve real proficiency in the art of *Aikido* as an arrest control technique *along with* emergency driving proficiency, firearms shooting proficiency, and other traditional law enforcement skills. Accordingly, one of my tasks was to develop a training methodology that made *Aikido* techniques part of a standardized arrest control course with quarterly qualification, proficiency testing, and certification. The course I designed covered all arrest control techniques ranging from those needed for the simplest misdemeanor used to persuade the perpetrator to "come along" to those required for complex felony arrest situations. The latter are the highly volatile situations in which a gun might be pointed at someone's head and the "bad guy" would need to be immobilized face down on the ground. Since statistics show that most law enforcement officers get killed by someone taking away their own gun in scuffles gone bad, one of my challenges was to learn how to adapt the martial art of *Aikido* to law enforcement applications where handcuffs, nightsticks, mace, and guns are involved that can, and do, get taken away and used against the "good guy."

Fortunately, I was well prepared. One of my previous *Aikido* teachers in Hawaii was Mr. Shinichi Suzuki who first exposed me to law enforcement/arrest control basics. Suzuki "Sensei" (meaning "teacher") was an Eighth Degree Black Belt (*Hachidan*) in the art of *Aikido*. He was one of the early students of Master Tohei when he first came to Hawaii in 1953. As a career law enforcement officer on the island of Maui, Hawaii, Suzuki Sensei was the first person to develop a program in which *Aikido* was an essential part of arrest control techniques. Even in his retirement, Suzuki Sensei continued to teach arrest control to the new Maui police cadets. And, listen to this... this was still when Suzuki Sensei was 90 years young!

In addition to this early exposure to arrest control when I lived and trained in Hawaii, I enrolled myself in a seminar with Mr. Robert Koga in California since he had also successfully adapted *Aikido* for use in law enforcement. By combining what I learned from Master Tohei, Suzuki Sensei, and Robert Koga, I was prepared to create an arrest control program compatible with Dick's vision of the "social trust contract" that would give officers "street effective" tactics for the wide variety of situations they would face. The final program included quarterly certification testing to ensure that each officer had acquired and retained proficiency and capability when executing each arrest control technique.

After designing this new arrest control program, I was ready to teach my peers (the three shifts of deputies of the Pitkin County Sheriff's Department) and to join them in active police work. Not only had I created arrest control training in alignment with our social trust contract, but also I received traditional law enforcement training so that I could fulfill my duties as a regular law enforcement officer. With this training, I was now qualified to carry a .357 Magnum sidearm. We had to use large pistols in Pitkin County in case we needed to kill ("put out of its misery") large deer or elk that had been hit and injured by cars traveling on the highways of the upper Rocky Mountains. This was a frequent occurrence, especially for motorists driving at night in the upper elevations. We carried .357 and even .44 caliber sidearms because a bullet from a "big city" police revolver would simply bounce off the skull of an elk!

THE ART OF COMPASSION

"...I received traditional law enforcement training so that I could fulfill my duties as a regular law enforcement officer."

Aspen, 1980.

In addition to the State Law Enforcement Training and required Detention Officer Training (we also ran a jail in Pitkin County), I learned the police radio "10 Code" necessary to communicate with police dispatch and fellow officers using both our car and mobile hip-side radios. I was #78 using our police 10 code! "Aspen 78," I'd say. "Go ahead 78," said the dispatcher. "I'll be 10-8," I replied. I thought this was so cool and all I said was that I was on duty in my front-wheel drive Saab police car and moving out on patrol. I was the peaceful philosopher ready for my first bad guy and ready to put the social trust contract into engaged action!

I remembered stories that Master Tohei would tell me about his younger years when he would purposefully walk in dangerous sections of Tokyo late at night just to test his martial efficiency. I was young with a bit of the downhill ski racer still inside me. So naturally I thought, "Here was my chance to do the same as Master Tohei and put my training to the test in potentially dangerous situations." It took no time at all, however, for me to remember Master Tohei's real point when telling me these stories about his youth. "You must walk with calmness and inner peace," he would say. "You must experience '*ki o dasu*' (*ki* extending) directly, and you must allow your energy to flow naturally *('shizen ni')*," he would say, "by simply calming the waves of your conscious mind." Master Tohei would then add, "When you do this properly and deeply, others will not attack you."

People sense your inner calmness when you have a relaxed, natural, and purposeful walk. When this happens, you exude confidence as well as compassion. This essential lesson from *Aikido* was central, not only as part of my regular shift work as a Deputy Sheriff, but also as the focus of my classes in *Ki* Development, *Aikido*, and Arrest Control with my fellow deputies. Clearly, the deputies needed to learn to be calm, confident, and compassionate under stressful conditions as well as be martially effective when the police work got nasty.

My teaching schedule included three shifts of deputies. First shift deputies received arrest control training from 3:30 p.m. to 5:00 p.m. at the end of their day shift; second shift deputies trained from 5:00 pm. to 6:30 p.m. before their evening shift; and graveyard shift deputies trained from 6:30 a.m. to 8:00 a.m. at the conclusion of their night patrols (they rotated to allow patrol coverage during training). In addition to teaching each of the sessions above, I worked a regular patrol shift that would start each evening after our second shift training class. Accordingly, from 6:30 p.m. to 12:00 p.m. each night, I served as a regular Deputy Sheriff. I later learned that this schedule was specifically designed for me by Pitkin County Undersheriff Don Davis because he wanted me to be on duty when it was more likely that the bad, nasty stuff happened in the evening hours leading up to midnight.

Now, with this band of merry men and women called the "peacemakers" of the Pitkin County Sheriff's Department, someone needed to know how to make us real police men and women. Dick Kienast surely could not do this as he was an academic, a "Great Books" humanitarian, a philosopher, a politician, and a teacher from Notre Dame and St. Mary's College. In short, Dick was known affectionately as "The Dove" because of his commitment to genuine "peacekeeping." Dick attracted high-minded idealists and he surrounded himself with like-minded people eager "to make a difference" in society. The real career policeman whom we all looked up to (and feared) was Don Davis, the so-called "Undersheriff" from Las Cruces, New Mexico. Don was about 6' 5" and a svelte 250 lbs. of rock solid muscle. He wore tight Levis and tight turtle neck shirts that highlighted the muscular bulges covering his body. Let's put it this way, only my father got away with calling me "Dave" (which I do not like – my name is "David" in case we meet) but Don actually got to call me "Davey." Don't ask me why he did this, but I was not going to correct my giant-sized police boss/mentor. His calling me "Davey" was actually a sign of affection that occurred immediately after our initial encounter where we really got to know and understand each other.

Have you wondered if you could pass a difficult test even though some people may not want you to succeed?

**Passing "The Test":
Deep Calmness and Conflict Resolution**

On the first day of our *Ki-Aikido* arrest control class, Don and I came to a certain understanding. Don's persona was to intimidate you and look down on you with his large physique. In addition, with all our diverse backgrounds, Don was the only deputy that actually knew how to be a real cop. Don knew that Sheriff Dick Kienast was my *Ki* Development and *Aikido* student at the Aspen-Snowmass Academy of Martial Arts. He also knew that Dick loved the "peaceful *Aikido* philosophy" and that Dick had hired me to teach arrest control as well as serve as a regular patrol deputy. Don, however, needed proof that all this "*Ki-Aikido* philosophy stuff" was a good idea in the *real world of street-effective law enforcement.*

On the first training day, I began teaching the most basic of all arrest control tactics – a wrist control technique called *sankyo*. Master Tohei first demonstrated this technique in 1953 when he considered ways to adapt *Aikido* to police work. This is a basic wristlock that can be secured from any position – it's that good. It is perfect when modified for use when handcuffing "bad guys" because you can control even a large person with just one hand leaving your other hand free to grab your handcuffs (usually worn behind your back on your belt). With a good *sankyo,* one hand holds the bad guy, the other hand secures your handcuffs from behind your back and, *voila,* you easily lock up the bad guy who is now completely immobilized in cuffs.

The dynamics of our first encounter were quite complex and involved a mixture of skepticism and resistance. Big Don, who was no dummy, was familiar with this *sankyo* wristlock technique already, and was preparing to resist me in the event that I tried to apply the technique on him. So, remember, Big Don knows this technique already and he is prepared to resist, *especially in front of all the other deputies,* so that he could feel secure in his position and in his personal identity using Don's own patented "macho power!" At the same time, Don's open resistance would enable him to pronounce his skepticism with respect to both *"peaceful Aikido"* and one *"peaceful philosopher"* turned cop (me, in particular). Add to all this one more dynamic—by testing me in front of other deputies, Don was also testing the judgment of his boss, *"the peaceful Sheriff"* (Dick "The Dove" Kienast), who wanted to hire me in the first place!

For my part, I was already prepared to expect resistance from people whose size alone made them intimidating. I had taken Master Tohei's *ukemi* (meaning I was the person being thrown by him) for years and years in the 1970s during the large public demonstrations he gave in Honolulu, Hawaii, up and down the West Coast, and in Japan. When he introduced and demonstrated the power of *Ki* principles, Master Tohei always chose the biggest, baddest looking guy in the audience. This was done by design because when the audience sees "the big guy" on stage being tossed around like a piece of paper, then they immediately become convinced of the power of *Ki* and Master Tohei's ability. The audience sees first hand the power of *Ki* (your life force) and they see Master Tohei demonstrating this power without using physical tension or physical strength. Instead, the audience witnesses Master Tohei's calm compassionate manner with his mind and body unified.

Following the lead of my teacher, I also choose the "big guy" (in this case, "Big Don") to demonstrate *sankyo* at the beginning of our first arrest control class. But, as I said, Don knew the wrist technique and was ready to apply his entire intimidating physique, persona (and then some) in order to show the first class of deputies how this little "Davey-boy" philosopher-type wasn't about to throw Big Don down to the ground, much less handcuff him as though he were as light as a piece of paper. So here we have a typical daily life conflict in the making! How do you show compassion in these daily life conflicts?

When you are deeply calm, you can easily sense where the person's energy is directed. In this case, it was obvious to me that Don was so intent upon me not applying this technique in one direction that I could easily move him in the opposite direction. Instead of applying the *sankyo* technique, I simply reversed it to another technique called *kote oroshi*, which moved in a completely different direction and used the powerful force of his single-minded resistance to my advantage. All I did was respect Don's power and moved with him (compassion) rather than against him (dissension). In the process of changing direction using the reverse *kote oroshi* technique, I used Don's own mighty power of resistance to throw him in a complete circle about three feet off the ground – like *a piece of paper*! Don landed flat on his back and looked stunned. This landing on the back scene lasted less than a nano-second because, at that precise moment, I simply lifted a little to help him bounce off the floor, a movement which had the immediate affect of flipping him over from his back to his stomach so that he was now face down on the floor. This time he was not bouncing. Instead, Big Don was effectively pinned face down with one arm raised like a "T" perpendicular to the floor, thus isolating his shoulder and immobilizing his entire body. At this point, I very politely instructed him to put his free hand behind his back and, *voila*, I proceeded to handcuff "the big guy" very nicely.

Don was shocked. Everyone knew the challenge of "the big guy" had been managed successfully, and the class was now most attentive and polite from that day forward. The process of using the biggest, strongest person in the class had the same effect as Master Tohei's public demonstrations using the biggest, strongest person in the audience. The most important message I demonstrated to the deputies on the occasion of Don's public challenge was that *if you are deeply calm and relaxed under stressful conditions,* even physically demanding conflict conditions, *then you can use the universal power that is always present at every moment.*

Don had joked previously that he didn't need *Aikido* training because he "already had a black belt." I asked him "In what martial art?" He replied *"Big Man Dō!"* After Don's quick fall and immobilization in handcuffs in front of the class, he stood up and humbly handed me the thick leather black belt (with a large Lone Star buckle) that he was wearing. Handing me his belt, he jokingly said, "I think I will try your style." From that moment on, we had great respect for each other and enjoyed our working relationship. I am very grateful for all the real world police lessons that Don taught me during my time as a Deputy Sheriff in Aspen, Colorado.

Have you ever wondered what it would be like to be threatened with a gun?

**The Power of Compassion:
Weapons, Hostages, and Violent Tempers**

Don and my Patrol Director, Bob Braudis, taught me how to be a cop, and I have great respect for them. I taught Don how to use his mind and his calmness so that he would understand that it is not necessary to throw around the weight of his powerful persona and intimidating physical stature. In this way, Don learned how he could use the power of compassion to resolve conflict instead of actually escalating the conflict and the felt separation between himself and others through his intimidating appearance. His real power was much more than physical might. Don and the other deputies learned that compassion and harmonizing with others in daily life was indeed a powerful tool that could be a most important resource in executing our shared vision of building "social trust."

I had many wonderful experiences as a law enforcement officer dealing with bad guys in bad situations. Experiencing these many difficult conflicts taught me that when you enter any situation, even violent ones, with compassion and calmness, you can move the Universe. That is, by trusting calmness and the depth of your own awareness, you can lead others even if they are very upset, angry, and physically violent.

Despite Don's *macho* persona, I must admit that I did feel grateful that he respected me and created many great learning opportunities for me. Perhaps this was appropriate since I was hired as one of the so-called martial arts "experts" in our group of Deputies. When a situation got really nasty, or potentially so, Don would call one of us martial arts types on the radio to assist, even if we were off duty at the time.

"—Davey, we have another little problem..."
Aspen, 1980.

As the Sheriff, Dick's 10 code radio number was "51" and Don's was "52" since he was officially the Undersheriff. [Don's official title sounds strange now that I think of it since Don at 6' 5" (in his cowboy boots) towered over Dick (in his preppy saddle shoes) who stood about 5' 9" or 5' 10"]. Anyway, Don

THE ART OF COMPASSION

would call me on the radio by saying, "Aspen 78, this is 52, go to Ajax." "Ajax" meant to change the frequency on the radio to one that was off the record in terms of not sharing the conversation with everyone going through police dispatch where all radio communication was tape-recorded. When he said, "78 go to Ajax," it always meant that he wanted to speak off the record and that always meant the same bad stuff – bad guys, nasty situations, and potentially violent encounters. So I'd switch to the Ajax frequency and say, "This is 78. Go ahead 52." Then Don would dispense with the 10-code police talk and say, "Davey, we have another little problem. Can you go to X, Y, or Z place and help fix it?" He always said the same thing. He just said, "Fix it." He never said HOW to "fix it"; he just said, "fix it!"

I learned "how to fix it" most often by observing a true professional law enforcement officer, Bob Braudis, who eventually served as Pitkin County Sheriff for twenty-five consecutive years. Bob is the embodiment of the maxim "Trust is a Social Good." To illustrate the power and effectiveness of the Art of Compassion, I will choose just one category of common law enforcement situations that need to be "fixed", as Don would say. Sheriff Bob Braudis also happens to be a very tall and large man. Sheriff Braudis was one of my teachers as he was a Patrol Director at the time I was a fledgling rookie Deputy. Bob always had a kind and gentle manner. In spite of his large physique, I never witnessed him raise his voice or express anger even in potentially violent situations. Whether it was a domestic fight, a kidnapping, a felony arrest, or a simple civil disturbance, Bob always seemed to lead the situation in the direction of sanity, non-violence, and calmness. In a hostage situation, for example, if police cars have lights blazing and if officers are using bullhorns to try to communicate with gun-toting, deranged kidnappers, then the energy of the volatile situation simply becomes too Rambo-like. However, with the calm, steady presence of Sheriff Braudis, I witnessed that everything could change. His mere presence would calm everything down—no bullhorns, no sirens, no flashing lights. Bob's focus in these situations would be to make the suspect (the bad guy) as well as potential victims less excited and more calm.

All Bob was doing in those times of crisis was getting the *Ki* (energy) of the entire setting to change. It may sound strange but, by taking the bullhorns, police cars, and flashing lights out of the picture, the entire conflict changes for all parties. When you change the mood or the energy of a situation, people feel differently – bad guys, hostages, and law enforcement officers alike all benefit when someone like Bob leads the energy of all parties in the direction of greater calmness.

This is no different than my theatrical example of the Furman University classroom when I purposefully created a tense atmosphere by pretending to be upset handing back the term papers. The point is that you can either escalate anxiety or you can reduce anxiety, conflict, and tension in your daily life by your *conscious action*. It's all up to you! Nothing is ever static in this ever-changing Universe. You simply cannot hide or be a neutral, passive observer. You cannot escape your role in the process of your life. No matter what you do, you are influencing (positively or negatively) every situation and every encounter of which you are a part. And here is the good news. You can always influence others positively by acting in accord with your own non-aggressive, compassionate heart/mind.

Dick, our Sheriff and leader, wanted to build "social trust" and we all believed in it. Therefore, these potentially violent situations were not a time to abandon everything we knew to be true about how compassion is key to building interpersonal trust. As a law enforcement officer, I have encountered violent situations by first introducing myself politely and then asking if I could be of assistance. I have purposefully entered situations unarmed and then, after a calm conversation, managed to verbally coach violent offenders into handing me their weapons. I have even politely asked if suspects would mind if I put handcuffs on them for their own safety. This is sometimes necessary when the people outside the arrest location, for example, police back-up and emergency responders, become pretty edgy and nervous themselves given the potentially violent situations. Misunderstandings and accidental shootings can be avoided if suspects of violent crimes can be coached into handcuffs BEFORE they come outside and into public view.

By having compassion for even violent assailants, I have known and could feel that sometimes basically good people do bad things under stress. When suspects of violent crime are clearly mentally and emotionally sick, disabled, or torn apart over a loved one, for example, then this is a time to remember our shared humanity. Sometimes, good people are simply depressed and despondent. In these situations, people act out exposing their greatest fear and anxiety. By relating to people in a way that addresses their fear and tension, it is possible to *change their mindset* first. Once this happens, the person's *behavior* can change completely, simply because you did not throw gasoline into the fire of the criminal's emotions. This process requires you to address apparent conflict and violence with compassion. The root cause (usually fear) of the suspect's violent temper and violent actions sometimes can be addressed quickly by simply not harming them (verbally, emotionally, or physically) and thus not treating them as your personal enemy.

By remaining completely calm, I have been able to help suspects to see that their current plan of action (with weapons and bloodied victims) would only make it more difficult for them in the future to see the light of day. However, by being coaxed to cooperate *now* and lower the level of excitement and violence, suspects can be encouraged to begin to turn their life around *now* and thus avoid even longer prison sentences.

I first witnessed Sheriff Bob Braudis' ability to talk calmly to suspects, and thus *change their state of mind*, simply because the suspect did not feel that Bob was eager to escalate the level of violence. Instead, at a conscious or subconscious level, the suspect sensed Bob's compassion and desire to simply put an end to the violent situation. Bob was able to change the suspect's consciousness *first*. And yet, changing the suspect's consciousness could only be achieved by a prior causal event; namely, Bob's own self-imposed mental and emotional clarity which started a process that, in turn, made the suspect feel more calm. Bob was able to extend a certain calmness that the violent suspect perceived as sincerity, friendship, and trust. Suspects instinctively feel this calm, large presence of Sheriff Braudis (even though the suspect's mind might be terribly clouded with nervous anxiety). Practicing the Art of Compassion in real life sometimes means cutting through conflict with the force of deep calmness and even spiritual connection. Compassion for one's fellow man begins (as Sheriff Dick Kienast would say) by realizing deeply that "Trust is a Social Good." All of this is ultimately related to a philosophy of, and commitment to, interpersonal connection.

The main point here is that in life you get what you give. When you unselfishly give others your compassion, affection, and love, they respond in kind. This works because of the constant exchange of energy that is your real Universe. If you want love in your relationships, then give love. If you want wealth, then serve others well giving them more than they ever expected. If you want to feel God's love, then look within yourself because it is there already and you can discover it when you learn *how* to look honestly and deeply within your true Self. Your true Self, as we have already seen, is the same as no-self, no-ego, and selflessness. Your true Self is not independent; it has no independent existence. Rather, your true Self is *interdependent* with the whole of the Universe. Not only are you not alone, you are surrounded by a world that is also an integral part of your Being. And so, you have within yourself the seeds of feeling love, affection, and compassion for all living things. All this is yours for the asking. Just learn to look deeply within and you will discover that you are the Universe and the Universe is YOU.

Have you ever wondered what it would be like to feel deeply connected to everything around you?

You Are the Universe and the Universe Is You

Any conflict in your life is thus an opportunity for you to creatively manifest new and unforeseen options that will enable you to greet your world each day with loving compassion. When this happens, your spiritual life, your interpersonal relationships, and even your overall well-being will change because the Universe and YOU are One. You will be giving and receiving energy (*Ki*) in a manner that is harmonious with the principles of the Universe. In every relationship, there is a natural rhythm of giving and receiving. To unnecessarily cause or intend separation and false influence upon others is to upset the natural rhythm of the Universe. This is due to the fact that the power you access in the Universe is really not "your power" at all. The power you access through trust, calmness, connection and compassion is a much, much greater force than you can manufacture through your own willpower. When you exert your own will and selfishly try to get what you want without regard to others or the Universe, then you actually cut your Self off from this wellspring of great power. The Universe gives you miracles everyday. To receive them, all you must do is become *awake* to this reality and merely acknowledge and accept these daily miracles in a most positive and grateful manner.

My teacher, Master Tohei, has written a poem that expresses this beautifully. The poem is carved into a block of wood at the *Tenshingosho dojo* at the *Ki-Aikido* headquarters in Japan. It reads:

Shinpo Uchurei Kanno Soku Genjo

The poem can be translated many ways. Its general meaning, or feeling, is that *you receive what you give to the Universe.* A more literal translation may help us to see the depth of this teaching.

Let's look first at what the individual words mean:

Shinpo – Blessed, Respectful

Uchurei – Universal Spirit

Kanno – Feeling, Reply

Soku

Genjo – to be present, to be in the "Now"

So what about the word '*soku?*' '*Soku*' is a word like the conjunction 'and' that does not refer to anything in particular. Rather, the word 'and' simply joins two words, phrases, or clauses in a particular way. In a sense, the word 'and' does not mean anything, it simply indicates how the speaker or writer is relating one thing to another. Similarly, '*soku*' indicates that a specific relationship holds between what precedes it and what follows it. '*Soku*' means that whatever words come before it and whatever words come after it in the sentence *mutually interpenetrate*. That is, '*soku*' means that the things or concepts before and after it are one and the same; they mutually interpenetrate into One seamless reality. We can say that the poem begins by asking us to have great respect for the Universe. It starts – Shinpo Uchurei ("Blessed Universal Spirit...") and then we can say, *Soku* ("immediately, in this very moment") [I can] *Kanno* "feel" [your] *Genjo* "presence." So, in this very moment, you and the *Ki* of the Universe are One. In sum, we can translate it this way:

"Blessed Universal Spirit
at this very moment
I feel your presence."

In reality, your true Self and the Universe are One – indistinguishable, no boundaries, no limits, and only infinite possibility. When your life force is attuned, when it is fully activated, and when you are most calm and aware, then you can experience this "mutual interpenetration" and know that you are indeed One with the Universe. Your life will be transformed and the Art of Compassion will be yours to *practice in service to others*. The quiet confidence and humility you experience will create a change in those around you. Since your intention is pure, not arising from a selfish mind (Jp. *shoga*), you naturally operate out of a Universal Mind (Jp. *Taiga*). The contrast between desires, thoughts, and actions that arise from a selfish mind and those that arise from a Universal Mind is expressed by the Japanese words '*shoga*' and '*Taiga*.' When you think and act with a selfish mind, or '*shoga*,' others are likely to resist you and complain. However, when you think and act out of a Universal Mind, or '*Taiga*,' then others around you will gladly follow your lead because they unconsciously sense that the lead is really coming from the Universe. Master Tohei captures this sense of having a Universal Mind in one of his beautiful **Ki Sayings**: *"You will feel that you are the Universe and the Universe is you. It will lead you to the supreme ecstasy of being One with the Universe."*

When you feel (in this very moment) that you are the Universe and the Universe is You, you also discover that what you receive from the Universe is precisely that which you give to others.

Shinpo Uchurei Kanno Soku Genjo

The Art of Compassion practiced in service to others is thus the second step on your journey toward wholeness occasioned by genuine spiritual and interpersonal transformation. Please practice the following second set of exercises that will help you to feel deeply connected to all things and all persons in your daily life.

Daily Exercises
to Facilitate The Art of Compassion

Have you ever wondered what it would be like to communicate without words?

Exercise 4:
Can You Feel the Energy of the Universe?

Now you expand upon Exercise 3 and move to the next stage, focusing on "awareness of others." Here you are cultivating another foundation piece to be built upon as the transformation process continues. You are learning to "notice in detail" all things around you. You are setting the stage for later development by learning to extend your mind without judgment.

In this chapter, I have spoken of the constant exchange of energy that sustains your life and influences your relationships at *every* moment. Learning to feel this "presence", this *Ki* of the Universe, Spirit, or God (used interchangeably) is only a matter of cultivating your mind, your emotions, and your total consciousness into ever-deeper states of awareness. In later chapters, I will discuss specific types of meditation, breathing, and relaxation exercises in order to help you experience this more deeply for yourself. For now, however, while still at the early stages of our Seven Arts process, you must begin to practice *daily* the Art of Compassion. Compassion requires sensitivity to the position, feelings, and situational context of other persons with whom you are exchanging energy.

Each day practice observing the dynamic changes of energy between two or more people. This can be experienced by calming yourself deeply such that you can *feel* the words, intonation, and body language used in the various exchanges.

Observe how different people react differently to the same thing during the course of the exchange. Observing human relationships deeply from a position of deep calmness and serenity can teach you much about the interactions of others. By being mindful of these interactions of others, you will *consciously* become more aware of your own reactions to others as well as ways in which you influence the world around you. Again, you cannot begin positive transformations in yourself or in others if you are not yet aware (and therefore do not yet understand) how the actions, emotions, and conscious states of one person affect others. Therefore, this exercise is focused upon cultivating your awareness of individuals as well as the overall context of human interactions/relationships.

Observing the *Ki* (energy) exchange between people in your daily life will cause you to focus your attention upon your own inner states of consciousness as well as ways of acting and being with others. When practicing this exercise, people begin to notice how they sometimes treat complete strangers with more respect than their own spouse or family members. Many people unconsciously take things for granted at home simply because they lose their own perspective of "freshness." You unconsciously assume that your home life or work life is not "fresh" – it has become boring to you and you begin to complete (usually incorrectly) the sentences of your loved ones. This is a form of discounting or judging people as well as your environment. When you discount the value of those around you and judge that they do not need or deserve your full attention, you fail to practice compassion at a fundamental level.

The root cause of your discounting others and your environment is your lack of sincere, fresh, and present awareness. You tend to judge others too quickly, you take others for granted, and you lose interest, focusing instead upon your own ego, your own agenda, your selfish mind.

You lose sensitivity, you lose awareness, and you lose your ability to calm yourself in the present moment. Instead, you work to impress the external world. You operate out of fear and the need for approval. As a consequence, you do not give your best effort in manner, appearance, and deed to those loved ones closest to you. In effect, people can learn through this exercise to extend energetically the same care, awareness, concern, and compassion to their own family as they do toward complete strangers. With this exercise, you will be learning to create the highest sensitivity within yourself such that you will be promoting love and compassion for all living things.

Your numbness toward others, or discounting others, or judging others is what causes within you a lack of compassion, yet *compassion and connection with others is your original and natural state of Being*. The mental conditions of numbness, discounting, and judgment are really caused by habits of conscious intentionality. These habits are caused by the history of your conscious life as being dis-connected from others and your environment. In addition, habits of conscious intentionality may be due to the presence of (perhaps deep) emotional baggage from your past that has been habitually repressed. You lose spontaneity and freshness in your daily life when discounting, numbness, and judgment occupy your mind. Your home life and work life become boring. The problem, however, is likely YOU, your ego, your selfish mind, and your conscious projections. Being unselfish is the same as becoming compassionate. To be compassionate, you must first see, feel, presence, and understand the ways others truly are, instead of seeing others through the "filter" or "intentional box" that your consciousness has created for them.

Let's review. This exercise will help you to *view* others, and then yourself, in a mirror-like, more authentic, less intentional light. Every day observe silently as many interpersonal interactions as possible. Do not participate. Just observe quietly from a position of deep calmness. At home, at work, and at play, there are many chances during the day to see and observe the energy exchanges affecting human interaction. After your observations, record them in your Seven Arts Journal.

By learning to observe closely, you will develop a natural sensitivity toward others. This is practicing simple awareness without conscious projection on your part. Practicing in this way will naturally make you more aware of your own patterns of interpersonal interaction in your daily life. When there is a lack of awareness of your own interpersonal patterns, there is ignorance. When there is ignorance, there is self-deception and blindness. And when there is personal and interpersonal blindness, there is separation. Finally, *when there is separation, there can be no connection and, without connection, there can be no compassion.*

True compassion must emanate first from compassion toward yourself. If your own self-talk or self conversation (that internal voice you hear when you think, reflect, and introspect) is deluded, or not honest, or downright negative, then *you* are causing separation and weakening your capacity for connection and thus compassion. The real transformation begins when you become *aware* of these negative intentional patterns in your conscious life. From this awareness of your own internal states of consciousness comes liberation, freedom, spontaneity, freshness, joy, and the ability to see your surroundings and your loved ones as a gift from God, Spirit, and the Universe. Enjoy this practice as the first step in the Art of Compassion.

Compassion for others occurs naturally when you understand and experience deeply that you are loved and embraced by the Universe to which you are connected and are an integral part. Such awareness leads to the third Art of Responsibility. As an integral part of the Universe, you are constantly influencing the direction of all *causal* forces in many realms - mental, physical, emotional, and spiritual. We will examine these interrelationships in detail in the next chapter.

Have you ever wondered what it would be like to give people your undivided attention?

Exercise 5:
Practice Compassion Through Mindful Attention

Now you are prepared to go deeper. This practice focuses on "noticing 100%." You are practicing in daily life how to give your "full attention to others."

Technology has provided us with many conveniences and ways to save time. The computer revolution has allowed us to communicate immediately with each other. All of this is good. However, as with all things, it does not seem to be enough. Oftentimes we trade our attention to the person right in front of us for the seeming glory of "multi-tasking." Exercise 5 is an experiential exercise that asks that you treat everyone that you encounter as a joyous and unique gift. A fundamental principle of the Art of Compassion is simply to be *mindful in the present moment*. A starting point for deep mindfulness is the simple practice of giving your undivided and sincere attention to others. Look at people when you speak and listen. Avoid multi-tasking when engaging people because, in the process, you tend to ignore, discount, or prematurely judge your fellow man.

By practicing *daily* these two simple exercises of compassion, in combination with the Art of Preparation exercises learned at the conclusion of Chapter One, you will be planting seeds, tilling the soil, and providing sunlight on your journey toward positive personal transformation.

In your Seven Arts Journal, explore the reaction that you receive from people when you give them your undivided attention and mindfulness. What was their response? How did you feel about them as you encountered each person? What did you learn from your encounters?

3

THE ART OF RESPONSIBILITY

> *"Two things fill the mind*
> *with ever new and increasing*
> *admiration and awe,*
> *the oftener and more steadily*
> *we reflect on them:*
> *the starry heavens above me*
> *and the moral law within me."*
>
> Immanuel Kant (1724-1804)
> **Critique of Practical Reason**

In the last chapter, we observed that the Universe is in a constant state of flux; everything is impermanent. The *Ki* of the Universe and your life force are flowing constantly through you as energy is exchanged. When you are tense, filled with anxiety, and judge others, you tend to cause separation and thus you feel weak and isolated from the world around you. In this state of being, there is no compassion. However, when you are calm, relaxed, and serene, you can see things clearly. Your compassion becomes a powerful positive force and you begin to see new options, new openings, new creativity, and new possibilities; in short, you are *"fresh"* and your environment gains your mindful attention. When you become attentive to your environment with an awareness of the positive ways in which you can serve, then you naturally respond to the world around you in ways that promote connection, compassion, and kindness in accord with the needs of others. Seeing your actions as *causal interactions* with the Universe leads to the next Art.

Have you ever wondered about the long term effects of actions taken today?

Free Will and Causation:
What You Sow, So Shall You Reap

Now we are prepared to learn a third Art. The Art of Responsibility arises naturally from knowledge of the Way of the Universe. The Universe is not only energy in flux; it also functions *causally*. The law guiding the universal rhythm is that there are no real accidents. The Buddha refers to this principle as his central doctrine of causation or more accurately: 1) the doctrine of "dependent origination" (Pali; *Paticcasamppāda*), and 2) the view that all things are "causally conditioned phenomena" (Pali; *Paticcasamuppanna dhamma*). This doctrine of causation means that for every effect, or event, or result (that is, for everything that occurs in the Universe) there are multiple causes that *in combination* lead to that singular effect, event, or result.

This process is not limited to only the material, physical world of nature. The arising and passing away of *all* things, including physical/material phenomena, moral phenomena, conscious phenomena, social phenomena, psychic phenomena, and even the process of reincarnation, are *causally conditioned phenomena*. Within this causal framework, your consciousness that initiates and leads all of your actions is but *one* of the causal influences contributing to any outcome or effect. And, it is always important to remember that your consciousness is indeed *one* of the causal factors influencing anything that occurs in your life. So, while you are truly free (that is, you have genuine *free will*) to influence the Universe through your consciousness and purposeful actions, *some of your life* outcomes, or results, or effects may have arisen (and thus occurred) due to causal forces beyond your immediate control. In Buddhist thought, the law that governs how events are shaped both by conscious and unconscious forces is called the law of karma. The causal law of karma (which is an integral part of this universal process) is always "measured"; that is, it functions in direct proportion to your *intentional* consciousness.

The law of karma is measured in accord with your entire consciousness. Your consciousness obviously includes your current conscious awareness of your environment, body, perceptions, feelings, desires, and the motives and intentions that are the basis of your actions.

Your consciousness also includes subconscious and unconscious motives and intentions that influence your action. All of your experiences and perceptions contribute and, when combined, form your entire consciousness. Although you may not be thinking currently about the conversation that you had with a friend yesterday, it is stored in your consciousness and can readily be recalled from memory. Such memories may act as subconscious motivation for action. When someone asks what you would like for lunch and you mention that Japanese food sounds good, you may at that point realize that yesterday you had been talking with your friend about some excellent Japanese food you had two weeks ago. Though you were not currently thinking about this conversation, it nevertheless was just beneath the surface of consciousness and influenced your decision to suggest getting Japanese food for lunch.

Unconscious motivations and intentions lie much deeper beneath the surface of your waking consciousness. They are not readily or easily called to mind, but still may influence your actions. Sometimes, in athletic competition or in work contexts, people do less than others. And, many who are honest with themselves will readily admit that they know that they are capable of much more. Such persons seem to have a fear of success and so this hidden trait hinders their actions unknowingly. While they may be aware that they are not giving their best, they are not able to say exactly what it is that stands in the way and is holding them back. At some unconscious level, there are motivations and intentions that are responsible for the way the person acts. Both subconscious and unconscious motivations and intentions may be reckless, defiled, or based upon ignorance. They may be based upon attachments to things, events, or psychic needs that ultimately cause harmful outcomes to your true Self.

Remember that your true Self is not a separate self. Since you are not separate, what you do has consequences whether you intend them or not. In short, the causal principles that guide the movement and function of the energy of the Universe operate in a manner consistent with the meaning of the old maxim, *"What you sow, so shall you reap."* There are thus causal consequences for which your divine Self (which is the same as no-self, no-ego) is *responsible*. Your every free action causes inescapable and necessarily interlinked effects upon the whole Universe. You and your actions are thus an integral part of the movement of the Universe. You are not separate and thus YOU are responsible. Since you are not independent of the Universe, you are necessarily bound (causally and karmically) by the universal laws that sustain your existence as well as the existence of all things. In other words, you are not only *in* the Universal Soup, you *are* the Soup.

This realization may seem like a heavy burden to bear. However, this same realization also can be the occasion to take real responsibility for yourself in this Universe. By understanding deeply the real karmic conditions and consequences that cause your consciousness to be continually unclear, you will also come to realize that you are infinitely free to change your consciousness, even deep consciousness, with mindful training over time.

Your choices are truly free. You do not have free will in the sense of acting wholly independently of everything around you or acting in a way in which you do not have to "pay" for the consequences of your actions. You do have "free will" in the sense that you are free to exercise your own volition as part of this universal causal process. Your choices also are codetermined by *all of* your mental motives – conscious, subconscious, and even unconscious. Since all levels of consciousness figure into your action, you must *take responsibility* for your whole conscious life. This whole includes thoughts, defilements, opinions, judgments, motives, desires, intentions, etc., and it is your entire consciousness that is connected *causally* to the entire Universe.

As the French philosopher René Descartes noted, the dilemma of the human condition is that we are infinitely free; however, at the same time, we have limited (not infinite) intelligence. In other words, the human predicament boils down to the fact that we are truly free, but we are too dumb to know exactly what to do for our own good and the good of others. We do not always make good, well-informed decisions. In order to know exactly what to do, we would need to know all of the consequences of a proposed action, but these consequences are infinite in number. It would thus require infinite intelligence to understand all causes and all the long-term causal consequences of our actions. *We do not have infinite intelligence,* however, *to go along with our infinite freedom.* To make matters worse, we cannot escape *(causally)* our responsibility as participants in this Universe – we will necessarily and without fail eventually reap the effects (even unintended effects) of our *choices.* These *choices* are the combined result of: *1)* our conscious intentions, 2) our subconscious motivations, 3) our unconscious desires, and 4) the influential causal effects of all of our past choices and actions that already have influenced the entire course of our personal life as well as the course of the Universe Itself.

To summarize, the equation goes like this: You are infinitely free to make choices; however, you have limited knowledge and intelligence to make the best choices. In addition, your consciousness may be significantly clouded by unwanted motivations and desires, making the best choices even more difficult. It is also the case that there are no real accidents (no uncaused effects) in the Universe. Therefore, you are bound by, and responsible for, the causal effects of all your choices and actions including those that may be based upon limited knowledge and subconscious motivations. This means that all of your choices and all of your actions are causally interconnected and causally conditioned; hence, *you are ultimately responsible for all your actions and all the levels of your consciousness, including your subconscious motivations and your unconscious desires.*

> *Have you ever wondered if you can ever really change?*

You Are Free:
You Can Change Your Subconscious and Unconscious Mind

Over time your consciousness (for which you are completely responsible) becomes filled with memories. It also becomes "habituated" causing you to see things and affairs as filtered by defiled conscious intentions as well as your subconscious and unconscious desires, motivations, and projections. Your habits of judgment and emotional reactions to others are all products of your conscious life, including the history of your causal conditioning and conscious interactions with the world around you. *Over time your subconscious mind is thus created and is continually fed by, and is therefore a product of, your conscious mind.* Since your conscious mind has developed as a result of your past and present conscious influences, you are karmically responsible for your entire conscious life, including your subconscious mind and unconscious mind. In short, your subconscious and unconscious minds have developed as *receptacles* of your conscious mind over your entire lifetime. The good news is that your *present* consciousness is free to change direction. You can cleanse yourself and create new conscious habits over time and thus "purify," as it were, your subconscious and unconscious mind.

We will learn in the fourth Art of Relaxation that deep meditation is a vehicle to clarify and purify your subconscious and unconscious states and thus *you can know that you have both the power and the ability to cleanse* **all** *levels of your consciousness.* When this sort of purification occurs, true transformation takes place. The key point to realize is that we are not only *of the Universe,* a lesson learned by the Art of Compassion, but also we have a role *in creating the Universe* for which all human beings are collectively responsible. The Art of Responsibility focuses upon understanding this relationship to the Universe and using this understanding to transform the Self.

Have you ever wondered why you "get what you need"?

The Seven Stages of Spiritual Development are Sequential and Need Based

This third level of spiritual development embodied in the Art of Responsibility is critically important. In many respects, this is the most important "Art" because it is really this "Art" that *fuels* and *feeds* the deeper levels of understanding and conscious transformation. The Seven Arts are really *stages* of development. Each successive Art (One through Seven) represents a deeper transformational stage on the journey. Since each stage prepares for and leads to the next, *it is impossible to skip stages of spiritual development, emotional development, and consciousness development.*

Another way to see the relationship between the Arts is to understand how each Art or each stage satisfies a *need.* Fulfilling that need is a precursor to going deeper with mindful understanding of the transformation process. In addition, once some learning takes place within an Art (and you notice a positive change in your consciousness and your Being), then unfortunately there is a strong temptation to become "attached" to the new learning and growth achieved that is relevant to each stage of development. Therefore, it is necessary to "let go" and free yourself of this newly acquired attachment so that you can comprehend new, deeper *"needs"* that will fuel and feed further growth and development. To "let go" of a stage is not simply to leave it behind, but to resist the temptation to see it as the end of the process. It fulfills a need, but it also enables you to see, perhaps for the first time, new needs and possibilities that serve as a critical part of the transformation process. The newly revealed "needs" become the "fuel" that feeds deeper and deeper levels of development and transformation.

Each developmental stage and each Art is one in which you must enter fully and precisely because you see, understand, and deeply comprehend a *"need"* for yourself. For example, the *honest self-talk* you learned in the Art of Preparation informs you to engage in daily practice. Once you begin to master the initial, daily exercises, then you *realize for yourself* (Jp. *ki ga tsuku*) that you must keep going deeper and deeper into the transformation process. That is, you must be clear enough and humble enough to see that the positive transformation you seek is still incomplete. This continually deepening awareness leads to a new set of previously unrealized *"needs."*

As these new, deeper needs begin to express themselves more clearly in your consciousness, you must learn to understand them and embrace them with a new, deeper, and commensurate level of authenticity and awareness. This new depth of awareness would be impossible to achieve without experiencing the previous foundational stages of sequenced development. Just as a tall building must be built upon a solid foundation, so your own tower of transformation must be based upon a solid foundation. Each prior Art provides the necessary foundation for the next Arts, and each subsequent Art builds upon the former Arts.

So now we are beginning to discuss the real work of emotional development, consciousness development, and spiritual development. This type of progressive spiritual development is illustrated beautifully in the classic Indian text, **The Bhagavad-Gita**. In this work, the protagonist Arjuna moves through four main stages of spiritual growth and development. Each stage necessarily builds upon the other stages. Knowledge (Sk. *jnana*), action (Sk. *karma*), devotion (Sk. *bhakti*) and duty (Sk. *dharma*) are all at work and occur in different combinations in *each* of the four main stages that facilitate ever-deeper levels of consciousness, awareness, and understanding. Each stage of Arjuna's spiritual development serves as a necessary prerequisite to subsequent stages. Each stage represents more clarity and deeper understanding.

The Seven Arts process of self-discovery is constructed similarly. Remember, you cannot skip stages, levels, or Arts that are all a part of the sequential transformation process. Each Art responds to a need and each need, once fulfilled, opens the gate for new needs to appear with greater clarity. Therefore, new Arts are *experienced* with greater clarity, *learned,* and then *performed* as they fulfill the *new needs sequentially.*

The third Art of Responsibility is the fuel for each successive stage of development because it teaches us to sacrifice and renounce (Sk. *yajna*) the fruits of our immediate desires, cravings, impulses, attachments, and actions. When you understand deeply that you, and no one else, are responsible for your own life, then you begin to stop blaming others for your life outcomes. It is true that your family, and specifically your parents, did exert a powerful influence upon your life, but *you are still free* to overcome whatever ill affects your early life experience may have imparted into your deep consciousness. And, yes, your genetics represent still another causal factor operating at the physical, material level that continuously influences the holistic you that you are at this very moment. Nevertheless, your choices about what goes into your current consciousness can exert a powerful influence to change your entire consciousness.

You must realize that you are still free to overcome the adverse effects of your personal history. It is possible for you to manifest the real you that you aim to BE. Your social and emotional past as well as your physical body and environment need not serve as a continual excuse for unpleasant or unsatisfactory conditions in your life. You must take responsibility for your entire Universe of lifetime possibilities. From the perspective of Buddhist thought, which asserts that our consciousness is formed partially by our past lives, we would say that you must even *take responsibility* for the past lives and past karmic dispositions (Sk. *sankharas*) that presently affect your consciousness in this world today.

Have you ever wondered if you are parenting well and preparing your children for life's most difficult challenges?

Eggaberth, the Mountain Goat:
Patience and Discipline

When the Art of Responsibility is understood *deeply*, you will begin to develop two critically important qualities that will serve as the powerful engine of your pilgrimage, your journey to positively transform your life. The two qualities that drive the process are: *patience and discipline.*

Patience and discipline are required in order *not* to see yourself as a victim of your deepest desires that often times lead either consciously or unconsciously to *dis-satisfaction* and suffering in your own life and in the lives of those around you. These deep desires can be changed over time but it requires patience and discipline. At some point, you must muster the sheer conscious strength *(discipline)* to act out of a new paradigm that will be your own creation along the journey. Actually, your new paradigm of consciousness will be in harmony with the universal paradigm that *is* synonymous with fulfillment of your true Self. This new paradigm or new "way of thinking" is really the work of the Universe Itself that happens *through* you. You must develop yourself enough to have conscious awareness of the movement of the Universe... to taste it, to gain a glimmer of it, to have some direct experience so that you understand that on the other side of your present suffering or unsatisfactory condition is a much, much better place. Once you have this conscious awareness, you must exercise patience and trust in yourself and in your connection to the higher powers, the Universe, so that you can exercise the discipline necessary to gain the strength and support you need to realize your full potential.

I have helped rear our five children with homegrown bedtime stories of my own making. I created some twenty-five years ago a series of stories that illustrate the two lifetime "tools" or "qualities" that I am describing to you now – patience and discipline. "Eggaberth, the Mountain Goat" is now a Shaner family character. Eggaberth, the Mountain Goat, has had many life adventures, all of which were shared at bedtime as stories of achievement in the face of adversity. In the first stories, Eggaberth was a Japanese mountain goat who lived on a farm with other barnyard animals. The problem was that Eggaberth was most *undisciplined* and he had *no patience*. He ate the farmer's crops, ate the other animals' food, and was continually bringing misery to himself and others through his own selfish actions. The farmer in my story decided Eggaberth needed positive self-transformation, so he sent Eggaberth to become an *uchi deshi* (that is, a "live-in student") with my own real-life teacher, Master Koichi Tohei.

The background material that I used to create the Eggaberth stories was my own experience as an *uchi deshi* serving Master Tohei. Since I was a foreigner (Jp. *Gaijin*), the opportunity to live with my teacher was a most rare opportunity because it was reserved for native Japanese *Aikido* students seeking to become professional instructors. In my case, Mr. Takashi Nonaka from Hilo, Hawaii, who was an island Chief Instructor, the President of the Hawaii Ki Society, and a personal friend of Master Tohei, smoothed the way for me to have this unique opportunity to serve as Master Tohei's *otomo* (personal assistant) in Japan. Otomo training is part of the regimen of an *uchi deshi* that focuses especially on the cultivation of awareness, patience, and discipline. In my opinion, the outcome of this special training is the *cultivation of awareness, patience, and discipline*. These three qualities are the "fuel" for personal and spiritual development. And so, the core of *otomo* training is the practice of selflessness, serving others while emptying yourself.

Let us pull all this together and understand how these three qualities will help you to sacrifice and renounce the fruits of each stage of your spiritual growth. Without the patience and discipline to renounce, to become unattached to your spiritual and interpersonal progress, you will not advance to ever-deeper levels of awareness, knowledge, understanding and consciousness development. You cannot underestimate the importance of these three qualities. It is obviously the reason why I wanted to share these qualities with my children (through Eggaberth bedtime stories) at a very early age.

"Eggaberth, the Mountain Goat" passed his *uchi deshi* training in our bedtime stories. He learned awareness, patience, and discipline and then he used these qualities to overcome any adversity, any challenge, and thus became the hero of our bedtime stories ever after. Eggaberth has been the hero of adventures in space, under the sea, in the jungle, and traveling through time with dinosaurs – you name it, "Eggaberth, the Mountain Goat" has done it using the three qualities of awareness, patience, and discipline. With patience and discipline (and conscious awareness), you can accomplish anything. With patience and discipline in your toolkit, you will have the strength to positively transform your life in service to others.

Have you ever wondered if you can ever really be selfless?

Otomo Training:
The Art of Awareness and Selflessness

Uchi deshi training is a helpful model for understanding how the Art of Responsibility enables you to sacrifice and renounce the fruits of your immediate desires and thereby understand more deeply that you and no one else is responsible for your own life. So what exactly is the purpose of *uchi deshi* (live-in student) training? What is *otomo* training? How are patience and discipline truly cultivated in daily life?

"During the late 1970s when I lived at headquarters, there were seven uchi deshi (including myself) of which only three are now actively teaching and training with Master Tohei."

The gala dinner, arranged in commemoration of the author's arrival as uchi-deshi in the old Haramachi HQ in Shinjuku, Tokyo. 1979. From left to right: Shimatani sensei, Koiso sensei, Otsuka sensei, Osaki sensei and author. Behind—Master Tohei's son, Shinichi.

In short, Master Tohei created a monastic environment for special students (*uchi deshi*) whereby their entire life would be *sacrificed* (Sk. *yajna*) so that they could immerse themselves in a monastic-type training environment twenty-four hours a day. *You sacrifice your freedom, you sacrifice your needs, you sacrifice your ego, and you begin to practice "selflessness" by serving others.* As an *uchi deshi*, you live at the headquarters *dojo* (training hall) with Master Tohei. During the late 1970s when I lived at headquarters, there were seven *uchi deshi* (including myself) of which only three are now actively teaching and training with Master Tohei. The seven of us slept on the floor and lived in one room above the *dojo*; it is very difficult training to say the least. There was Morishima *sensei* ("*Sensei*" is an honorific term meaning "teacher," or literally, "one step ahead."), Koiso *sensei*, Shimatani *sensei*, Oshima *sensei*, Osaki *sensei*, Otsuka *sensei*, and myself. Otsuka *sensei*, who was in charge of us *deshi*, is now 9th dan (Ninth Degree Black Belt) and senior instructor at the *Ki-Aikido* Headquarters near Utsunomiya in Tochigi Prefecture, Japan. Osaki *sensei* is the second person still training. He also resides in Japan and is teaching *Ki-Aikido* professionally and positively leading his many students. I am the third survivor of this group and presently serve the International Ki Society (*Ki no Kenkyukai*) as the Chief Instructor of the Eastern Ki Federation in the United States, and as Japan Headquarters' Advisor to the Eastern Europe/Russia Ki-Aikido Federation. I have taught *Ki-Aikido* annually in Russia since 1999.

*Have you ever wondered
why you seem to be late when it matters most?*

**Be an Invisible Mirror:
Move Quickly on the Letter "N" of the Word "Now"**

Everyday and at every moment the life of the *uchi deshi* could be turned upside down. We already had sacrificed our freedom upon admission into this twenty-four hour a day monastic environment, and thus we had office duties, cleaning duties, special training classes to attend, as well as classes that we were responsible for teaching. However, the point of "selflessness" service training was that we were to be completely unattached to any selfish motivation, completely available to serve others, and always prepared to change our direction, our anticipated schedule, and our responsibilities at any given moment. If Otsuka sensei or Master Tohei said the plan of the day is changing, then you had better be quick to adjust immediately. We were taught to move on the first letter *"I"* of the Japanese word *"Ima"* which means *"Now."*

In order to do this, your mind must be both calm and extended *(awareness)* so that you are ready to adapt to new conditions and thus change direction as early as the pronunciation (in the English wording) of the letter "N" in the word "Now." Anything less than this swift mental action would mean that your mind, your consciousness was LATE! This is the same mental preparation (Art of Preparation) or life force (*Ki*) extension that is required in performing effectively the martial art of *Aikido*. The aim is to be so calm and *aware* that your mind is like a mirror and so you can react very quickly as if your opponent/attacker is actually moving in slow motion.

"Early each day someone would be assigned as Master Tohei's otomo. The training is to assist him in whatever he is doing, wherever he is going..."

Author helps Master Tohei to attach microphone before appearance.

Otomo training is a real gift for learning patience and discipline. Your role as *otomo* is simply to *anticipate* the needs of the person you are attending and serving. In order to anticipate these needs effectively you must have the patience necessary to allow this person's actions to direct your responses and the discipline necessary to put your own needs and desires into *their* service. In this case, that person being served was Master Tohei himself. Early each day someone would be assigned as Master Tohei's *otomo*. The training is to assist him in whatever he is doing, wherever he is going (you travel with him), and to do so without calling attention to yourself. *Your aim is to be invisible in your selflessness.* This type of training is exhausting to your consciousness as you must pay attention constantly to every interaction and every nuance; however, you must do so without staring and without making Master Tohei or those around him feel uncomfortable. Your *otomo* duties include everything from taking Master Tohei's *ukemi* (that is, being thrown as his *Ki* and *Aikido* demonstration partner when he teaches), to driving his car as chauffeur, to pouring tea when visitors arrive for meetings, to preparing, packing and carrying his luggage, to helping him dress, to proactively, silently, and, preferably invisibly, attending to his every need. All this must be done early by *anticipating the need* and *performing the service* without being asked and without calling attention to yourself.

My favorite small, symbolic example of *otomo* awareness training is the need to watch Master Tohei's eyes. Suppose Master Tohei is sitting at his writing desk at the back end of the office (at the old Headquarters in Haramachi). A postal employee brings in the day's mail and sets it on the counter near the door. Master Tohei simply glances at the bundle of mail – he sends his *Ki* to the mail. This is his intention. If I am aware, I should (without being asked) attend immediately to the four things that I have learned already. These four things should be done in sequence, they should be performed smoothly, and the overall process should start moving invisibly on the "N" of the word "Now" (or, in this context, on the "I" of the Japanese word "*Ima*"). In order not to be "*late*," my four activities should begin precisely on the "I" of "*Ima*" as signaled only by the *visible* movement of Master Tohei's eyes and the more powerful movement of his *Ki* (life force).

The four activities are:

1. Swiftly, yet calmly, go and pick up the bundle of mail without calling attention to myself.

2. Go to the special drawer near Master Tohei's writing desk that contains his reading glasses.

3. Go to yet another desk that has another special drawer that contains the Master's favorite letter opener.

4. Collect all three and neatly place them in front of the Master. If you can figure out a way for all this to happen invisibly, then that course of action should always be preferred and executed seamlessly.

This sequence of activities is but one small example of selfless attention where the training focus is to give up ALL of my needs and instead exercise the patience and discipline necessary to serve others twenty-four hours a day. If Master Tohei had to *ask* me to collect these four things, or if I were *late*, or if I were too *visible* in my execution, then it would be the same as being scolded (which he did) for not being mindfully attentive. It would also mean "losing face" for not executing my duty at the high level that the Master requires and that I am supposed to be capable of performing as the

Master's personal assistant. The only way to manage this kind of twenty-four hour a day pressure to be so attentive is to *embrace serving others completely with deep calmness and mindfulness.*

The martial art application of this exercise in selfless service is to avoid being *late* in observing physical movement or *Ki* movement when someone is attacking you. If you do not *"feel"* their *Ki*, their mindful energy to attack you, then you are *late* in your ability to react and defend yourself. This type of twenty-four hour training has the cumulative affect of training you to *"see"* things simply through your extension of *Ki* (your life force which is the energy of the Universe) and not necessarily *"see"* through your physical eyes alone. You learn early to anticipate actions, attacks, strikes, events, and outcomes well before others by merely relying upon your cultivated sensitivity as developed through twenty-four hour a day *otomo* training.

In a martial setting, this has the affect of your attackers seeming to move in slow motion – you should never be *late*. In fact, you can develop your consciousness to *anticipate endlessly* and this is exactly the point of *serving others selflessly. Otomo* training is the Art of Selflessness. It is training related to the practice of the seventh Art, the Art of Service (which we will discuss in detail in Chapter Seven). Practicing selflessness toward others requires patience because the person that you serve controls the tempo of all action. Practicing selflessness toward others requires discipline because you learn to redirect your own needs and desires in service to others. Awareness is the result of serving others twenty-four hours a day using patience and discipline.

*Have you ever wondered
if you can change things at your core?*

Deep Down...You Know the Things You Need to Change: Redirection, Not Suppression

This last point is important. Many people think that to be selfless you must just "stop" or "suppress," or "repress" your desires completely. Because your mind and *Ki* are always moving, it is impossible to "stop" your mind, or completely "suppress," or "repress" your emotions; attempting to do this is a big mistake. Your conscious motivations and short-term desires are sometimes very powerful. Think of addictions of any kind. Think of substance abuse. Think of clouded priorities and the attraction of people or things that "you know" do not have your best interests at heart. Think of the power of subconscious motivations and unconscious desires stemming from years of repression due to your emotional and interpersonal history.

    To practice the Art of Responsibility you cannot simply suppress or repress to ever-deeper layers of consciousness the destructive habits that "you know" you possess and "you know" that you wish you had the power and the discipline to change. You have desires that you know you would like to control. You do things you know are wrong. You think things and do things you wish you could change. The best you can do is to first honestly acknowledge the existence of these destructive habits, desires, and attachments and, then, like an *Aikido* art in motion, *redirect your conscious energy* to alternative outcomes about which you can positively *take responsibility*.

At this point, we have come full circle in a discussion of the Art of Responsibility. Since we have discussed the causal process that is operative in all dimensions of the Universe, you are now deeply aware that *you cannot escape real karmic responsibility for your life.* You must develop your internal strength through training; you must discover your true potential and practice patience and discipline in your daily life in order to improve yourself in a step-by-step fashion. You must honestly acknowledge your defilements, latent desires, and unethical or immoral actions that you know are wrong. You must begin the process of transformation by acknowledging your past, all levels of your consciousness (even the unpleasant parts), and you must work positively each new day to transform your subconscious and unconscious mind. All this is made possible by exercising your freedom at the conscious level of your mind in each present moment – twenty-four hours a day.

No doubt the idea of exercising your freedom twenty-four hours a day may seem confusing. Let me illustrate again. When you dream, do you not notice how your dreams frequently reflect what you are dwelling upon and thinking about just before you go to bed? It is especially true if you are grappling with anxieties. You can probably relate to your school day experiences when you had the classic "test anxiety" dream the night before the exam and you had been "cramming" information into your brain for a full twenty-four or forty-eight hours just prior to the course final examination. When you dream, your subconscious mind takes over. And, your subconscious mind, as you can now see, is a receptacle that is fed daily (and literally is created at every waking moment) as a direct result of what your conscious, intentional, working, and active mind puts into it in daily life. *Your subconscious mind is both the receptacle and reservoir for your conscious mind* that dominates your attentive, daytime, waking states of being. You are thus responsible for the subconscious mind and unconscious mind that your conscious mind has fed and created over your entire lifetime. The good news is that you are free to change your conscious mind using patience and discipline and thus create anew the future receptacle and reservoir that is your subconscious and unconscious mind.

*Have you ever wondered if
you can really know your subconscious mind?*

**You Can Choose to Live Mindfully:
Take Responsibility for All Levels of Your Consciousness**

The truth of how our experiences influence and form the subconscious mind was convincingly brought home to me nearly forty years ago. In 1976, I had the misfortune of watching the movie, *The Omen. The Omen* was a dark, scary movie about the devil, including themes from the biblical *Book of Revelations* (666), etc. Certainly, one might expect to be scared going to a scary movie ... right? But, for me, this served as a significant turning point in my understanding of the way all of our experiences form our consciousness and how we can take control over the formation (and transformation) of our entire consciousness. One of Master Tohei's **Ki Sayings** (Jp. ***Shokushu)***, included in this small lessons handbook that he had written a few years earlier, helped me to see this clearly.

> **The Subconscious**
>
> The subconscious mind acts as a storehouse of knowledge and past experiences. The materials stored in the subconscious mind form the conscious mind.
>
> Henceforth, let us cease putting any minus materials into the subconscious. Let us always extend plus Ki and live our life with a positive attitude.
>
> —Koichi Tohei

The **Ki Saying** entitled "*The Subconscious*" describes the relationship between the conscious mind and subconscious mind and also prescribes the way to positively transform one's entire consciousness.

Here is what I realized in 1976. After actually paying money to go to a movie theater and *choosing* to expose my conscious mind to scary stuff (*The Omen*), and then actually experiencing nightmares repeatedly reminding me of the horrors occasioned by the receptacle of my subconscious mind (that followed as a *causal* consequence of my attending the movie), I decided to stop, as Master Tohei says, "putting any minus materials into my subconscious." What I did was to *take responsibility* for my subconscious mind by *choosing* (with my present conscious mind) NOT to go to see scary, violent, and otherwise negative movies again. I basically asked/told myself that "if I am for peacemaking, then why should I purposefully inject violence into my being through my present conscious choices and conscious actions?"

As a result of this experience and subsequent conscious choices and actions, I have not seen a violent or scary movie since 1976. I can choose to take responsibility for what goes into my subconscious mind by acting responsibly with my present conscious mind. Besides, I do watch the news, and there is enough real world violence and suffering in daily life and world affairs to more than fill my conscious mind with negative information. I wish this were not the case in the world today but at least you can know, and be empowered by the fact, that you are free to choose what you put into your subconscious mind.

You can choose to live mindfully and consider the deep affects of your conscious choices. You can choose how you wish to engage your present world by attending responsibly to your conscious mind. Once you choose to stop putting negative materials into your conscious mind, you cannot expect an immediate transformation. A glass of dirty water (like your mind) is not immediately purified by adding a few drops of clean water. Over time, however, the cumulative daily effect of adding clean water drop-by-drop gradually becomes noticeable and eventually the water does become clear. Patience and discipline are required to affect the same sort of changes in your mind/consciousness, especially at the early stages in which no obvious change may be noticeable. Patience and discipline are both keys to spiritual progress because you can use them to learn how to take responsibility for your whole Self, including the whole of your consciousness.

Each successive stage (of the Seven Arts) requires patience and discipline to fully execute the lessons learned. There are no "quick fixes" – personal development and spiritual development require attention; it is work but it can be pure joy once you can apply patience and discipline in your pursuit of a higher calling. Habits of the heart and mind need to be confronted honestly. These habits may have a tenacious grip upon all the levels of your consciousness including your conscious mind, subconscious mind, and unconscious mind. However, by embracing patience and discipline as your friend and ally, you will succeed in your effort to positively transform yourself to become your highest Self. Your highest self is revealed when you live your life with a Universal Mind and you become that wonderful, giving person that you know is waiting to blossom deep within you.

*Have you ever wondered
if you can stick to a plan over the long haul?*

Seven Arts Mean Twenty-One Phases of Personal Development: Make Patience, Discipline, and Awareness Your Silent Friends

The exercises that I have given you for the practice of the first two Arts, the Art of Preparation and the Art of Compassion, require patience and discipline in order to continue your practice on a daily basis. More importantly, however, we have learned how each Art builds successively upon the previous Art. As new knowledge and awareness arise, new questions and higher levels of potential understanding make themselves apparent to you. In order to enter into a new, successive stage and develop a new, deeper level of awareness made possible by learning and practicing a new, successive Art, you must first exercise the patience and discipline needed to actually *sacrifice, renounce, cast off, and abandon the very same skills and tools that helped you to reach your present level of understanding.*

This may seem ironic, but the skills and tools you use to achieve one level of understanding must be challenged and sacrificed in order to enter the next, more advanced, "deeper" level of sequenced development in the successive, process of consciousness transformation. You must not become attached to previous learning and training in order for you to develop new skills and new tools that are appropriate for the new, more advanced level of development that you are seeking in all realms of spiritual, interpersonal, and material well being. *This process is akin to climbing to the top of a flagpole within each Art or stage of development.* This process is thus repeated seven times for each of the Seven Arts. In order to go to the next stage, you must have the courage to keep climbing and "let go" of your desire to cling, clutch, and feel the support provided by your "present" flagpole. By continuing to climb, even though you have reached the top of a particular stage, you will be making possible the next steps toward ever-deeper levels of knowledge and understanding. You must *trust* that new awareness and new tools will present themselves to you so that you can once again climb to the top of a new, successive flagpole represented by the next stage (or Art) of development.

If you cannot exercise the patience and discipline necessary to jump into new unforeseen territory (new Arts), then you will be forever stuck in your current place. Your own attachment to your progress thus interferes with your ability to go deeper, to examine yourself with even greater honesty, and to begin to explore more deeply the attachments at work in the depths of your subconscious and unconscious mind.

Remember that these attachments are yours to own; you must take responsibility for them precisely because they originated from, and were created by, *your choices* (conscious choices as well as subconscious and unconscious choices). Think of this as a kind of "tough love" directed at your whole self. Acknowledging these attachments, and even making friends with them, serves as the fuel that will feed your continued growth and development. There is no place to hide. The reason that you want to embrace deeply these attachments and this entire transformation process is not because you are holding up a mirror in order to judge yourself negatively, but because the opposite is true. At this point in your journey, having compassion for yourself is key. Indeed, self-compassion holds the key to taking responsibility for not only your choices but also the events and circumstances that, in combination, have served to define the person that you are today. Blaming past events and circumstances beyond your control for the condition of your present life is simply a foil for living in the past. It can lead to depression. In the same way, having anxiety about future events and circumstances (that have not even occurred) is another kind of foil for not living in the present. Being in touch with the present (that is, being open and honest with the present) is truly the way to engage true positive self-transformation. This is because the present moment is truly the only time that actually exists; it is thus the only time to truly take responsibility for the conditions that are blocking you from further progress on your journey.

Let us delve into this matter even more deeply. Each of the Seven Arts has three dimensions or phases (twenty-one in all) that you must "live in" and "work through" without skipping any phase. Each Art has a beginning *(nascent)* phase, then a middle *(enduring)* phase, and finally each Art also has an ending *(cessation)* phase. The beginning *nascent phase* occurs when you first perceive and understand a *need* AND you are both willing and able to try new things in order to gain new insight or new knowledge on the path of present transformation. For example, you may have started the first Art of Preparation because you understood at some level of consciousness that you possessed a *need for personal transformation* with a focus on spiritual development, or emotional development, or interpersonal development, or material development. Acknowledging this newly perceived need is precisely that which occasions your entering the beginning *nascent* phase of any of the Seven Arts of personal and spiritual development.

In the next, middle *enduring phase* of each Art, you learn to practice regularly and even enjoy the daily exercises which you may perform for a very long time. Perhaps you will remain in the middle phase of a particular stage or Art for years. Some schools of thought suggest that this kind of growth occurs over a lifetime with seven years being the incremental time frame to truly digest the middle phase of each stage of development. Significant transformational ages, based upon this model of seven-year increments, are 7, 14, 21, 28, 35, 42, and 49. Perhaps coincidentally or not, the first draft of both of my Seven Arts (personal development and business development) books was written in my 49th year.

At some point on your journey, you begin to see changes in your life and so you begin to think that this journey can proceed to ever-deeper levels of knowledge and awareness. Accordingly, you begin to see an entirely *new set of needs* emerge. When this happens, you begin pointing toward the third phase of the Art with which you are currently occupied. In this ending *cessant phase*, you recognize that there are other Arts beyond the present Art or stage that you are presently practicing. You realize that something (or perhaps everything) needs to change for you to advance. At some moment, the ending *cessant phase*, for example, of the first Art of Preparation, leads you, perhaps even unconsciously, to the new, beginning *nascent phase* of the second Art of Compassion. The three-phase process continues again and again through each of these Seven Arts. A total of twenty-one phases (moving through all Seven Arts) thus will occupy your work and attention occasioning ever-deeper layers of consciousness development.

*Have you ever wondered
if you can let go of the things making you stuck?*

Renouncing the Fruit of Your Labor

The reason that the third Art of Responsibility is really the fuel and engine for all of the positive transformative movements necessary to work and progress through each of the three phases of each of the Seven Arts (thus twenty-one process transformations) is because you ultimately must take responsibility for the entire process of progression. And, since this journey of positive transformation is not easy nor is it a quick fix, you will need the tools of patience and discipline all along the way.

The deeper you go into the transformation process, the more you tend to become attached to the higher stages of development that you are experiencing. You begin to feel satisfied with your development. This satisfaction, however, ultimately will cause an attachment that will make you stagnant and prohibit you from understanding more deeply and honoring your true gifts. Being too "satisfied" and too "proud of yourself" will only invite hubristic pride allowing your "selfish mind" (Jp.*shoga*) and ego to begin to take over again causing your developmental progression to come to a halt. Accordingly, personal sacrifice and renunciation (Sk. *yajna*) are the keys that will enable you to creatively enter new ways of being by gradually entering new phases and practicing new Arts for being in the world in accord with your highest Self.

Renouncing your "selfish mind" (Jp. *shoga*) and actualizing your unattached "Universal Mind" (Jp. *Taiga*) means putting your consciousness on the path of selfless action and service toward others. "Selflessness" arises spontaneously when you understand deeply that you cannot escape the causal consequences of your thoughts, deeds, and actions. Therefore, the Art of Responsibility begins with knowledge and understanding of the causal processes and transformation processes at work in the Universe. It is true that you are not separate from the dynamic, ever-changing Universe; hence, you are an integral part of the larger, grand, Universal causal process. When you become attached to your present level of development, then you become stagnant, which leads to selfishness, which leads to the false, and ultimately illusory, feeling of separation. However, your present conscious transformation is on a path of connection, not separation. Your mission is to become One with the dynamic Universe which is a most honorable, selfless path. Indeed, following this path of selflessness is the most important thing all human beings can do with the gift of their dynamic, ever-changing life.

Have you ever wondered what would happen if everyone changed with you?

Choose for Yourself, Choose for the World

Consider for a moment the following reality. Psychologist J. G. Jung and philosopher G. W. F. Hegel both expressed ideas about the *collective* MIND, or *collective* CONSCIOUSNESS, or *collective* SPIRIT of all humanity. All humans possess a consciousness that is One with the spirit or energy of the Universe. We are all, therefore, a part of a greater consciousness that reflects the combined whole of present human consciousness in this world. In fact, all humans alive today are presently acting out of their personal life history. This includes every person's subconscious motivations and unconscious desires which have been developed by, and are expressed in and through, a community of human beings each influencing the other "drop-by-drop," one drop at a time with each human interaction.

What would happen if everyone set out on a journey of mindfulness and personal transformation? What if everyone made a commitment to himself or herself to take responsibility and put into practice the Seven Arts? The leaders of religions, nations, local communities, universities, businesses, and the like are the real "consciousness influencers" and are thus the ideological leaders of our civilization. These "thought leaders," if you will, are making decisions every day (drop-by-drop) that necessarily and inescapably contribute to the universal causal process that creates the entire collective consciousness that truly is the whole of humanity. A state of global peace and prosperity, for example, cannot be achieved without a change in the consciousness of those whose position is one of power and influence. To understand our collective (Art of) Responsibility for our nation state relationships around the world, and for protecting the ecosystems that sustain our planet and our species, it is necessary to understand first that our Universe is driven by the collective consciousness and personal choices that each human being is making today and at every single present moment going forward.

"The leaders of religions, nations, local communities, universities, businesses, and the like are the real 'consciousness influencers' and are thus the ideological leaders of our civilization."

A meeting with the Ambassador of Japan, Ryozo Kato at the Embassy of Japan, Washington DC, 2006.

Every one of the seven billion humans alive today is operating in their conscious life and making important decisions within a cave, as it were, as expressed by the limited window of each person's knowledge and past experiences – me included. Each person can choose freely to understand and experience their *original connectedness* to God, Spirit, the Universe or they can continue to operate out of *separation* as lived and experienced in accord with their present conceptual box. This "box" is represented by the habitual patterns of thought and limited awareness that make up each person's conscious mind that, in turn, serves as the master of each person's daily life decisions. Accordingly, the path you are following through these Seven Arts is a path that truly can make a positive difference in this world. There is no escape. You cannot *choose* not to be a part of this global, causal, even universal process. Even if you *choose* to do nothing, to opt out, or to be neutral, you are still contributing to the causal condition of the Universe. You cannot run; you cannot hide. However, *you can make a difference* for yourself and for others by practicing the Art of Responsibility. Make patience and discipline your friends and you will be able to move through each of the three phases of each of the Seven Arts with beauty, elegance, and humility.

Practicing patience and discipline will help you to redirect conscious motives and desires that you know are destructive to you, your family, and the Universe. Simply listen to yourself and you will feel instinctively when a conscious motive is not healthy for you, others, or the Universe. Acting on motives that you *"feel"* (usually in your solar plexus or stomach or heart) are wrong or injurious to others will simply propel the negative spiral of your life into deeper levels of separation, isolation, and despair. You must *trust deeply* that you have the energy, the power, the patience, and the discipline to turn your life around for the better.

Practicing the first two Arts well will give you confidence in your transformative ability. It also will give you a taste that the great power of the Universe is actually behind you at all times; it is *the wind at your back* working to support your growth and development just for the asking. You can open your heart and mind and draw from the *Ki* of the Universe, God, and Spirit whenever you open yourself, free yourself, connect yourself to the divine that is already within you. Remember that each day, each waking moment, you are creating yourself and that there are causal consequences all of your own "making."

Practicing the Art of Responsibility means to understand more deeply that your existence is your creation and that you are affecting the entire Universe simply because you are alive and that you do exist as an integral part of the Universe. You are One with the Universe even if you have not yet personally discovered or experienced this for yourself. Your influence upon others, positive or negative, is unmistakable. By mindfully attending to your deepest responsibilities that you know need to be honestly addressed in this transformation work, and mindfully recognizing that you have both the freedom and power to change, no matter what your past experience, then you will begin to personally experience the pure joy and abundance that surrounds you at every moment.

Please use patience and discipline to practice the exercises below and begin to delve more deeply into the Art of Responsibility. Do not dishonor your higher Self. "*Choose*" for yourself; *"choose"* for the world.

**Daily Exercises
To Facilitate The Art of Responsibility**

Have you ever wondered if you could be more patient, tolerant, and "bite your tongue"?

**Exercise 6:
Take a Deep Breath - Introspect Before You Act**

This is the second stage of self-honesty; you are building upon Exercise 3. You already "notice" where you are at all times and so now is the time to begin "acting with purpose"; that is, not simply re-acting or acting mindlessly. Here the practice is to act with purpose in accord with your PDA.

In this third chapter, I have emphasized purposefully the phrase "you know." You know when something you are doing is self-destructive. You know when your motives are not in the best interests of your well being, your family's well being, your organization's well being, or your business's well being. You know when you are taking advantage of others. You know if you have cheated someone else, or cheated a process, or even cheated yourself. You know when you have acted on short-term desires that you know are not good in the long run. You know when all of the above are present because you *feel* differently. You may even become sick to your stomach as this knowledge expresses itself in your physical, emotional, and spiritual being. You feel a small twinge in the small of your back, in your solar plexus, or in your heart. You know when your mind gets nervous, busy, and anxious for your actions are simply not right. You know when you are hiding something from others; you may even be hiding something from loved ones. Or, you may even be so blind at present that the time has not yet come for you to realize and experience that you are even capable of hiding something from yourself. Eventually, you know that you want to change, but you just feel powerless to break the cycle of destruction for you, your loved ones, and even others who are more distantly related, but are nevertheless affected by your actions.

To give you some mental and emotional "space" for your consciousness to truly consider all of the above, to give you some sense of true responsibility as well as empowerment to effect positive change, *"take a deep breath and introspect"* in order to acknowledge the existence of all of these "you know" feelings. Have a dialogue, make friends, make peace with all of your "you know" feelings. Instead of having these feelings and feeling bad about them and then ignoring, suppressing or repressing them, confront them with honesty. Realize that your transformation must begin with self-honesty and personal integrity. That is, introspect and feel deeply these things that *you know* to be true.

By acknowledging deeply and making peace with these unwanted desires, emotions, and actions, you will be taking the first step toward managing them. By acknowledging and taking responsibility for these habits of the mind and heart that are in fact a part of you, you will be shown a place to go (to them actually) for they serve as the starting point for transformative redirection. To be clear, you cannot make these "you knows" just go away. If you try, you suppress them more deeply and they will rise to haunt you another day. Simply confront them, take a breath, and talk to them. Acknowledge that all these thoughts, feelings, and motivations are in fact a part of you. They exist in you for a reason. Each "you know" has an original series of causally conditioned predecessors that collectively occasioned the feeling to arise, exist, and remain within you.

The first step is acknowledging both the thoughts and feelings you have as well as the causal conditions that gave birth to them in your conscious mind, subconscious mind, and unconscious mind. The second step is developing your patience and discipline to manage the transformation process that began with your honest self-reflection, honest introspection, and honest acknowledgement. The third step is using your skill to redirect the energy behind these aspects of your consciousness to new and positive ends.

You can truly change yourself over time. By simply waiting, breathing, and acknowledging these real "you know" aspects of your consciousness, you are likely *not* to act them out. When you do not act out the negative desire, the negative addiction, the unwanted motivation, or powerful short-term emotion, then you are no longer acting out of fear and anger which contributes negatively to the causal Universe that surrounds you. If you feel odd about something you are about to do – listen to your inner voice, acknowledge both the feeling and the issue behind it; above all, do not discount your feeling and proceed to act out your desire, addiction, or unwanted outcome. By truly acknowledging that you not only have these "you know" feelings, but also that they are an integral part of you, you then can take the first step toward *taking responsibility* for your new positive transformation "in-the-making."

This exercise is about taking the first critical step in breaking the cycle, breaking the negative paradigm, which you have created for yourself over time. The true process for deep transformation must start with *self-honesty*. Self-honesty will serve as the cornerstone necessary to build for you a solid foundation for personal, interpersonal, and spiritual growth and development. You must not begin a supposed transformation process by *covering over* (Sk. *samvrti*) your deepest flaws. Start at the true beginning, take a deep breath and introspect deeply and honestly before you act. Consider all the ways that you can change yourself for the better by first acknowledging, then accepting as your own, and then redirecting the energy behind your unwanted desires.

In sum, each day acknowledge your deepest, darkest desires. Take a deep breath in order to give you time to reflect more deeply before you act. Create new possibilities that are desirable possibilities which will make you feel good about yourself, your loved ones, your friends, as well as others in this world. Recognize that you are not only responsible for you, but also recognize that all your actions are causally linked to those around you.

Act so that your loved ones, co-workers, friends, and relatives will be proud of you. If you are at first proud of yourself, you will then realize that others will follow you gladly. When this happens, your spirit becomes open and inviting, not guarded, scared, and hiding something. When you open your heart, the Universe rushes in to serve as *the wind at your back*. The universal wind at your back has always been there for you, but you must honestly acknowledge that it was *you* that was *causing* your own feeling of separation and disconnection. Trust that you are the Universe and the Universe is you. Begin your positive transformation at its base by acknowledging both *who you truly are* (with all of your imperfections) and *who you truly want to be*. Let the power of God, Spirit, and the Universe lift you from your present position and inspire you to rise from the mud like a lotus flower basking in the warm sunlight.

If you do this exercise, every time you *feel* a *"you know"* throughout the day, then you will be nourishing your being with truth and honesty. From such a solid base of honest self-reflection and honest introspection regarding the causal "seeds" of your unwanted desires and motivations, you will be creating for yourself very deep and positive roots necessary for truly successful spiritual, interpersonal, and material transformation. Simply stop performing the deeds and deceptions that you know in your heart of hearts are destructive to you, others, and the Universe.

I am asking you to muster the courage, fortitude, patience, and discipline NOW in this present moment and thus begin to put into practice this third Art of Responsibility simply because, at this point in the process, you should have the confidence to succeed. You should have great confidence because by now you have already learned much and already made positive changes based upon your daily practice of the first two sets of exercises (Exercises 1 through 5) associated with the first two Arts – the first Art of Preparation and the second Art of Compassion. Now you are prepared to succeed at practicing the third Art of Responsibility. "Take a Deep Breath and Introspect Before You Act."

In your Seven Arts Journal, externalize the "you know" desires that emerge. List them one by one. Explain first why you think they are not constructive. It may be that they don't fulfill you. It also may be that they contradict what you've stated in your PDA. Or it may be that these actions hurt others. Explain the ramifications of these actions. After you've explored this, explore why you believe you have these desires. Ask yourself, "When I desire this, what am I really wanting to achieve? Do I want to escape? Be accepted? Avoid failure?" There are no simple answers here. Exploring these issues honestly is the first major step in channeling your energy elsewhere; that is, toward more positive outcomes consistent with your PDA.

Once you have determined the unconscious, subconscious and conscious reasons for your thinking and behavior, then you can begin to channel the underlying mental formations and desires through more positive means. In your Seven Arts Journal, record ideas about alternative and healthy approaches to transform and reshape your deepest desires so that they eventually align with and ultimately serve your PDA, your highest good. As with all of the other exercises, through successive practice, you will be building the foundation for, and basis of, the possibility for reaching ever-deeper states of clarity and awareness. In this case, Exercise 13 (entitled "*Be In and With Your Emotions*" to be discussed in Chapter 6, The Art of Living Naturally) will help you to take the practice of this Exercise 6 to ever-deeper levels of true Self understanding leading to the actualization of your PDA.

Have you ever wondered if you could serve your loved ones better?

Exercise 7:
Be an *Otomo*: Empty Yourself and Serve Others Selflessly

This exercise combines, and builds upon, your prior practice of "awareness/ noticing" (Exercises 2, 3, 4, and 5) and "intentional action" (Exercise 6) in daily life.

I have explained that *Otomo* training is really about serving others selflessly. My story in this chapter (and continuing in Chapter Seven) is about a monastic-type setting designed to capture your consciousness for twenty-four hours a day. However, in the Art of Preparation, we discussed the fact that *your world, your twenty-four hours, IS your life monastery* as well. Your monastery is wherever you are, however you feel, however you perceive, however you think, however you are – truly and deeply. It is much easier to experience deep relaxation and the seeds of transformation while on retreat or on your vacation than in your daily life. However, the real life challenge is bringing deep relaxation and mindful action back into the world of the stresses and strains of your everyday life.

In this exercise, I am asking you to practice emptying yourself of your own agenda each day. That is, by focusing upon serving others, you will not only be creating positive influences in this world, but also you will be intentionally transforming your "selfish mind," or ego-driven tendencies, into a "Universal Mind" with true selflessness serving as the base of your innermost consciousness.

Again, you must exercise patience and discipline to do this intentionally with a present, purposeful, and *awake* conscious mind. The more you train yourself in this manner in daily life, the more you will realize that this redirection from a selfish mind to a Universal Mind can happen in an effortless fashion without conscious intention. *This is because selflessness and selfless service to others is the natural Way of the Universe.* This experience of deep connection and selflessness already exists at the base of your original consciousness.

The universal power of love and protection for all things will eventually be directly experienced within you and suddenly you will also experience that *the wind of the Universe is now at your back*. When this happens, your actions are performed to serve others *without effort*. You will create abundance *without trying*. You will feel as though the more you give to others the more the Universe shines upon you. By serving others you extend your energy away from yourself. Just as you push water away from you in the ocean or in a bath, you realize that without your conscious effort, intention, or desire, the Universe (like water) naturally flows back to yourself with more love and protection, abundance and joy. The more you give, the more the Universe gives back to you. However, it is important for you to honestly confront your true intentions. You must give to others without expectation of reward and without expectation of abundance coming back to you. To give in this fashion without expectation is the meaning of true selflessness.

This exercise is really a follow through from Exercise 5, "Practice Compassion Through Mindful Attention." Being an *otomo* requires not only giving each person undivided attention, but also selflessly serving those in your direct sphere of influence.

We live in a *causal* "something for something"/"this for that"/ "*quid pro quo*" culture. And in the realm of interpersonal interactions, community relations, and business relations, situations are created by using *quid pro quo*. This is not about *expecting* things in return for services provided. I'm talking about something different. This is about positively, energetically *anticipating the needs* of others and *serving* your friends, partners, and even adversaries, in a *selfless (otomo)* fashion.

With each person you meet each day, give them your attention, your kindness, your love. Serve others as you wish to be treated and you will be cultivating truly the Golden Rule, the Silver Rule, as well as the Art of Responsibility. Enjoy!

4

THE ART OF RELAXATION

*"The tongue is soft and remains,
the teeth are hard and fall out."*

Ancient Chinese Proverb
Author Unknown

I ended the previous chapter (and daily exercises) discussing the mental and emotional state of moral consciousness referred to simply as *you know*. It is the state of consciousness where you have a deeply felt intuition that something is wrong. You do not feel good about your desire, your addiction, or your attachment to something that you believe to be improper. You simply *know* or *feel* or *acknowledge* that what you are doing or thinking of doing is not in your best interest nor is it in the best interest of loved ones, friends, co-workers, teammates, and so on. Building upon this theme, let's examine another type of *"you know"* experience: STRESS.

Have you ever wondered if you could learn to relax?

Transforming Stress into Relaxation

You know when you are under stress. You can feel your anxiety, your tension, and your nervousness. You know or you can feel that your mental, emotional and/or physical state of being is under stress and, consequently, you wish it would simply go away so that you could face your day, or your specific task, or a certain person with a different, stress free, anxiety free state of mind and state of being.

Also, while you know that you wish to have all these negative feelings go away, you do not know *how* to transform yourself. In this fourth Art of Relaxation, we will tackle the first obstacle that is likely to arise as you acknowledge problems and challenges in your life stemming from the self-honesty work and daily practice that you already are experiencing in accord with the third Art of Responsibility. By directly facing and taking responsibility for your real causal influence in this Universe, and by directly facing and taking responsibility for your real and deep destructive tendencies, desires, and motivations, you open yourself to what may be a new source of stress. Specifically, you will experience directly and become more acutely aware of a good deal of anxiety that may have been repressed for years by your refusal to face, acknowledge, grapple with, take responsibility for, and ultimately manage your destructive tendencies.

By first becoming aware of (and then confronting the real depth of) your conscious, subconscious, and unconscious destructive tendencies, you will realize that you are about to face your most difficult work. When you practice daily the third Art of Responsibility and truly decide to take responsibility for your entire Self, you can easily feel overwhelmed and intimidated by the new challenge that faces you. The Art of Relaxation then becomes an important tool that, like patience and discipline, will help you to feel strong and empowered as you tap into the power of the Universe Itself.

When you relax very deeply, you can experience directly the reality of your true connectedness to the Universe. In reality, you are not separate and you have no independent existence. You are One with the Universe. Relaxation can enable you to experience this connectedness. What prohibits you from feeling and experiencing this unitive power is your own mental and emotional state of being. Your busy, attached, judging, opinion riddled, intentional consciousness is *causing* the false, illusory experience of separation. Your own "tense" state of mind literally covers over *(Sk. samvrti)* your true Self, the Self that is no-self (Sk. *anatman)*. Your true Self is not independent and isolated and filled with tension. Your true Self is the same as "no-self" because you are without ego. Selflessness is one and the same as experiencing deeply the reality that you truly have no real independent existence apart from the *Ki* (life force) of the Universe.

When you face true self-examination, your darkest shadow elements will appear, causing further anxiety and despair. These subconscious and unconscious aspects of your consciousness and personality must be embraced lovingly in order to be redirected and transformed, thus fueling your positive spiritual and interpersonal well-being. The Art of Relaxation will give you a source of strength that is truly available to you at any time. The Universe that sustains your life when you are filled with tension, anxiety, and despair is the same Universe that will lift you out of your despair if only you allow it to happen. Deep relaxation is the pathway for you to experience directly your connection with your Original Self that is One with the Spirit of the Universe.

> *Have you ever wondered if it were possible
> to truly see things differently?*

**Rediscover Your Original Self:
Relative Thinking and Absolute Thinking**

The Art of Relaxation is about rediscovering your Original Self and the natural energy or power that arises from your experience of absolute connection to God, Spirit, and the Universe. Your life, your mind, your emotions, and your body are all *one energy*. And, although there is a sense in which this energy is yours, it is clearer and more accurate to say that this "energy" or "natural power" that arises with your rediscovery of your Original Self *is not really "yours" at all*. When you experience your Original Self as no-self, no-ego, and no separation, then your energy and your experience of abundance, power, and empowerment is the result of accepting your natural connection to the Universe Itself. When this happens, the power and dynamic energy (Ki) of the Universe are yours to tap, to *ride like the wind*, and to embrace, but never to "own" or "possess." They are not "yours"; they belong to the Universe.

Your own judging, intentional consciousness creates the illusion that you have an independent existence. Accordingly, you conceptualize and, as a result, you perceive your mind and body as separate and distinct. You may think of your mind as airy, ethereal, or more *spiritual in nature*. You also may perceive and think of your body to be quite different, judging it to be *material in nature*, made up of molecules and atoms that have substance. Unlike the mind then, you might view your body as existing in three-dimensional space having length, breadth, and depth. This, however, is a big mistake and merely contributes to the worldview that we have called *relative thinking*. Relative thinking is a form of perception and consciousness that treats conceptual distinctions as though they were actual or absolute with an equivalent counterpart existing in the "real" world. For example, this sort of attachment to the *concepts* of mind and body is the basis of the notion of mind-body dualism that has been part of western thought for over 2000 years.

In reality, however, your mind and body are One. Ultimately, both are merely appearances or manifestations of a single energy – the *Ki* of Universe. By learning and practicing the Art of Relaxation, you will discover and experience *Absolute Thinking*, which is a unitive consciousness that is always present. *Absolute Thinking* is, as they say, "right in front of you," "right before your eyes," "right before your very nose." There is nothing mysterious about such talk once you can learn to experience for yourself (Jp. *ki ga tsuku*) your true Self, your true potential, and your true transformative power. This energy that results from *Absolute Thinking* can lift you like a Phoenix rising from the depths of your honest confrontation with your darker self, a confrontation occasioned by your sincere daily practice of the third Art of Responsibility. When you learn to experience the original unity of your mind, body, and spirit, you can ride the wind; that is, ride the great power that is the Universe. The Art of Relaxation, which enables you to experience this unity, is thus a key to your own empowerment. It will provision your transformational journey by instilling in you the ability to tap into your full potential at any moment in time.

Have you ever wondered if you are going through life with your emergency brake on?

Release Your "Life Brake": Crafting Your New Life-in-the-Making

I will take two approaches in sharing with you the artistry and benefits of the Art of Relaxation. First, I will share a few personal stories about how any type of performance is enhanced significantly by having a relaxed state of mind. I will draw from my experiences and associations with athletes, musicians, martial artists, and business leaders to illustrate the power and performance-enhancing qualities of relaxation. I am sure that you have some of your own stories about this as well. Second, I will describe the actual mental, emotional, and physical frame of reference associated with relaxing deeply. To emphasize the fundamental importance of this new frame of reference associated with consciousness that produces deep relaxation, we will call this real relaxation a "new paradigm of consciousness."

Adopting this twofold strategy will help me to explain exactly *HOW to practice* and, therefore, *HOW to experience for yourself* deep relaxation. To truly calm the waves of your mind so that you can enter into a transformational state of consciousness characterized by non-intentional thinking is to experience and realize for yourself a new way of being. The liberation that you will experience is capable of moving you so deeply that you will embrace your life, and even your darker shadows, with a spirit of renewal and redemption. You will embrace the Arts of Compassion and Responsibility with a divine wind surrounding you and you will experience a new sense of creativity, new possibilities, and new ways of crafting your new *life-in-the-making.*

This liberating process not only creates new life possibilities, but also reveals new aspects of your true Self that until now have been distorted. Through the process of relaxation you will be rediscovering your true Self by uncovering the already "connected" person that you are. You will work to peel away layers of viewing fields and distortions that have systematically and habitually served to *cover over* (Sk. *samvrti*) your truer, deeper, connected Self. By unveiling these masks and filters of direct perception, you will walk out of the cave of your own mind. The mental and emotional emergency brake that has covered over your Original Consciousness and has held you back from directly experiencing and realizing your true potential and your true Self finally will be put into the release position. You will directly experience liberation and you will realize for yourself that the emergency brake preventing your life from moving forward positively has been *of your own making,* the product of long-habituated patterns of consciousness. The Art of Relaxation will serve as a catalyst as it will stimulate in you a rebirth of the higher and greater possibilities for your whole life and for the lives of those you touch. So let's begin.

---

*Have you ever wondered
if there is something more, something beyond you,
yet you keep getting in your own way?*

**It's Not Your Power:
"Throw Away" Your Separate Self**

Citing my teacher, Master Koichi Tohei, once again, I would like to draw upon one of his famous "Four Basic Principles for Realizing the [Original] Oneness of Mind and Body" in order to communicate how one can learn to relax and experience mind and body oneness. I should clarify that the view that mind and body are originally one is not unique to the belief system of Master Tohei. My first book entitled **The Bodymind Experience in Japanese Buddhism** and second book entitled **Science and Comparative Philosophy** (written with Shigenori Nagatomo and YUASA Yasuo) documented that the worldview of mind and body oneness is a basic characteristic of Indian, Chinese, and Japanese Buddhist philosophical and religious traditions. Master Tohei's gift, however, is teaching people ***how*** *to experience these truths for themselves.*

Principle number two of his "Four Basic Principles" is translated into English as "Relax Completely." This phrase is quite famous to the English-speaking *Aikido* world. However, a significant part of the message is missing without taking a closer look at Master Tohei's actual principle number two in the original Japanese. "Relax completely" translates the Japanese sentence: *Zenshin no chikara o kanzen ni nuku.*

"*Zenshin,*" the first word, means your "whole self" including your mind, body, emotions, spirit, dreams for the future, past history, and even karma. It means the totality of your entire being. The second term *"no"* is a grammatical term showing the "possessive" relationship, and *"chikara"* simply means "power." So, the first part of the phrase, *"Zenshin no chikara,"* means "the power of your whole self." This phrase refers to all the things that *you believe* to be so great, so wonderful, and so powerful about yourself. For example, your past accomplishments and experiences; your hopes, dreams, and ambitions for the future; your great physical prowess perhaps; your superior intellect; your superior talent in something; or maybe your supreme emotional stability. All of these combined internal beliefs about yourself, when considered deeply, make up your whole self—*Zenshin*. Combine all these beliefs about yourself with the conscious or unconscious belief that these are the source of your power and you have the *"great power of your whole self identity."* The power of your *"zenshin"* must be great indeed!

Well, not so fast. *"Kanzen ni nuku"* means to pull or slide something out (like a card from an envelope). A simpler interpretation that is closer to what Master Tohei means is "throw it all away"—like junk mail! The term *"o"* is another grammatical term indicating the relationship of the direct object. So, in combination, Master Tohei is saying, "consider deeply the power of your whole self ... and then... *throw away this sense of yourself completely"* (Jp. *Zenshin no chikara o kanzen ni nuku).* The English translation and phrase "Relax Completely" (famous as it may be to Master Tohei's students) does not do this important concept justice. Indeed, the idea of "relax completely" actually "covers over" (Sk. *samvrti*) his teaching about how to relax deeply/completely. It is not merely a physical concept as in releasing tension from your body alone. You relax by taking *all of your attachments* to the concepts you have (related to the power of your self as an independent being) *and throw them all away!* These attachments and conceptions arise from the "relative thinking" of a selfish mind (Jp. *shoga*). You must "surrender," "let go," and "release" these concepts in order to experience your connected Self through "Absolute Thinking."

The emphasis here is on your ego, your sense of a separate self. The power you normally think of as your *personal* power is weak, so weak that you might as well abandon it completely. Real power, the power of the *Ki* (life force) of the Universe, is vast and it can be tapped by abandoning your attachment to your own separate, isolated, independent, selfish, ego-based consciousness. To relax completely, therefore, means much, much more than mere physical relaxation. It means relax your mind, relax your emotions, relax your own attachment to physical power and every other kind of *personal* power based upon your internal belief system about yourself. In short, *"throw away"* or *"cast off"* (Jp. *datsuraku*) the notion that you are a separate self. By throwing away this notion you can *embrace the experience of connection afforded to you by relaxing deeply.* This experience of connection enables you to relax any time even, or perhaps especially, under pressure.

Have you ever wondered what it would be like to be one of those people skiing fast and crashing on the Wide World of Sports?

Applying Deep Relaxation in Daily Life: The Case of Downhill Ski Racing

In the martial arts, stressful situations can be created for training purposes. Many people attack you at once, for example. In these moments, in order to respond effectively, you must relax deeply thus drawing upon the power of the Universe. When you relax deeply, your attackers seem to come for you in slow motion simply because of the depth of your calmness. You see or feel their attack by sensing their *Ki*, their mind, their energy even *before* the physical strike or kick begins. All of this, of course, can be cultivated by serious training in the martial arts. Since not everyone can nor desires to pursue martial arts training, it is important to figure out how to relax without having to defend yourself against multiple attackers. But *how do we translate these experiences into our daily life? How can we apply relaxation for stress relief, for executing at work, for improving our musical or athletic performance, or for improving our interpersonal relationships? In short, how can we apply relaxation for improving the clarity of our entire consciousness, especially for spiritual development?*

We all know stories of people performing well under stress by relaxation. For example, the clutch baseball hitter Reggie Jackson, known by baseball fans as "Mr. October," illustrates well someone known for relaxing under pressure and performing his best during the stressful fall baseball playoffs. Somehow, certain people instinctively know *how* to draw upon their full potential when the stress of the situation would make most people crumble.

I first discovered the lessons of relaxation as a young teenage downhill ski racer. My hero was Jean-Claude Killy, winner of three gold medals in the 1968 Winter Olympics in Grenoble, France. My training coach was another Frenchman named Jean-Pierre Pascal. In the early seventies, he invited me to live with him and his wife, Helenka, at their home, in Squaw Valley, California. Jean-Pierre coached the Olympic Valley USA Ski Team of which I was a member. We traveled extensively looking for the best snow so that we could train year round. We trained in Europe and Argentina in the summer months. In May and June, we would travel to Red Lodge, Montana, and then to Val Thorens, France, where we would ski high altitude glaciers that retain snow for training even in the summer heat. At these two high altitude locations, we focused our training upon the shorter slalom and giant slalom events. In July and August, we would travel to Argentina in the southern hemisphere (where it was winter) allowing us to focus exclusively upon the very long "downhill" event. The downhill event was my favorite – the faster the better!

In some international downhill events you can go over three miles from start to finish in less than three minutes. Do the math and you can see that, including the slow start out of the gate, you are averaging over 60 mph. In some World Cup Downhill courses you are going 90-plus mph at the finish. When you are skiing, say up to 45 mph, you feel as though you are pretty much in control. However, at speeds of 50-plus mph, a new feeling arises that is more like you are *a passenger* on a pair of fast moving boards. At higher speeds, you are "floating" so *you must relax* everything in your upper body to feel the skis on the snow. At 50 mph and up, you cannot just turn or stop on a dime whenever you feel like it. Downhill ski racing becomes more like a high-speed dance as you search for ways to *work with the mountain* to produce more speed. If you are tense, and your ski edge "chatters" and "grabs" the snow, then you certainly will lose speed and precious seconds in your race down the mountain. Worse, "chattering" can also cause you to enter a high-speed cartwheel that is disastrous.

During these three minutes of dangerously high speed, your mental focus must be on relaxing, floating, and looking far ahead of your present position. You must maintain concentration on your line or path of descent in order to properly position yourself, especially as you enter the most dangerous sections of the course. Focusing on your aerodynamics is yet another critical component because of its impact upon wind resistance and, therefore, your overall speed. Once your speed exceeds 80 mph, if you just accidentally lose your balance and stick out one arm, the force of the wind impacting your tight synthetic body suit not only slows you down significantly, but also this aerodynamic error can impinge upon your ability to remain "centered" and "balanced." Losing your balance can cause you ultimately to flip completely upside down like the skier in the famous clip illustrating "the agony of defeat" for **ABC's Wide World of Sports** opening and closing credits from 1961 to 1998.

Have you ever wondered what it would be like to do scary things and overcome your fear?

**Let's Do Scary Stuff:
Rock Climbing, Jumping Out of Airplanes, and Speed Skiing**

In order to learn how to relax in the midst of stress, I can remember three things we young and crazy downhillers would do. Please try to remember that, while all these things seem a bit crazy, each of the activities described in the three stories below really did have (at least *in my mind*) a training purpose – to *teach* us to relax under extremely stressful conditions, to let us *experience deeply* for ourselves the power and performance enhancement qualities of relaxation, and to help us *practice* the art of relaxing under extremely stressful conditions. I will describe for you three activities – rock climbing without safety ropes, jumping out of airplanes, and the relatively unknown sport of speed skiing.

First of all, if you are old enough, take yourself back and remember that we were ski racers, *downhill ski racers*, in the early seventies. My downhill coach was yet another Frenchman, Phillipe Mollard, who was a past FIS (Federation of International Skiing) Downhill World Champion skier. I was young and impressionable and would do anything to become a World Class Downhiller. Phillipe's first coaching tip was to encourage us to do things scarier than our chosen

"...we were ski racers, downhill ski racers, in the early seventies..."

Bogus Basin Ski Area, Idaho, 1972.

discipline of high-speed downhill ski racing. Even when we were "free skiing" with Phillipe at our training center at Lake Tahoe in Squaw Valley, California, he would remind us each day that "if you are not seeing the whites of your own eyes three times a day, then you are not pushing yourself." By this comment, Phillipe meant that we should "free ski" fast enough to *scare ourselves to death*, thus *"seeing the whites of our own eyes."* "OK, that's easy," I thought. "I can even make up new scary things to do outside ski racing and surely this will help me to be even more mentally prepared for the high-speed, high-risk downhill event." This was the thinking of a very hungry teenage downhiller eager to be the best in the world. My teammates and I wanted to create experiences that, like downhill racing, involved high speeds and/or dangerous situations in which we could practice "seeing the whites of our own eyes" by staying relaxed in high stress circumstances.

For example, my teammates and I decided that even though we did not know how to rock climb (we were training in the high altitudes of the French Alps at the time), we would just play Spider Man without ropes, without proper training, without proper equipment, and without rock climbing footwear. I vaguely remember once being scared to death hanging from my fingernails at the top of a high ledge only to see some unknown man in full gear with ropes, karabiners, and even lederhosen scaling up the mountain wall from the opposite side of the high shelf from which I was hanging by my fingernails. He scaled the peak from the opposite side before I did (thankfully) and so he was in a position to pull me over the ledge to safety. Do you think I believe in guardian angels?

Now I thought Coach Phillipe Mollard was my hero. If he said, "Do things scarier than high speed downhill in order to prepare yourself mentally," then I said "Yes Sir, of course, let it be so." So, when we were back in Squaw Valley, our next scary venue that my teammates and I dreamed up one night was sky diving. One of the nation's best sky diving programs was near Carson City, Nevada, and it was just on the other side of Lake Tahoe. About eight of us decided that jumping out of airplanes qualified as scary, so surely we should experience a free fall or two high above beautiful Lake Tahoe. I chose to jump out of airplanes only once as I received my fill of scary the first time I jumped! On the positive side, I can say that I am also a quick learner so *one* jump out of an airplane was just fine, thank you. I can also say that by exposing myself to new and challenging experiences (rock climbing and sky diving), it did help me to relax more as a ski racer. Phillipe was correct in the sense that exposing myself to new experiences helped me to be at peace with the dangers of high speed downhill racing with which I was much more familiar. Rather than focusing solely upon relaxing during high speed racing, I learned to face other dangers with greater awareness simply due to the fact that I was willing to face them. It is like the old saying, "you can't learn to swim without getting your feet wet."

At this point some other Squaw Valley downhillers thought of a different scary exercise for relaxing under pressure that, at the same time, enabled one to work on downhill aerodynamics! Unlike today's U.S. Ski Team, we did not have access to NASA-type wind tunnels in order to practice and improve the racing aerodynamics of our downhill "tuck" position ... so some Squaw Valley-ites decided to be creative!

Two of my fellow Squaw Valley residents, Paul Bushman and Steve McKinney, proceeded to take "scary" a little further and seriously pursue the relatively new sport called "speed skiing." [By the way, later, Steve's younger sister, Tamara, became America's best female ski racer winning eighteen World Cup races including the prestigious overall World Cup in 1983, the slalom World Cup in 1984, and the giant slalom World Cup in 1981 and 1983.] During my time in Squaw Valley, Steve broke the world land speed skiing record going over 117 mph (in Italy) at a special course designed for such high speed events. He would break the world record three more times over the next decade, eventually going nearly 125 mph on a pair of skis!

Speed skiing through a radar detector goes something like this: Imagine getting ready to approach the speed trap by first going about 70 mph as you enter the top of the special course.

After reaching 70-plus mph, you drop into a very, very steep pitch that is like skiing down a vertical elevator shaft. The speed trap is located at the bottom of the steep, nearly vertical shaft. It's like jumping out of an airplane with skis on and you point yourself straight down taking advantage of your very best aerodynamic position.

Special equipment for this kind of speed skiing is needed like wrap around (the body) ski poles; ski clothing with an outer space look made of high tech, skin-tight, stretchy vinyl plastic; extra long, ultra-wide, extra heavy skies with no front tip to avoid wind resistance and four deep grooves running down the center of the ski (rather than one center groove typical of all other skies); and, for added stability, a helmet shaped like a cone with long wind foils covering your upper back. The aerodynamic bullet shape of the helmet with wind foils extending below your neck and down your upper back is designed to keep you from rising up off the snow. This occurs because the physics of the air movement mirror an airplane wing; that is, your body in a high-speed tuck position is like an airplane wing that creates lift. Incidentally, creating too much lift with your body position at very high speeds is a great way to lose control and flip over! Now this "speed skiing" sort of thing is definitely scarier than traditionally scary World Cup downhill courses, so it certainly qualified in Phillip's system of experiencing deep relaxation and calmness under stress.

Rock climbing, sky diving, and speed skiing – you see, we would do anything to learn to relax under stressful conditions. For us, being relaxed meant having a particular sort of mindset in the face of these stressful conditions. In these circumstances, you just have to have a mindset that is free and easy as if you didn't care about or think about the danger. You have to trust that some *other power* (Jp. *tariki*), not your *self power* (Jp. *jiriki*), will help you to accomplish important tasks.

Another ski racer friend, Ken Corrock, from Sun Valley, Idaho, typified this free and easy attitude. [Another "by the way," Kenny's sister, Susie Corrock won a bronze medal in the downhill event in the 1972 Winter Olympics in Sapporo, Japan.] Kenny left the U.S. Ski Team and "turned pro" in order to join the newly formed, dual, head-to-head, pro racing format designed by former U.S. Ski Team Coach Bob Beattie. The head-to-head, parallel course format was created to be more spectator-friendly and even incorporated multiple jumps in each course to add to the fan excitement. These were the early carefree years when Spider Savage, the Palmer brothers and colorful personalities like Dan "Moondog" Mooney and Otto Tschudi "ruled the roost." I went over to Heavenly Valley, Nevada, on the other side of Lake Tahoe (from my place in Squaw Valley living with Jean-Pierre), to watch one of Kenny's early pro races. Kenny was from Sun Valley and I knew him from my college days in Idaho when I raced for my college ski team. Bill Dyer was a college roommate and ski team buddy who was also a member of the U.S. National Ski Team. He was my mentor and college skiing cohort with whom we had many fun-filled weekends in such places as Sun Valley, Alta, and Snowbird.

"Bill Dyer was a college roommate and ski team buddy..."

Author (left) and Bill Dyer (right) in Bogus Basin Ski Area, Idaho 1973.

THE ART OF RELAXATION

It had snowed *a lot* over Lake Tahoe the night before Kenny's race, which favored his relaxed style. If it snowed heavily, then the course would develop deep ruts around each gate as a result of many racers skiing the exact same course. In the pro racing format with dual courses, racers would have to race many times over the same course throughout the day. As the day wore on and people were eliminated from competition, the finalists had to possess extremely relaxed knees (as "loose as a goose," you might say) in order to quickly navigate the deeply rutted, head-to-head racecourses. These course conditions truly favored Kenny who grew up skiing the deep powder snow characteristic of his home in Sun Valley, Idaho.

Kenny won this colorful pro-circuit event and, with it, came more money than any of us had ever seen before. Kenny took home not only a place at the top of the winners' pedestal, like we amateurs, but also he received a check for $8,000 as I recall. Ultimately, it was a relaxed state of mind and body that enabled Kenny to succeed and win the event by navigating the very difficult terrain under most stressful conditions.

In the context of downhill skiing, we have seen how important relaxation is to producing and managing the high speeds that are characteristic of the top competitive levels of this sport. In this sport, as in other sports and almost every other human endeavor, *relaxation equals better performance.* At this point in my story, I have no doubt that you have been thinking of your own episodes and life experiences in which you or someone you know has performed well because they were able to relax. A second way in which relaxation is a key element to improved performance (not only in skiing, but also in other activities) is the advantage that relaxation gives you in handling unexpected change. This key element was brought home to me clearly and early in life by yet another experience as a young and aggressive ski racer.

Have you ever wondered "why me," "why now"?

**Prepare for the Unexpected:
Argentina, the Army, a Misplaced Gate, and a Whole Lotta Trouble!**

In Argentina in the early seventies, Juan Peron was in power and the Americans were not in good graces. I have forgotten the particular crisis of the day, but I do remember that, "for our own protection", we had military guards with machine guns standing at attention outside *each one* of our hotel rooms. This military guard situation not only put a damper on our nightlife but also it was a little scary in and of itself. (Coach Phillipe would have been happy.)

While in Argentina during August and early September, we only trained for downhill events. We used the winter climate in the southern hemisphere to run what we called "non-stops" all day long. This meant skiing our legs into shape by skiing the mountain from top to bottom without stopping; hence, the phrase "non-stops." Our coaches would stand at various sections of the downhill racecourse, videotape us, and relay (by walkie-talkie radios) their coaching suggestions to other coaches standing at other strategically critical sections of the course. At night, we would watch the film shot during the day and listen to the coaches' audio taped comments as they watched us speed by them at various critical sections of the course. Basically, we were spending time in the evening being critiqued by our coaches in order to improve our overall performance for the next day of training on the *same* downhill racecourse.

I mention "the *same* course" purposefully. You see, racers typically memorize the course. Since you are traveling at very high speed and cannot see around the next turn or over the next pitch, you must learn and even memorize your preferred line of descent; that is, the optimal place you want to be positioned in order to safely and swiftly negotiate the dangerous terrain at 80 or 90 mph. However, racecourses change not only due to new snow conditions, but also due to new tracks laid down by the skiers preceding your descent throughout the day.

In World Cup races, *a lot* of attention is paid to properly grooming and even icing downhill racecourses. The purpose is to protect the snow base, the racetrack as it were, so that the base remains compact and does not break up simply due to the friction caused by razor-sharp ski edges turning at high speed. When this happens, it creates unwanted new snow tracks, and sometimes deep curves that can cause the next racer's skis to "chatter." Chatter can cause friction that reduces speed (that's bad enough), but much worse is the fact that chatter also can cause a CRASH!

Large diesel engines, tank-like Caterpillars, are used in North America and Europe to groom ski slopes and racecourses. This is especially necessary for downhill racing events where fresh, powder-like snow must be compacted and iced down after a big snowfall.

In Bariloche, Argentina, and Portillo, Chile, however, there were no tank-like Caterpillars for grooming the ski slopes and creating downhill racetracks where North American and European ski racers trained. Instead, the Argentine military would come out and "boot pack" the course. This means having about sixty to eighty strong military men in ski boots who are ordered to walk straight up the three-mile long downhill racecourse packing down two feet of fresh powder snow that had fallen the night before with nothing more than the strength of their legs and their ski boots. These strong men would try to stomp down the new snow and recreate what was the day before our icy fast racetrack. After the boot packing comes "side-slipping." This means the same sixty-plus army folks would finally get to put their skis on and then drop down the course side ways, hence, the term "side-slipping," in order to recreate a smooth racetrack surface after the initial boot packing phase of the new course preparation.

So, now we are prepared to put all this information together and get to the punch line related to practicing the Art of Relaxation in a sometimes stressful, constantly changing world. Learning to relax and anticipate new problems is difficult enough in daily life, but try doing this at 80 or 90 mph "standing on sticks," as we would say. The problem, you see, is that all the work the military did to prepare the course (after the night snowfall), also significantly changed it from the way the racecourse performed the day (and week) before during our training. At the time, I was not as aware as I should have been to the critical significance of changing snow conditions and the degree to which things can change on the so-called *same* race course day-to-day. My ignorance here almost cost me my life (or at least the possibility of severe injury).

At the end of this particular racecourse in Bariloche, Argentina, you come to a steep down hill pitch that can significantly increase your speed to the finish line. To take advantage of what we called "the waterfall to the finish line", you needed to avoid catapulting off the ground at the crest of the pitch and to land quickly on the downhill side aiming

THE ART OF RELAXATION

yourself to the finish line. By staying on the surface of the snow as much as possible, you could ride "the waterfall" and increase your speed rather than being slowed by the increased air resistance while being airborne. To avoid sailing off the crest into the air, you need to "pre-jump" the crest, to come off the ground just before reaching the crest so that you drop over the crest and immediately onto the downhill side of it. Relaxation is key to being able to time your pre-jump correctly because the relative time difference between a perfectly executed pre-jump and one that sends you flying out into the air is so small that you cannot wait a bit longer or jump a bit earlier. You simply have to feel and know exactly the right "present moment" in order to execute when exactly the right time to jump actually "is."

A second complication to negotiating this last part of the course is the problem of visibility. The crest of this steep pitch really is like the edge of a waterfall in that you cannot see over the crest to know where you need to land. As a result, it is necessary to fix in your mind a line or position on the crest that you are going to use as a reference point. Each time you go down the course you have in your mind this marker point that will enable you to land on the "under-hill" in the best smooth section of "good" snow. This enables you to avoid hitting "bad" snow that can send you crashing head over heels.

Let me explain. On this particular course, most of the area beneath the crest was an extremely dangerous washboard type of bumpy terrain. Such terrain on the under-hill, as we called it, is incredibly difficult to land on in the best circumstances. What makes this virtually impossible is that your legs are also numb and burning with pain by the time you reach the end of a three-mile racecourse. From previous runs and detailed study/memorization of the exact features of the course, I (and the other racers) had identified a narrow four-foot alley on the under-hill suitable for landing the pre-jump. Bear with me now...this is hard to explain! The narrow alley on the under-hill was twenty feet left of a gate that was placed on the right side of the course at the lip of the crest. Hitting this twenty-foot mark was essential to avoid landing on the bumpy washboard terrain that made up the entire under-hill (except for the targeted four-foot alley of smooth and safe under-hill terrain). If you miss the twenty-foot mark, and thus miss the safe alley, then you will hit the washboard with nearly numb legs. With numbness comes tension (not relaxation to absorb the bumps) and the result is a certain recipe for a high speed CRASH! Since the safe under-hill alley itself was hidden from the ski racer's view, the key is to align yourself exactly left of the gate at the twenty-foot mark while screaming by the last steep waterfall drop at a high rate of speed while pre-jumping the waterfall at the exact precise moment! The exact position for hitting the pre-jump successfully was fixed in my memory of the course and the twenty-foot mark relative to the gate. If you think that is difficult to explain, read, and comprehend; imagine the difficulty of actually doing it!

I was soon to learn a valuable lesson: do not trust the Argentine army to return the gates back to the same spots where they were prior to the snow storm! *Anticipation, mental attachment, and mental projection can all get you into trouble in a world that changes constantly.* The morning began as usual with skiers lined up for training runs on the course. I was the third in line of racers who would be starting at one-minute intervals. Racer number one was already on the course and missed the twenty-foot mark because *the critically important right-hand gate at the crest of the waterfall was not returned to its original location by the Argentine military "boot packers," "side slippers," and "course preparers."* The first ski racer on the course flew over the crest, aimed himself into the last waterfall pitch as planned, but skied right into the washboard under-hill terrain traveling at eighty-five mph. The poor guy blew right out of his skies and crashed his broken body into the scoreboard located at the finish line of the racecourse. Immediately, coaches with walkie-talkie radios sent word of the serious injury to officials at the starting gate and instructed them to *stop all racers* from coming down the course. The problem was that racer number two was already halfway down the course, and I had just left the starting gate completely unaware of the crash of racer number one nor the impending doom for racer number two just ahead of me.

Of course, neither racer number two nor I (the third racer on the course) knew about the accident or the actual "cause" of the crash at the finish line. No one could have pieced together that the cause of the crash was actually related to everyone's previously established "mental mark" – the twenty-foot relative position from the (now moved!) ski gate at the crest of the waterfall. No one could have predicted what was about to unfold. Racer number two also crashed since he was the second "unknowing" and "falsely cued" person to ski directly into the washboard under-hill terrain of the waterfall finish. The narrow four foot safe path was nowhere to be found with our "mark" (the right course gate) standing (who knows where?) out of position. When the second racer crashed in the washboard under-hill terrain, both skis immediately exploded out from under him (the bindings pre-released ejecting ski from ski boot) and, in that nano-second moment, the razor sharp edges on his skies sliced open the inside of his left knee like a sushi chef cutting sashimi. As I speedily (and unknowingly) approached my second friend on the course, he was still lying on the waterfall pitch flat on his back in a heap, pulsating blood. I was rapidly approaching the last section of the course in full concentration, only thinking about the upcoming pre-jump to be timed precisely at the lip of the crest while eyeing my twenty-foot mark.

Fortunately, coaches, spectators, and Argentine army men all started waving at me from both sides of the course signaling me to stop. The problem, however, was that you feel like you are a "passenger" going over 50 mph on a pair of skies. Furthermore, at 85 to 90 mph, you do not just turn sideways and stop unless the terrain allows you to pull off such a stunt. Fortunately, the air resistance created by just standing up at 90 mph was enough to slow me down considerably! I managed to reduce my speed just enough not to kill myself going over the waterfall. Like the first two skiers, I hit what was now an incorrect mark so I also skied right onto the washboard under-hill terrain following my fallen compatriots. However, since I had slowed down to 50-ish mph before the lip, I managed to negotiate the washboard bumps with my knees pounding my chest as I held on for dear life! I flew by and narrowly missed hitting my fellow ski racer who was lying in a pool of red snow.

At that moment, I learned a valuable life-long lesson related to the Art of Relaxation. *I learned not to "expect," and not to be "attached" to anything.* My expectation and attachment to the relative position of the critical right flagpole on the course almost caused me serious injury. My assumptions and lack of preparation with the *new* racecourse was a formula for disaster. *The Universe is changing all the time. It is in a state of constant flux. At every moment, your best avenue to success is to relax, expect the unexpected, and trust that your inner-Self will prevail, provided that you remain calm under stress. Calmness means clear thinking, clear thinking means preparation, and preparation (like the Art of Preparation) means building a solid foundation for personal success.*

THE ART OF RELAXATION

*Have you ever wondered
if you are really stronger relaxed?*

The Power of Relaxation

There are other stories and events that have proven to me the power of relaxation.

Over the years, I have had the pleasure to work with many talented individuals and championship coaches. For example, I have worked with the late great Hall of Fame football coach George Allen, who never had a losing season as a Head Coach for twelve years in the National Football League (NFL); the late performing artist, singer/songwriter John

"I have worked with the late great Hall of Fame football coach George Allen, who never had a losing season as a Head Coach for 12 years in the NFL."
At the Conference on Sport Psychology for Coaches. Miami, FL, 1989.

Denver (with Tom Crum); as well as Metropolitan Opera House star tenor Tony Stevenson, Japanese Sumo champion Kurosagawa, World Champion skiers, professional soccer players, professional golfers, National Hockey League players and coaches; and I also had the particular pleasure to work with Ileana Shaner, and her partner, Eric Harrell, who together won the Overall "World Cup" at the first International *Aikido Taigi* Competition in Japan in 1996. With all these people in all these different settings, I witnessed again and again how relaxation is essential to peak performance.

All these people wanted to learn to perform to the best of their ability. In all cases, whether you are a musician, athlete, or a coach, the key to helping others perform to the best of their ability is to help them achieve the optimal state of mind necessary for them to draw upon their full potential, especially under competitive pressure. Ironically, drawing upon your full resources means to empty yourself, to throw away completely (Jp. *kanzen ni nuku*) your attachment to your own prowess. Instead, you must learn to draw upon the Universe to help inspire you and guide you to levels of achievement and peak performance not previously realized.

Now we come to the crux of the matter. Exactly *how* can you learn to develop a skill or craft that enables you to relax under pressure? I would not recommend the Phillipe Mollard approach for young, teenage downhillers and suggest that you practice "scary things" such that your daily life will seem like a breeze in comparison. Nevertheless, I have shared these personal experiences because important elements of them are applicable, not only for athletic peak performance, but also for spiritual development. It all comes down to training yourself and developing your consciousness. Unfortunately, stress and anxiety rule many people's lives, and it causes them to become blind to (or to deny) the gift of their full potential as infinitely creative beings in this world.

Deep relaxation, deep calmness, and achieving ever-deeper states of meditation is not a mystic exercise. Training the mind to achieve transformative states of consciousness has been a part of western and non-western cultures for thousands of years. There are pedagogies for consciousness development that are applicable to all human beings regardless of their cultural background and religious commitments. I started meditation early in life as a form of sport psychology, if you will. When I was introduced to the teachings of Master Koichi Tohei at an *Aikido* demonstration, I was already on the path of serious skiing and ski racing. My hero ski racer, Jean-Claude Killy, declared after the 1968 Winter Olympics that his key to success (three Gold Medals) was the practice of yoga. Breathing, meditation, and self-conscious relaxing were his keys to success. Therefore, when I heard at an early age the same concepts being discussed in *Ki* and *Aikido* training, I immediately jumped at the chance to improve my mind and, therefore, my ski racing ability. Today I realize, however, that the depth of relaxation that is possible fuels not only athletic performance, but also fuels spiritual development as well as all other areas of personal and interpersonal development.

Have you ever wondered how consciousness works?

Intentional Consciousness Explained:
Three Orders of Awareness

Breathing and meditation are the key activities that enable you to learn how to relax, how to transform consciousness that is stressed and anxious into a consciousness that is relaxed and calm. The benefits from such a transformation are well known and range from better athletic performance to better health. In what immediately follows, I examine some of the details of what happens as you learn to relax and move from one state of consciousness or awareness to the next. Although I believe you will find this discussion interesting and most likely helpful, it is the *practice* of (not mere description of) breathing and meditation that produces a new paradigm of consciousness characterized by a state of deep calmness and relaxation. So, if you find the explanations below unhelpful or difficult to understand and follow, then please do not despair since you can simply go straight to the exercises at the end of the chapter and learn through your own direct practice. The explanations below are but one way I have used to try to *describe* what is going on when a person moves from "relative thinking" to a new paradigm of consciousness characterized by physical relaxation, heightened awareness, emotional stability, and deep, deep mental calmness.

Let's explore the basics of consciousness development through deep relaxation, breathing, and meditation. Over thirty-five years ago in 1979, I began writing a book explaining three modes of consciousness. Discussing these modes of awareness is just as relevant today as it was when I first created the three-tiered interpretive device in order to explain the basics of consciousness development in the context of writing my doctoral dissertation, **The Bodymind Experience in Japanese Buddhism.** This work was eventually published as a book in 1985; however, this version was intended for an academic audience of professional philosophers interested in understanding both exoteric and esoteric Japanese Buddhist traditions. Today I can draw upon the same three modes of conscious awareness in order to explain to a wider, more general audience the basic structure of our experiential life. While my teacher, Master Tohei, does not use the word "bodymind", I have used it to translate the original Japanese word *"shinshin"* in order to clarify to both academic and general audiences the meaning and significance of different states of conscious awareness.

The three "modes" or "orders of awareness" describe the "directed" or "intentional" structure of our consciousness and experience of the world. That is, you and I experience the world as directed from inside our head to the external world outside our body. If you structure the world "intentionally," starting "from" your location or place in the spatial world, it then feels as though you "direct" your attention "to" things and events outside yourself. Even when you engage in introspection of your own internal states of feeling and/or thinking, the structure of your experience is as though there is a "you" deep down somewhere that is somehow the real author of your conscious attentions. You are free to direct your attention *from* you, as the subject and author of your consciousness, *to* objects outside yourself, or *to* internal states of feeling or memory, or *to* ideas themselves "inside" your own consciousness.

The three modes of awareness I use to describe the structures of consciousness are based upon levels of intentional complexity. I can say that since the publication of **The Bodymind Experience,** I have used this model or template of intentional consciousness to help many people over the last thirty-five years to practice the Art of Relaxation and improve their performance in a great variety of fields and endeavors from music to athletics, to business development, and to organizational development.

Have you ever wondered why your thoughts are always "of something"?

Third Order Awareness

Let's examine briefly the basic differences between the three orders of directed experience (that is, levels of intentional complexity) as they will help us to explain the Art of Relaxation more fully. In daily life, 99.9% of the time our conscious life is changing rapidly and moving directionally/ intentionally at different objects or things at a high rate of speed. I call this Third Order Awareness and it is typical of our constantly changing and moving our attention to different thoughts, sensory impressions, people, concepts, opinions, judgments, problem solving, etc. The simple act of getting out of bed, showering, dressing, eating, gathering your belongings, and driving to work or school has thousands of different changes of intention and attention. Each idea and each sensory process represents a flow of concepts and impressions that serve as the constantly changing environment of your consciousness that is composed of the objects of your attention.

If you were to measure the electrical activity of the brain using an electroencephalogram, then this Third Order Mode of Awareness would look like constantly moving blips up and down the recorder paper as new thoughts and impressions get measured as spikes of constantly changing electrical activity. Your mind is busy moving as you manage all of your various responsibilities. Throughout the day you feel as though you engage the external world as the author or director of your various private attentions. Even your experience of time is a function of the passage of a constant sequence of thoughts and sensory impressions. For example, time seems to "fly by" (Lt. *tempus fugit*) when your attention is fully engaged. Conversely, time is experienced as moving slowly when you are bored, disengaged, and your attentions are scattered and unfocused. This stream of various attentions and commensurate mental activity is the most complex and yet most common form of intentional, directed consciousness, and I will refer to it as Third Order Awareness.

Have you ever wondered if you could truly focus your mind?

Second Order Awareness

The second intentional structure of consciousness is quite different and rare. In Second Order Awareness, your consciousness is capable of directing and sustaining its concentration and focus upon a single object. For most people, learning to hold your attention on one thing for even one minute is a very difficult, seemingly impossible task.

I frequently demonstrate the difficulty of maintaining concentration with groups of students, athletes, academics, musicians, business leaders, and martial artists using a very simple exercise. For example, imagine that you are in a class and I am standing in front of you holding up a coffee cup. I then ask you and the other participants to "get a good image of the coffee cup 'in your mind' and then please close your eyes. Continue to concentrate only on the cup until I say stop. Please do not open your eyes until I inform you that the exercise is over." After only one minute I say, "OK, please open your eyes." Then I ask, "Tell me some of the things you thought about and we will make a list together."

Participants are eager to share the following kinds of thoughts and impressions about the coffee cup as I go around the room looking for responses to my question. Participants eagerly chime in saying things like "In my image of the cup, I thought of its color." Another says "I saw its shape as you turned it in your hand before we closed our eyes." Still another adds "In my mind, I saw the shiny corner of the cup in the light." Now many participants jump in and say things like "I wondered if you were still holding the cup up over your head while we had our eyes closed?" Someone else adds "I heard the street noises more clearly when I closed my eyes." Another confessed "I wondered how long we were going to have our eyes closed?" Another confesses further "Yeah, and I wondered if I was the *only* one with my eyes closed? I kept wanting to open my eyes and look at the others in the room." Still another adds "I thought, *why* are we doing this?" Finally, another says "I just wanted some coffee as I got sleepy."

You can see that, for each person participating in this one-minute concentration exercise (remember I had asked them to concentrate *only* on the coffee cup), there was a stream of consciousness with many different thoughts and impressions bouncing all around in the privacy of each person's mind. However, the assignment was simply to maintain concentration on the cup itself for just one minute. The difficulty of sustaining single-minded concentration on just one object for even one minute is evidenced by the sequence and variety of things and impressions that came into each participant's mind.

This exercise was simply a request to try Second Order Awareness, directing and sustaining concentration upon a single object. But, in reality, everyone in the room was engaged in Third Order Awareness where their attention was constantly changing from color, to shape, to light, to cup position, to my position, to outside noises, to the passage of time, to thirst, to sleepiness, etc. This type of response is very typical because people are not usually taught *how* to relax their mind or consciousness so that it can remain in a state of calm, single-minded attention characteristic of Second Order Awareness. Remember, Second Order Awareness is characterized by sustained, focused concentration upon a *single* object of our attention.

Have you ever wondered if you could really empty your mind?

First Order Awareness

Let us now turn to the next mode of awareness. First Order Awareness can be experienced only after you master Second Order Awareness. In First Order Awareness, there is no intentionality; that is, there is no experience of the directed nature of consciousness from here to there. In First Order Awareness, you experience your world by merely presencing. You and your world are not separate. You do not *cause separation* through your conscious intentional activity. In First Order Awareness, there is no judgment, no analyzing, no defensiveness, no blaming, no criticizing, and no teaching. There is no adding on, or projecting, or intending any of your own conscious, subconscious, or even unconscious formation states on to the field of sheer presencing.

Once you learn to experience the world from this viewing place, which is more like a place of witnessing, then you will be confronted with the pure, non-intentional background or horizon of your consciousness experience. You will experience, perhaps for the first time in your life, the pure foundational stage or arena within which all your conscious projections (of a Third Order and Second Order type) take place. The intentional or directed nature of consciousness is thus laid bare because, for the first time, you see (that is, you presence, you are confronted with) the *pure field of experience* upon which *you* have been adding a lifetime of *your own private projections*. These "formation projections" were caused by your culture, your personal history, your emotions, your likes, your dislikes, and your institutional memory of all the significant events that happened to you in your lifetime that were still affecting your consciousness up to the present moment. You must first *claim as yours* all that has happened to you as a result of your deep consciousness formations and then you must "let go," "release," and "free yourself" of the negative affects of your formation projections that have been defining your deeper self, most likely without your conscious awareness. To discover your deeper Self, you must experience the relationship between intentionality (Second and Third Order Awareness) and true non-intentional presencing (First Order Awareness).

This base of pure, non-intentional consciousness can be likened to a mirror that reflects things as they truly are, not as they have appeared to you filtered, colored, and tainted by your personal projections acquired over a lifetime of experience. Your conscious projections reflect your subjectivity that can be likened to dust *covering* the mirror of your consciousness. When you experience First Order Awareness for the first time, it is as though you are coming out of the cave of your past consciousness and habituated projections. Rather than viewing the world as you always have (filtered by your projections), you now see the world, people, events, and states of affairs without the intentional formation or pre-arranged dust *covering* the mirror of your consciousness. Without your *subjective* intentional frames of reference, you experience the world as *objective*. At this moment, the cave or consciousness prison of "relative thinking" gives way to "Absolute Thinking" characterized by a unitive experience with God, Spirit, the Universe Itself. You experience and realize that you have been One with the Universe all the time and that you, through your subjective projections, have served to create *causally* a false, illusionary view of not only the external world "around you," but also the world "within you" characterized by your silent introspections and internal formation projections.

Seeing the world or "being in the world" from the standpoint of Third Order and Second Order Awareness is characterized by intentional, directed experience. The intentional nature of these modes of experience serve as a filter or dust upon the mirror of your consciousness prohibiting you from ever seeing yourself truly. Your Original Self, your unadulterated Self now can be presenced perhaps *for the first time in your life.*

Have you ever wondered if you could calm yourself through meditation or prayer?

A Pathway for Genuine Transformation

The task before us now is to explain a pathway for transforming your consciousness *from* the habit of Third Order Awareness *to* the focused, single-minded attention characteristic of Second Order Awareness, and only then will you be able to experience and discover for yourself (Jp. *ki ga tsuku*) the qualitatively different, non-intentional experience characterized by First Order Awareness. Only by mastering Second Order Awareness (so that it becomes a habit of consciousness) can you discover the gift of presencing your Universe from a First Order Mode of Awareness.

I believe that the great traditions of meditation and personal development in both East and West share this structure. Teaching people *how* to relax and *how* to focus their mind is really a matter of patience and discipline. It means learning *how* to view the world from a Second Order mode of awareness so that your consciousness is directed to a single thing, concept, or image while you sustain this focused concentration over time. This does require special mental training in order to maintain focus upon a single thread. But this type of awareness is not mystical; it is most logical, rational and, above all, experiential. Your practice must be daily, and so, patience and discipline will serve your experiential journey very well.

Given this background, we are now prepared to understand that the Art of Relaxation has everything to do with learning *how* to calm the busyness of your mind characterized by Third Order Awareness that occupies 99.9% of your conscious life. The pure field of your experience in this Universe (First Order Awareness) is never fully experienced by most people simply because the common Third Order mode of intentional consciousness is constantly "covering over" (Sk. *samvrti*) your true Self, it is coloring your view of others, and it is altering your opinion of yourself, others, and the world around you.

Layers of habituated conscious projections accumulate day after day, month after month, year after year until finally it is as though we are viewing the world through the distortion of tinted glasses, prohibiting us from not only "presencing" the world as it really is, but also we are prohibited from ever realizing that, in fact, our view of the world has become systematically tinted and distorted. It seems as though we cannot get out from behind the tinted glasses of our consciousness. We perceive and think that the world actually is tinted and we have no way of knowing/experiencing that our internal and external worlds could be otherwise. This is the cave we live in until we can peel back the layers of our conscious projections learned since childhood.

Let's return now to the basics. Schools of meditation, breathing, and relaxation of both East and West share something in common. When pursuing single-minded and sustained consciousness (Second Order Awareness), practitioners are encouraged to choose an object of meditation that is *dynamic,* not *static*. My concentration exercise using a coffee cup (or sometimes a classroom board eraser) is difficult precisely because the object of concentration that I choose is static. Of course, at an atomic level, the coffee cup is moving and dynamic but, at the visual level, people *see* a static, unchanging coffee cup. The problem (and the opportunity in disguise) is to recognize that your conscious mind is dynamic in nature.

Your mind is always moving (in a Third Order mode) from object to object, or concept to concept, or image to image, and so on. If the electrical activity of your brain were to stop completely (static), then you would be "brain dead" with a flat line on the monitor instead of the dynamic activity registered by the blips and spikes described earlier. Since your mind is active and wants to move, it is difficult for you to force it to slow down, much less sustain mental concentration with a single dynamic rhythm focused upon one thing or one thread over time. The reason the mind jumps around in the coffee cup exercise is because the mind is dynamic and wants to move, but the coffee cup appears static. Therefore, the mind creates new images and concepts moving through our class-generated list. In our example, the mind moved from the coffee cup's shape, to color, to light, to its position in my hand, to outside noises, to awareness of the passage of time, to sleepiness, to thirst, etc. While our class list (above) was generated by many participants, the key point is that each individual mind moved through his or her own private mental list of stream of consciousness images during the one minute concentration exercise.

To compensate for the mind's desire to move, the great meditative traditions choose (as the object of meditation and focus) something that shares the mind's dynamic tendency to move. If the object of your meditation is dynamic and not static, then your mind can move in harmony with it. The sustaining, single-minded focus of Second Order Awareness thus can be facilitated by working with a dynamic object (as the focus of concentrated meditation) that matches the dynamic quality and movement of your consciousness. The mind wants to move and so you can satisfy that need by using objects of concentration that also move; that is, they possess a dynamic quality.

Have you ever wondered why meditation seems so strange?

Mantras, Mudras and *Mandalas*

In the Eastern traditions, we can cite three examples of objects of meditation that possess this dynamic quality conducive to single-minded attention over time – *mantras, mudras,* and *mandalas*. After discussing these three examples, you will be prepared to understand the actual practice of your own Dynamic Meditation. At the conclusion of this chapter, I will guide your Dynamic Meditation and Dynamic Breathing practice through the exercises recommended for the Art of Relaxation.

Mantras are simply sounds. Sounds are dynamic because the sound waves continue infinitely moving through space and time. A *mantra* can be a temple bell ringing over time, or a sound that you recite and hold in meditation (usually a vowel and consonant combination, for example – OM), or a *mantra* can even be the sound of the wind or ocean waves breaking on the shore. Each of these sounds can serve as the object of your sustained concentration over time. Since your mind wants to move as is its habit, you simply satisfy the mind's craving and allow it to dwell over time on something that is itself dynamic. Sounds can be uttered with dynamic, rhythmic, sustaining power if only for thirty to sixty seconds. Learning how to produce and sustain your focused attention upon a *mantra* can quickly help you to calm the waves of your mind that reflect the busy, intentional habits of consciousness that characterize your daily life (Third Order Awareness).

Mudras are symbolic hand postures that are performed in dynamic, rhythmic succession. The practitioner memorizes and practices the sequenced series of hand postures in order to be able eventually to perform them without conscious intention. Of course, in the beginning you must have conscious intention in order to learn the series of intricate postures, but it is the actual single-minded performance of the continuing series of postures that represents the dynamic quality that serves as a positive vehicle for meditation and Second Order Awareness.

Mandalas are visual diagrams that symbolically represent a dynamic flow of representational themes and meanings that are based upon a single thread of concepts considered in succession. A *mandala* picture may contain multiple images arranged in a circle that the practitioner initially learns and memorizes with conscious intention. However, during the meditation practice, the practitioner becomes familiar and more comfortable with the predetermined dynamic flow of images and symbols that at once satisfies the mind's desire to move dynamically, while at the same time providing a continuous single-minded thread occasioned by the "theme," as it were, of the *mandala* representation.

Mantras, mudras, and *mandalas* share the dynamic quality that serves to satisfy the mind's desire to move its attention continuously. In the western tradition, reciting a rosary or prayer continuously has this same calming effect. The conscious mind wants to move, so the use of something that is itself dynamic has the beneficial effect of marrying the mind's desire to move with the practitioner's desire to learn to focus and sustain concentration over time.

Have you ever wondered if you could change mental and emotional habits?

The Process of Transformation

Among the many ways to experience the Art of Relaxation using this understanding of the mind is to learn Dynamic Breathing exercises. I have found that this method is extremely successful because breathing, by definition, is a dynamic activity. Breathing exercises can be learned by anyone and they need not have any specific religious connotation. For some people, the imagery of, and symbolism of, *mantras, mudras,* and *mandalas* may serve as a religious deterrent to their journey toward personal transformation. However, everyone breaths; breathing is always a dynamic activity, and breathing mindfully is an easy way to begin a practice that facilitates the Art of Relaxation.

Before we start to explore mindful Dynamic Breathing more deeply, let us review some important themes based upon the three orders of experience defined thus far. The transformation process is one that moves from Third Order Awareness to Second Order Awareness and then, finally, to First Order Awareness. The first step is simply to practice observing the Third Order intentional structure of your own conscious life. Simply learning to recognize patterns of projections that cause you to view the world in certain ways is itself an enormous undertaking that occasions a tremendous opportunity to fuel your personal growth. During the day, from our Third Order mode of continuous intentional projections, we spend a lot of time judging, criticizing, blaming, and instructing others, as well as being defensive when others do the same to us. Bringing about an awareness of the frequency, scope, and depth of these patterns of conscious projection is itself a worthy first goal in the Art of Relaxation.

As you gain insight into the patterns of your conscious life as experienced through the dust, the filters, and ultimately the cave of Third Order Awareness, you will want to experience yourself and your environment more calmly and more deeply. This can be accomplished by training yourself to view the world in a more focused, single-minded manner occasioned by cultivating Second Order Awareness. Patience and discipline will help you to mindfully practice Dynamic Breathing and Dynamic Meditation on a daily basis. This, however, is not an end in itself. By mastering Second Order Awareness, you will find that, without any conscious intention on your part, you will grow to experience non-intentional consciousness characteristic of the unitive experience of First Order Awareness.

The process of moving from Second Order, single-minded attention, to non-intentional First Order Awareness is not unlike learning anything so well that it becomes second nature. You memorize, for example, a piano piece so that you eventually perform it without consciously thinking of the individual phrases and fingering positions as you once did in practice. Or, you initially learn all the individual mechanics of a golf swing – stance, ball position, left arm straight, head down, etc. All these golfing instructions were at one time a mass of confusing Third Order points to remember. However, once your golf swing became "natural," you could perform a shot being mindful of only a single (Second Order) mental instruction – perhaps visualizing the target or imagining the flight of the ball as you plan to execute the shot.

Another good "process of transformation" example is learning how to drive a standard stick shift car. In the beginning, you may recall a mass of Third Order instructions given to you perhaps late at night by your brave instructor in the Wal-Mart parking lot away from anyone or anything that may get in the path of your car! Initially, your instructor needed to teach you about the coordinated and confusing movement of the gearshift, the clutch, the gradual release of the clutch and simultaneous depression of the accelerator. Only then (hopefully without losing the car's transmission) were you instructed to execute the entire series of coordinated movements again, but this time the process was for the purpose of entering second gear, and then again for third gear, and so on.

This mass of Third Order intentional directions, accompanied by physical movement in traffic, is enough to terrify the novice learning to drive a manual transmission stick shift automobile. The key of this "learning how to drive" illustration is that, at some point in time *without your conscious attention* or knowledge, you started driving your standard stick shift car *without intention*. This does not mean you entered a First Order mode of awareness, but it does demonstrate that it is possible to learn to perform tasks so well that you are able to perform even complex mental and physical activities without conscious intentionality.

Doing things without intentional thinking is common. It is also common that, when we free our mind of intentional thinking as in piano performance, golf, skiing, and driving an automobile, we usually simply add on some other acquired habit of thinking or emotion and thus we remain in a Third Order mode of awareness. For example, we are now free to drive the stick shift without thinking of our own physical mechanics moving through the gears, but our mind is now thinking (daydreaming perhaps) about some other problem or opportunity while we are supposed to be focused upon driving the car in traffic. We drive non-intentionally in terms of the mechanics of clutch, accelerator, and brake, but our conscious mind is now consumed by problems at work while talking on the cell phone, for example. Hopefully, your mind is not so distracted that you completely disengage your present awareness and find yourself in an automobile accident.

Our goal in the Art of Relaxation is to learn through Dynamic Breathing and Dynamic Meditation *how* to develop and sustain a Second Order mode of consciousness so well that we become free of even the single-minded conscious focus that characterizes the Second Order Awareness. Just as you once learned to drive the standard shift automobile without thinking, it is also possible to learn to be so comfortable in Second Order meditative consciousness that you similarly neutralize, as it were, the only directed, intentional focus that is operating in your Second Order consciousness. When this "molting," "letting go," "casting off," or "neutralizing" happens naturally without conscious intention, then a new qualitatively different experience emerges.

First Order Awareness is *qualitatively different* from Third and Second Order Awareness because in First Order experience there is no intentionality, no subject-object, no here to there, no directed-ness of conscious energy. In contrast, Third and Second Order Awareness are *quantitatively different*. Third Order Awareness is filled with many directed and intentional "stances", both mental and emotional, that occur in a never-ending sequence. Second Order Awareness is *quantitatively* empty by comparison. Second Order Awareness consists of only a single focused intention that exists over time. However, it is still an intentional and directed experience nonetheless. On the other hand, First Order Awareness opens the door to an entirely new, *qualitatively* different dimension of our experience.

Cultivating First Order Awareness means coming out of the cave of a lifetime of judging, craving, blaming, filtering, valuing, instructing, etc. When you train yourself thoroughly to be able to perform Second Order meditative experience without intentional thinking, then you will finally enter a new field of consciousness possibility. You will, perhaps for the first time, presence your true relationship with the Universe Itself – you are one with the Universe. This state of experiential awareness is in marked contrast to the way in which you have become accustomed to experiencing the world as conditioned by the filtering habits and activity of your intentionally based consciousness.

The key to entering First Order Awareness is to allow the single intentional focus of Second Order Awareness to fade away naturally. This will occur unconsciously without intention and you will experience a laying bare of the field of pure, unadulterated consciousness that is the underlying basis of your conscious life. For the first time in your life, you will confront directly and experientially the ground beneath all the acquired habits of your intentional life. You will see clearly the filtering habits of your mind simply because you will be present in the world without subjective distortion.

In this experience/mode of consciousness that we earlier called "Absolute Thinking," the objective reality you experience is the same objective reality that is in common with anyone else viewing the world without conscious, subconscious, or unconscious formation projections. Here the objective ground of our shared human condition is presenced perhaps for the very first time. The truth of the Golden Rule, for example, is now experienced directly as you naturally empathize and sympathize with others in response to your fundamental connection to, and identity with, your fellow human beings. With your subjective projections out of the way, you begin to experience your original connection with the Universe. In this original connection, there is no separation, no ego, no independent existence.

The Art of Relaxation cultivates First Order Awareness and thus serves to deepen your appreciation for, and practice of, the Art of Compassion and Art of Responsibility. That is, since your deep connection to all living things and all of creation is made manifest, then genuine *compassion* and real *responsibility* occur naturally without conscious intention. When you are transformed experientially in the process of true spiritual development, then your actions will be seen by your true Self in a new light against the background of deep calmness and insight. This insight is related to your direct experiential awareness of the basis of conscious intentionality. That is, you become directly aware of the myriad ways and possibilities of compassionate and responsible action. This insight, in turn, naturally gives rise to the next door in the process of personal transformation.

The Art of Conscious Action, which is the next and fifth Art, can only be truly appreciated once one has embraced true First Order Awareness. Against the background of experiencing your own mind "as calm and still as the surface of the water that reflects the moon and the flying bird," you will gain an entirely new appreciation for pure Conscious Action. At this point in your development, your conscious intentions (and the directed structure of your mind – Second and Third Order Awareness) will take on new meaning and significance. It is for this reason that the fifth Art of Conscious Action lies at your doorstep. Understanding and practicing deeply the Art of Conscious Action represents the next *need*, the next challenge, and the next level in the process of your transformation journey.

THE ART OF RELAXATION

**Daily Exercises
To Facilitate The Art of Relaxation**

> *Ki Breathing*
>
> *Breathe out so that your breath travels infinitely to the ends of the Universe, breathe in so that your breath reaches your one point and continues infinitely there. Ki breathing is an important way of unifying mind and body.*
>
> *At night when all is quiet and calm, do this alone, and you will feel that you are the Universe and that the Universe is you. It will lead you to the supreme ecstasy of being One with the Universe. At this moment the life power that is rightfully yours is fully activated.*
>
> *—Koichi Tohei*

Have you ever wondered if you could calm yourself quickly in the midst of a stressful day?

Exercise 8:
Dynamic Breathing

Now you are prepared to "go deeper." In Exercise 2, you were first introduced to the simple experience of stillness and calmness. At this point on your journey, your practice (Exercises 1 – 7) has prepared you for longer periods of silence and stillness. The breathing exercise will enable you to calm the waves of your mind much more deeply. This is mindfulness practice for mindful living.

The Art of Relaxation is about deep inner calmness. Your practice of breathing and meditation over time will enable you to master your mind rather than being its slave. Instead of being cast about like a bobber on the surface of a stormy sea, your mind will feel like the deep solid keel of a sail boat enabling you to navigate a clear life path amidst the rough current that others may throw in your path. Calmness means great strength of action.

Whether your aim is simple performance improvement or deep spiritual connection and development, your first steps must be to become aware of your own mental states as well as the process of true mental, emotional, and physical relaxation. The voice of God, Spirit, and the Divine is loud and clear once you calm yourself to a level where the silence is deafening with *teachings and instructions from the Universe* (Jp. *Kaiden*).

To begin your Dynamic Breathing practice, please follow the following instructions...

Each day choose a quiet place without distraction. Sit in a chair with an upright posture, knees at right angles, and the bottoms of your feet squarely on the floor. Relax and draw your shoulders first up and then roll them gently backwards. Open your chest fully, and arch (take the "slack" out of) the small of your lower back so that you feel long, stretched, and floating upright in the chair. You are preparing to open your chest, to breathe fully, and to maximize your awareness of your surroundings. You wish to feel large, positive, and full of energy. Allow the weight of every part of your body to fall naturally to its most "underside," completely relaxed position.

THE ART OF RELAXATION

"Breathe out so that your breath travels infinitely to the ends of the Universe, breathe in so that your breath reaches your one point and continues infinitely there..."

Photo by T.R. Smith

Soften your face and relax your mouth and jaw. Inhale slowly through your nose and exhale calmly through your mouth making the sound of AHHH. After your lungs have expelled almost all the air, ever so slightly bend forward at the waist (only an inch or so while keeping your back straight and shoulders square) until the air is exhaled completely. When all the air is expelled, softly close your lips and begin to slowly inhale through your nose. After you feel your lungs expand and become almost full of air, gradually bend again at the waist (only an inch) returning calmly to your upright position as the air is inhaled completely. Repeat for each breath.

As you begin this practice merely watch, observe, and become aware of your natural breathing process of inhalation (expansion) and exhalation (contraction). As you practice, naturally allow yourself to gradually increase the duration of each inhalation and exhalation. Do not attempt to force prolonged breaths as this will merely make you tense and will undermine your progress in the Art of Relaxation. Your goal is calmness and complete mental, emotional, and physical relaxation. Therefore, do not attempt to slow your cadence to longer time spans until you can remain deeply calm in the process. You can begin by merely being mindful of your natural breathing rhythm. This may be only twenty-second, ten-second, or even five-second inhalation and exhalation intervals. Soon you will discover thirty or forty-five seconds for each inhale and exhale is common and feels most calm and relaxed.

You can sit and perform Dynamic Breathing for ten minutes *each* day to begin. Gradually, you will learn the pleasure and benefits of longer sitting. You can easily work up to one-hour sessions where you feel most calm and relaxed. The best time for longer, uninterrupted breathing sessions is early in the morning (at 4:00 a.m. or 5:00 a.m. or 6:00 a.m.) when all is quiet and calm. I have taught beginners and even led entire families in this kind of Dynamic Breathing practice for three consecutive hours the very first time they practiced. Even five consecutive hours with my students is not uncommon.

In five-hour sessions, I call it the 600 breaths training. In this breathing, we count our breaths as a singular focus for concentration – 120 breaths for the first hour (thirty-second intervals), 240 breaths after two hours, 360 after three hours, 480 breaths after four hours, and 600 breaths after five hours. Every time I have breathed for five consecutive hours, I have never reached more than 480 total breaths before the five-hour time period. This simply means that during the five hours of Dynamic Breathing, the inhalation and exhalation intervals become much longer than thirty seconds. At my home, we have invited practitioners to breathe from 1:00 a.m. to 6:00 a.m. and then share a marvelous home-cooked breakfast!

You can practice as much as you like. If you feel pressured by *external* factors, then it will not be enjoyable and it will be difficult for you to maintain your practice each day. *Internal* motivation is always best. You can practice everyday for three consecutive hours from 2:00 a.m. to 5:00 a.m., if you like, then take a deep sleep "nap" until 6:30 a.m., and then go on with your day - calm, refreshed, clear and energized. The depth of calmness you receive from the Universe between 2 a.m. and 5 a.m. more than compensates for your lack of sleep. Deep, Dynamic Breathing practice is actually much more restful than sleep, especially if your sleeping habits include tossing and turning with anxiety-riddled dreams.

You can practice each day until the physical breathing action and rhythm are most comfortable. Once you no longer need to consciously and intentionally think about the mechanics of the breathing process, simply feel your connection to the Universe around you.

Breathe out imagining that your breath travels infinitely to the ends of the Universe. Breathe in imagining that your breath comes from the ends of the Universe into your deepest, truest Self. Be at peace with the dynamic rhythm of the breathing process. If you continue this process of inhalation and exhalation, you will eventually and unconsciously cease the act of "imagining" as your *Ki* (life force) extends naturally (Jp. *ki o dasu*) in all directions. Allow even the smallest waves of your mind to become deeply calm until you experience that You are the Universe and the Universe is You. Once you directly and experientially presence your connection with the Universe Itself, you will see yourself in new ways, with new possibilities, and you will experience a new appreciation for, and interest in, the Art of Conscious Action, the next and fifth level of your developmental journey.

Have you ever wondered how to meditate and whether or not it would truly make a difference?

**Exercise 9:
Dynamic Meditation**

Now you are prepared to "go deeper" still. By learning to empty your mind of needless clutter, you will begin to experience the pure stage upon which your intentional life has been cast. This experience of First Order Bodymind Awareness will serve as the foundation for "conscious action" in daily life.

> **The Definition of Ki**
>
> We begin with the number One in counting all things. It is impossible that this One can ever be reduced to zero. Because just as something cannot be made from nothing, One cannot be made from zero.
>
> Ki is like the number One. Ki is formed from infinitely small particles, smaller than an atom. The universal Ki condensed becomes an individual, which further condensed becomes the one point in the lower abdomen, which in turn infinitely condensed never becomes zero, but becomes One with the Universe. Thus we understand the definition of Ki.
>
> —Koichi Tohei

I will begin to describe Dynamic Meditation by making reference to a classic contradiction in the western philosophical tradition. My discussions of relative thinking versus Absolute Thinking can also be clarified through this example. The ancient Greek philosopher Zeno observed a series of paradoxes that cause us to question the validity of our everyday frames of reference (relative thinking).

Imagine a simple line segment from you (sitting in a chair) to a wall in the same room. Your task is to rise up from your chair and proceed to walk toward the wall and touch its surface with your finger. Simple enough? Now follow along with me. Once you stand up from your chair, look at the distance on the floor from your toes to where the wall meets the floor. See the distance as ONE line segment on the floor.

Now walk to the place on the floor that represents the halfway point between you and the wall. (Just to be clear, this is the same as the halfway point of your imagined single-line segment.)

Repeat this process again first noticing and then walking to the next halfway point continuing to move in the direction of the wall. Notice that from your present position moving by halves in the direction of the wall, you have created (each time) another new, singular line segment *albeit* one half its previous length. At this point, you will have traversed three quarters of the original distance between your chair and the wall (first going halfway to the wall, then halfway again).

Repeat this exercise moving closer to the wall again by half. If you repeat this exercise again, and again, and again, will your toes ever be able to touch the wall? At very close distances, you are an inch away, a half-inch, a pinhead, a molecule, an atom, a nucleus, an electron, a quark, etc. If you consult your rational mind following this logical progression, will you ever be able to touch the wall? No.

The point is that ONE can never be reduced to zero. This dynamic mental exercise of reducing ONE by halves demonstrates that ONE can never ever be completely erased to zero. You can imagine ONE as something that is never ending and so your mind can continue infinitely (by halves) in this Dynamic Meditation. If you only rely upon your logical, rational mind (your reasoning ability), then it should be apparent that you will never be able to traverse the infinite number of points contained within the ONE single line segment from your chair to the wall. Similarly, you will never be able to traverse the infinite number of points contained within the ONE single line segment even one inch from the wall, to the wall, and so on.

Zeno concluded that there was something odd or even wrong with our everyday experience *(relative thinking)* of space, time, and motion. Using logic and our rational thinking, Zeno believed that we should not be able to traverse space or a measured distance composed of an *infinite* number of points with our *finite* bodies. He concluded that this world that we can see, feel, taste, touch and move in, must be unreal; it must be an illusion of sorts. In the language of my teacher, Master Koichi Tohei, the problem is that our everyday experience is characterized by the learned and habitual bias of relative thinking. Absolute Thinking, by contrast, can occur naturally for anyone not attached to these relative frames of reference.

It is possible to imagine the same paradox in reverse in order to demonstrate that you should not even be able to move (at all) out of the chair in the first place. That is, how can your *finite* physical body traverse even the first twelve inches (itself ONE single line segment) required to stand up if the twelve inches represents a line segment of ONE that itself contains an *infinite* number of points? In either example of the paradox, your logical mind concludes that you can neither touch the wall (by traversing the infinite number of points contained in the distance comprising the ONE line segment across the floor to the wall), nor can you ever even move because your finite limbs cannot traverse the infinite number of points (by half) contained within the first centimeter or millimeter of your initial movement. Zeno declared that our experience of this world (empiricism) and our reasoning about this world (rationalism) create a real paradox. My point is that attachment to relative thinking is the real culprit; yet, we can learn a valuable lesson to assist our Dynamic (that is, never ending*)* Meditation. The concept that "ONE can never be reduced to zero" can help us to personally experience true, deep relaxation.

Begin your daily Dynamic Meditation just like your Dynamic Breathing practice – quiet room, early in the morning, upright in the chair, etc. (as described in italics in the Dynamic Breathing Exercise 8 above). In fact, you may wish to practice these two Art of Relaxation exercises interchangeably depending upon your mood and comfort. The most important thing is that you should feel comfortable and positive about your practice so that you will continue to train and develop yourself daily. Mental training has no quick fix; therefore, you must approach your practice as a process without attachment to the "results" or "fruits" of the real positive, life changing transformation that will surely come your way when you are truly ready to receive these fruits from God, Spirit, or the Universe. In other words, *attachment* to even the fruits of your positive progress (as you proceed through the successive stages of the Seven Arts development process) will cause your progress to be halted. In order to advance ever deeper on your Seven Arts journey of positive self-transformation, you must be willing to "give up" and "sacrifice" or "renounce" (Sk. *yajna*) even the benefits along the way. If you become attached to the benefits of one level of understanding (or Art), then you inhibit (or even prohibit) your ability to "give up" or "let go" of the clinging that causes you to remain stuck and thus fixed at the same level of experience, understanding, calmness and, ultimately connectedness to the Universe Itself.

As you calmly sit for the first few minutes of your Dynamic Meditation practice, simply observe and become aware of your own breath, your own heartbeat, your own state of being. Gradually relax yourself to the point of breathing without "observing," without "noticing," or having "intention." After you are calm and relaxed, begin the Dynamic Meditation process by feeling your positive Ki, positive energy, positive life force extending outward naturally and expanding sequentially in all directions. You

THE ART OF RELAXATION

begin by feeling your physical self first and then experiencing your energy expanding all around you until it fills the room, your home, your town, your state, your country, the globe, etc. The dynamic process of expansion continues infinitely as your awareness extends beyond the limits of your imagination. This continuing process of expansion eventually includes the earth, the solar system, the Milky Way, many spiraling galaxies, and continues until you cannot consciously think of any particular *thing* that is bigger. Your feeling of infinite expansion continues larger, larger, and larger. Eventually you cannot "imagine" anything larger than what appears in your mind as bright stars (which are actually entire spiraling galaxies traveling rapidly and moving apart

"After you are calm and relaxed, begin the Dynamic Meditation process."

from each other against the background of deep, dark space). When you can no longer "think" of or "imagine" anything *in particular* (that is, no *individual* thing or concept is the object of your directed intention), then simply allow the *feeling* of outward energy expansion to continue infinitely. You can allow this continuous progression to occur for minutes at a time if you like. By practicing this Dynamic Meditation, your mind will be satisfied, as it will be able to move along a path that is without end.

This Dynamic Meditation exercise shares with the Dynamic Breathing exercise the same dynamic qualities of meditation that we discussed previously. The concept that "ONE can never be reduced to zero" provides a continuous, never ending, dynamic rhythm that allows your mind to move in a constant progression or thread of infinite expansion, thus calming the waves of your mind.

After you have reached the outer limits of your conscious, intentional mind where you are simply feeling an expansion beyond any imagined thing or conceptual point of reference, then simply reverse the process again by halves. Instead of *expansion*, you are now practicing *contraction*, and your conscious mind can now be on a new dynamic path (reducing by halves) beginning with the outer galaxies and then moving all the way back to yourself. When you reach yourself, continue the process by concentrating your energy (again by halves) to the physiological center of your body which is located about four inches below your navel just above the pubic bone. From this single one point, which is your center of gravity, continue your concentration by halves to even smaller categories further reducing/contracting your ONE center point. Continue your concentration to the size of a pinhead, to the size of a molecule, an atom, an electron, a quark, and so on until again you can no longer "imagine" or "conceptualize" any thing smaller. As before when you experienced infinite largeness, simply let the *feeling* of concentration by halves continue infinitely – smaller, smaller, smaller.

THE ART OF RELAXATION

At this point, you will realize that your experience of infinite expansion and infinite concentration or contraction is the exact same. Once you move through the attached frames of reference (expansion as well as contraction) characteristic of relative thinking, you will be experiencing no *thing* or nothing *in particular* at both extremes of the Dynamic Meditation process. At this moment, you will realize for yourself that the experience of *"no thing"* or *"nothing in particular"* is the exact same as the experience of *"everything."* In this way, you will be preparing your mind, your consciousness, and your WHOLE being to experience the world in new and remarkably transformative ways. With time and continuous practice, you will not even need the "sustaining focus" pedagogical tool of moving through the expansion and contraction "half, half, half" imagery. Instead, you will quickly be able to simply go to the place where *nothing in particular is the same as everythin*g - - the Universe Itself.

Please practice Dynamic Breathing and Dynamic Meditation using the half, half, half continuation model. This singular focus of half, half, half will become (over time with continuous daily mental training and practice) the object of your Second Order Experience. And, with even more training and practice, this Second Order sustained focus, that is, this singular concentration upon the dynamic process of universal expansion and contraction, will eventually be "neutralized," "let go," (Jp. *kanzen ni nuku*) or "cast off" (Jp. *datsuraku*) unconsciously and without intention. At this moment (in this mode of First Order Awareness), you will presence you and the Universe as One. By experiencing the world as neither directed or intended, you will come face to face with a new level of awareness and consciousness development.

The fifth Art of Conscious Action will take on new meaning and significance as you experience directly the pure base, the horizon, the ground of consciousness itself; that is, you will experience the stage, the arena, the backdrop, the field upon which all of your conscious intentional life is cast. You will presence the entire context of your experiential life. You will walk out of the cave of your subjective, intentionally directed, consciousness that heretofore *covered over* objective reality. The new enlightening experience will serve as a new paradigm of consciousness and will liberate you so that your every day, intended Conscious Action will now take on new meaning and significance. Enjoy.

5

THE ART OF CONSCIOUS ACTION

"When the wind blows through the scattered bamboos, they do not hold its sound after it is gone. When the wild geese fly over a cold lake, it does not retain their shadows after they have passed. So the mind of the superior person begins to work only when an event occurs; and it becomes void again when the matter ends."

Hung Tzu-Ch'eng (fl. 1596)
Saikontan ("The Roots of Wisdom")

> **Plus Life**
>
> The Absolute Universe is One. Then two opposing forces appeared, and the relative world was born.
>
> In the Orient, this dualism is called yin and yang, in the West, plus and minus.
>
> A bright, happy life is called plus life, and a dark gloomy one is called minus.
>
> Let us eliminate every minus thought and strive for plus life henceforth.
>
> —Koichi Tohei

> **Willpower**
>
> An old Oriental saying tells us, "When our willpower is in harmony with the Universe and focused upon a stone, it can pass through it. In such a state, the mind can command the wind, rain, and thunder."
>
> But from where does our willpower come?
>
> Those who understand and answer this question are those who accomplish important tasks.
>
> When we coordinate mind and body by stilling the waves of our mind to imperceptible, infinitely decreasing ripples, we can send forth our great willpower that can move the Universe.
>
> —Koichi Tohei

The Art of Conscious Action directly follows and is based upon the Art of Relaxation. By exposing yourself to the depths of non-intentional First Order Awareness, you will experience directly the wellspring of infinite possibility that is your life. By presencing the very foundation of your directed, intentional experience, you simultaneously become aware of how your intentional life (the energy behind your directed behavior) is truly a function of your own will. You can be the author of very clear, purposeful consciousness (Conscious Action) that can move with the Universe; *you can live with the wind at your back*. The key to practicing Conscious Action is selflessness, for you must live in the present moment and "sacrifice" (Sk. *yajna*) or "renounce" the fruits of your intended actions.

Have you ever wondered what it would be like to "live with wind at your back"?

Selflessness, the Universal Mind, and the Way of the Universe

When you *choose* to act out of selflessness, you harmonize with the Way of the Universe. In reality, when you live in this manner, you realize that "YOU" have no "willpower" with any real substance or impact upon the world (see above). True Conscious Action springs from the Universe itself; hence, Conscious Action means that you are intending, behaving, and fulfilling your life's work in harmony with the Will of the Universe. Since you and the Universe are not separate, you can tap your full potential by embracing your connectedness to the Universe.

In the passage above entitled *"Willpower,"* the riddle – *"But from where does our willpower come?"* – is answered when you realize that *"those who accomplish great tasks"* do so by leading others with a Universal Mind. A Universal Mind (Jp. *Taiga*) is the opposite of a selfish mind (Jp. *shoga*), a mind that ignores our connection with others and with the Universe. Acting consciously with a Universal Mind means that you realize that you will not succeed in life by forcing your selfish will upon others using only your power, your position, or your authority.

Turning your *"Life of Work into a Work of Art"* means practicing the Seven Arts and trusting in the *Willpower of the Universe* to guide you. This power is tapped when your selfless intention to do good for others is grounded in the present moment. Conscious Action that arises from a calm mind moves with the Universe. When you are present in First Order Awareness, your consciousness reflects all things clearly like the calm still surface of a beautiful mountain lake. When a selfless intention for purposeful action arises from this kind of serenity and conscious clarity, it taps the power of the Universe. Others perceive that your sincerity and calmness is genuine and soon they are *sharing your work* in order to *actualize your shared dreams*. Others surrounding you feel your clarity, purposiveness, and passion, and they wish to serve the greater good by first embracing a greater vision of themselves and their true potential. This is the Way of the Universe.

If your Conscious Action is clear, purposeful, and in harmony with the Way of the Universe, then your actions will be supported by the power of the Universe. Obstacles will be removed and people will work in new ways to share and fulfill the vision that brings greater kindness into the world. In short, when you act out of a selfish mind, using your own personal effort or willpower, then you move against the Universe, causing hardship and failure and even ill health for yourself and possibly others. However, when you act out of a Universal Mind or universal consciousness, then the purity of your present (Jp. *ima*) now-mind and now-heart (Jp. *kokoro*) leads to Conscious Action. Accordingly, Conscious Action arises from a deep calmness that connects your true Self to the Universe. When this happens, you can transform yourself, transform your surroundings, positively influence other people, and even rally a team or an entire organization or nation to serve the greater good.

This is the true meaning of the Japanese concept of *nen*. *Nen* combines the ability to be "present now" (Jp. *ima*) [the top half of the written *kanji*], and to do so with your complete "mind/heart" (Jp. *kokoro*) [the bottom half of the written *kanji*]. Thus, *nen* is literally "living presently with the mind/

heart of the Universe." *Nen* has also been translated into English by my teacher, Master Tohei, as "Willpower." The Willpower about which Master Tohei speaks is really "the Power of Nen" (Jp. *Nen no Chikara*). The "power" (Jp. *chikara*) is thus the result of living in accord with the Will of the Universe (Universal Mind, Jp. *Taiga*). This is contrasted with your limited, ego-based, selfish willpower (selfish mind, Jp. *shoga*) that ultimately must be cast off, renounced, let go, and thrown away completely (Jp. *kanzen ni nuku*) in order to live in accord with the Universe; in other words, *living with the wind at your back*.

Have you ever wondered if the past and future really exist because you can't actually go there?

Reconsider Time:
Present Memories, Present Dreams, and Present *Conscious* Action

The reason the "Power of *Nen*" (the power of your present heart/mind) works in daily life is because we are all already One with Universe. The problem is that you don't realize that you are already One with the Universe because you have not yet experienced it directly. People who are motivated by a clear, positive vision that serves the greater good can move mountains or any real or perceived obstacle in the path of their dreams. By living in the present moment of First Order Awareness, you are not held back by your negative or perceived memories of the past or your anxieties, real or perceived, about the future. *The past and future do not really exist. The past and future have no independent reality apart from your present consciousness, your present heart and mind* (Jp. *Nen*). The past and future are only representations in your present state of mind. The past is only your *present* memory; the future is only your *present* hopes, dreams, and ambitions.

By practicing the Art of Relaxation and living more and more in the present moment without attachments to past memories or future results, you begin to live in accord with the Will of the Universe and you will tap the great power of infinite possibility that is naturally yours.

The power of consciously acting and living in accord with the Universe is a gift that is yours as long as you are alive. As long as you are alive, you are, by definition, already connected to and sustained by God, Spirit, or the Universe. Great tasks require great leaders, and great leaders are those who can inspire, articulate a clear vision in which everyone can participate, and can help people to succeed through their positive attitude and service toward others.

Whether you are *leading yourself* (as the Chief Executive Officer of your own life), *leading a business, leading an athletic team, leading musicians,* or *leading a class,* your Conscious Actions will enable you to succeed simply because the energy behind your effort will be far greater than yourself. Remember that the universal energy that ultimately brings about positive causal outcomes is ultimately not "yours" in the first place. Humility, therefore, in the face of enormous challenges, brings you back to the center of your consciousness. By making First Order Awareness the basis of your conscious life, all your actions will become Conscious Actions. That is, the type of intention that arises from a clear conscience and a calm spirit is the type of intention that is brought to fruition through Conscious Action.

Your present mission or dream or vision first must be experienced and understood deeply. It can be actualized when your initial vision or dream arises from the clarity that springs from having a Universal Mind. With a Universal Mind, you become completely committed to the execution of your intention or plan or Conscious Action. By living in the present moment, you also are completely flexible in the manner of determining exactly HOW you and others will bring about the intended result. With a Universal Mind, you are focused upon the purity of your vision with conscious resolve yet, at the same time, you are free to change the course of present actions required to bring about and execute your dreams.

Have you ever wondered if you are "wasting your time"?

**This May Not Be a Rehearsal:
Applying Conscious Action in Daily Life**

In order to examine *how* the Art of Conscious Action can be actualized, let's return again to real events and situations that illustrate the powerful impact of the Seven Arts. In this chapter, I once again will provide testimony by offering examples of practicing Conscious Action in my own life. I will begin with personal illustrations of the power of Conscious Action when applied to an individual action. Later, I will expand the discussion of real life applications so that you will become familiar with the power of the Art of Conscious Action when applied to team action, and even the actions of large multi-national corporations.

I first became familiar with the concept of Conscious Action from my father. The son of a steel mill foreman growing up during the Depression in the hills of western

Pennsylvania, my father put a high priority on hard work; "work before play," he would say, and "act with a sense of urgency" (including being punctual). His famous lines to me growing up were: (a) *"Money does not grow on trees,"* and (b) *"You may get hit by a bus tomorrow."* I never quite pieced it together but the theme was: (a) Do your work well, and (b) Fill your life with all that life has to give in the present moment because life itself is valuable. In other words, you should appreciate the time and the opportunity that each day brings because if "you may get hit by a bus tomorrow," then each present moment counts; you cannot predict what tomorrow will bring to your life.

Later in life I learned to create my own maxims for my own family's consumption. My version of "you may get hit by a bus" (which seemed to me to be a bit too negative) is "this may not be a rehearsal." When people ask me how I have managed to accomplish so much in different fields including athletics, martial arts, academia, and business consulting, I respond, "well ... this may not be a rehearsal." Life is precious; we cannot repeat each day, and so even each minute or second is an opportunity to be truly grateful, and to be positive, or to try a new experience, or to love a family member or fellow human being more deeply. All this is really about living in accord with the Art of Conscious Action.

The philosopher Friedrich Nietzsche (1844-1900) has a theory called "Eternal Recurrence." He suggests that you may have to relive your life again and again. If so, you should examine your choices carefully because you may have to relive them forever. The downhill ski racer in me says, "if this eternal recurrence idea is true and I must relive my actions again and again, then I choose courageous and challenging goals, bold action, and Conscious Action, believing that I have the strength and power of the Universe at my back." By "living consciously and intentionally," I mean crafting your life as though you do not have a second chance. *The time for Conscious Action, purposeful and selfless action, is NOW – "this may not be a rehearsal."*

Have you ever wondered if you could act without thinking "what will everyone else think"?

Begin with Small Steps:
A Seventh Grade Confirmation Class Dropout Leaves High School Early

I believe that most people need to practice everything in "small steps." Since small steps lead to meaningful and significant changes in conscious awareness, you can begin to use the tools of patience and discipline to form new habits of the mind and heart that are essential for lasting change and real personal transformation. Over the years, I have encountered many people who think and declare that they have had an immediate life-changing experience. However, without conscious awareness and Conscious Action to follow through, the so-called "personal transformation" proves to be temporary.

Again, I will say that there are no short cuts, no skipping steps, and no skipping the successive stages of the Seven Arts (as well as the three phases within *each* Art). Each phase within an Art and each of the Seven Arts build upon one another step-by-step to achieve solid and sustainable personal transformation for spiritual, interpersonal, and overall well-being.

My first step toward Conscious Action was choosing purposefully not to go through the seventh grade confirmation class at the family Methodist church. This "confirmation" tradition was one of Methodist religious education where, at the conclusion of the summer study, you "officially" became an "adult" member of the church at an elaborate church ceremony on an appointed Sunday in the early fall. To me, even as a seventh grader, I realized and understood well that my so-called *choice* to join the church was not "intentional" enough because my choice was actually vacuous; that is, I knew that I was "just a big kid" and I knew that I was not yet qualified to be an "official" "adult" member of the church. I also knew very well that I had no other "clear" options (that could lead to other "intentions") in order to purposefully join, for example, other Christian churches in our town or even to purposefully learn about other religions. Let's face it, if you are only exposed to one thing and it is the *only option, the only game in town,* then even a seventh grader can see that it is a meaningless choice.

As I shared in the first chapter, an example of a "small step" in the direction of Conscious Action was my seventh grade tutorial summer study "course" in World Religions. My mother and I spent the summer studying world religions such as Hinduism and Buddhism and comparing them to Christianity. This lifetime "course", starting with my mother as tutor, finally terminated when I was an adult completing my doctorate in Comparative Philosophy at the University of Hawaii. I now see the entire road (from my summer study of World Religions as an 11 year old to my completing the Ph.D. program in comparative philosophy as a 26 year old) as an educational process in Conscious Action meant to satisfy my own conscious intention, my own spiritual curiosity. My decision to attend graduate school in philosophy was not a career-oriented employment decision to be sure. Instead, my action sprang from the innocence of a seventh grade Methodist church Confirmation School dropout already thinking deeply about spiritual matters and choices that I already knew to be of supreme significance and importance.

That the educational path was so enjoyable tells me (in hindsight) that all the energy expended to complete the journey was occasioned by the *universal life force at my back* and the backs of other teachers and supporters who were moved by innocent spiritual curiosity and the overall spiritual journey. In reality, the simple and sincere motivation was simply to know other cultures, know other religions, respect all humankind, and look for ways to *grow and develop together* on a global scale without prejudice and without dogmatic judgment of others. When one's purposeful intention and Conscious Action spring from the desire to *serve* humankind (the Art of Service), then the Universe responds to both your true connection and to the connection you have with others that share your vision. When this happens, you feel as though you are led by the force of the Universe; that is, you feel as though you are *living with the wind at your back*. This is in direct contrast with the burden of feeling led by "*your*" own will; that is, living with only "*your*" own limited willpower. Under your own limited willpower, you feel as though you are always swimming upstream, trying feverishly to accomplish "*your*" goals that spring from a selfish mind and selfish desires.

The next example of Conscious Action experienced early in life was simply embracing my desire and intention to start college early and get on with my life with a sense of urgency and purpose. By leaving high school early, I completed my first year of college, competed in intercollegiate athletics (ski racing), and traveled widely in the process, all before my peers finished high school. I just thought that I was ready to move on, but I was also worried about the opinions of my friends (and girlfriend) that I would leave behind.

In Plato's dialogue, the **Crito**, Socrates is in jail and has to convince his friends (who want him to escape) that one should always do what is right and not be swayed by public opinion. What "everybody else thinks" is just not important if you are committed to Conscious Action in service to that which will bring about greater good. I knew that I wanted to get to the mountains and get started with college and ski racing. The only thing that was holding me back was *my own mind*. Like Socrates' friends, my mind was too preoccupied with a concern that "others," in this case my high school peers, might think ill of me. Since leaving high school early, I have learned over and over again that the most powerful action that springs from Conscious Action is often unpopular. However, if *you know* that the seed of intention behind your mission is one of service for the greater good, then by all means stick to your plan of action and execute your mission to the very best of your ability.

As soon as my senior high school football season was over in suburban Chicago, I left for ski racing and college in the Pacific Northwest. Out of a graduating high school senior class of over 800 students, only two of us left high school early with advanced credits and headed off to college. Oddly enough, the girl that joined me in this act of Conscious Action was the niece of astronaut Neil Armstrong, the first man to walk on the moon. We were between our freshman and sophomore year of high school when on July 20, 1969, Armstrong uttered his famous phrase, "That's one small step for a man, one giant leap for mankind." Later, I remember thinking that if Armstrong's niece somehow justified leaving school early, then maybe I was not making some kind of big mistake (which honestly was my greatest fear at the time.)

Another student in my high school senior class was Gary Fencik. I was proud to be on the same football team with Gary as well as my other teammates. We had a winning tradition as members of the Barrington Broncos football team. Gary later went to Yale as a wide receiver and eventually played for the Chicago Bears. In four years of high school football, we tied one game (in our freshman year as I recall) and won *all* the rest *except* for the very last game of our senior year played in a torrential rainstorm at night under the lights in Zion Benton, Illinois. I remember the feeling of loosing that game and riding home on the team bus after four years of success. It taught me to never ever think your trophy is "in the bag." Without Conscious Action and team action at every present moment, even the best talent will not prevail without the correct attitude and purposeful intention.

My high school relationship with Gary also has provided me with a silly but fun story that I am able to use when I instruct professional athletes. On our high school team, I was the defensive free safety and Gary was the wingback in our offensive scheme and sometimes cornerback in our defensive playbook. This fact is not remarkable in itself but it is significant because defensive free safety is the position Gary eventually played with the Chicago Bears. So when an audience of professional athletes wants to know what my athletic credentials are beyond ski racing and *Aikido*, I get to have fun with them. I ask, "Who is the Chicago Bears' all time leader in tackles and leader in interceptions?" The audience almost always says "Dick Butkus!" first. "No," I reply. "Mike Singletary!" they say and I shake my head "No." "OK then, Brian Urlacher!" they say. "No, again," I respond. And so they shout out more and more names from past and present football "eras." Finally, I say with pride that my friend, Gary Fencik, is the all-time Chicago Bears leader in these two vital statistics. In fact, I say, "Gary not only intercepted Joe Namath's last pass, but also he was the defensive team captain and led the Chicago Bears defense to win Super Bowl XX in New Orleans." I can then jokingly add, "On our high school team, I played defensive free safety and taught Gary everything he knows! He wasn't up to playing defensive free safety for the Barrington Broncos but, with my instruction and some college experience, he went on to become the all-time everything with the Chicago Bears!" All joking aside, you do have to believe in yourself, have a sense of humor, and have a positive "plus life" attitude in your practice of the Art of Conscious Action. If you do not believe in yourself and your own possibilities, then how can you expect to positively lead others?

Have you ever wondered what it would be like to face your fears with greater confidence?

When Facing Adversity
Return to Deep Calmness in the Present Moment
The Hand on My Shoulder

Conscious Action is something that you can draw upon at any time by simply returning to the "power of the present moment" (Jp. *nen no chikara*), that which we have been calling First Order Awareness. No matter what challenge you face, no matter how prepared you may think you are, sometimes "life" (the Universe) places you in situations that seem overwhelming. Each time this has happened to me, I have found solace and calmness in the fact that the Conscious Action I am performing is serving the greater good; hence, I know that I can count on the Will of the Universe to help me through the moment. This is not isolated only to my experience. I have taught many others to do the same over the last thirty years. Once you practice thoroughly the exercises in the fourth Art of Relaxation, you will learn how to change your state of being to the present moment without effort. The deep calm of non-intentional First Order Awareness is the place to which you want to return, especially when faced with an adversary or an unexpected challenge. Three brief examples from my own life experience of "The Hand on My Shoulder" will serve to illustrate the point as follows:

Have you ever wondered what it would be like to represent your country?

Representing My Teacher in Japan

In 1979, I resided as a "live-in" *(Jp. uchi deshi)* Ki-Aikido student with Master Tohei at the old *Ki no Kenkyukai* (Ki Society) headquarters in the section of Shinjuku in Tokyo known as Haramachi. This headquarters is only blocks away from the Aikikai Headquarters, which is another *Aikido* school. Master Tohei was once the Worldwide Chief Instructor of the Aikikai School under *Aikido* founder Morihei Ueshiba. In 1953, Master Tohei was the first to bring the art of *Aikido* outside of Japan. O-Sensei (title for Master Ueshiba) died in 1969 and his son (the late Kisshomaru Ueshiba) later was arranged to succeed his father and lead the Worldwide Aikikai School when my teacher, Master Tohei, founded the International Ki Society in 1972. Master Tohei's international fame is due, in part, to his own Conscious Action to selflessly spread *Ki* and *Aikido* principles around the world.

The author with Tohei Sensei, during a summer when he lived at *Ki no Kenkyukai* (headquarters) in Tochigi. This was soon after *Tenshinkan dojo* was built. 1991 or 1992. Photographer unknown.

Master Tohei honored me when he asked me one day (in 1979) if I would represent the International Ki Society by participating in a demonstration at Aikikai Headquarters the very next day! I was shocked. "Why me?", I asked. Master Tohei calmly told me that many different Japanese cultural arts and martial arts would be represented from all over Japan. Master Tohei wanted to respect the school he formerly headed and send someone to represent the *Ki-Aikido* school he founded three years after his *Aikido* teacher's death. I asked, "Why not ask one of the Sensei (an honorific term meaning 'teacher' or, literally, 'one step ahead') who are clearly my senior? Why not ask Maruyama Sensei or Tamura Sensei?", I pleaded. "Surely they would perform *Aikido* arts much better than I," I added. After all, these teachers were Master Tohei's most senior instructors.

As you can see, I was trying my best to get out of this incredible pressure. "How could I properly represent my teacher, and his entire school, and his worldwide organization at such a prestigious, high level demonstration?", I thought. Master Tohei put *his hand on my shoulder* and looked me in the eye and said, "You are a *gaijin* (a foreigner). You can represent me well by showing them that all people around the world can learn *Ki* and *Aikido* without regard to race or cultural difference. You are the best example of what I am really about. Please just *Relax Completely* and do your best." Literally he said, "*Zenshin no chikara o kanzen ni nuku.*" In Chapter Four, I explained this phrase in detail. It is translated as "Take the power of your whole self and throw it away." I thought I would faint actually, but then a great calm and peace came over me as soon as my teacher placed his hand on my shoulder.

Master Tohei's life work is about selflessness and service. His mission is spreading the Way of the Universe and universal teachings (Jp. *Setsudo*) of *Ki* Development as well as teaching others *how* to apply *Ki* and *Aikido* principles at work and in daily life. He has successfully spread this teaching throughout the world. Master Tohei's life mission is an example of Conscious Action based in selflessness – it is all about going through life with what he calls a "Universal Mind" (Jp. *Taiga*), rather than a "selfish mind" (Jp. *shoga*). I knew that when he said to me, "Relax Completely and do your best," I had the *Ki* of the Universe behind me (the wind was at my back) and so there was no need to fear. He trusted me and believed in me. I knew at that instant I should respect my teacher's wishes and represent all non-Japanese people training in *Ki-Aikido* around the world.

The next day at Aikikai World Headquarters the *Ki-Aikido* demonstration went over very well. I demonstrated mostly *Jo* (wooden staff) Arts and *Taigi* Arts (*Aikido* techniques performed in a series [Jp. *tsuzuki waza*] from a variety of attacks). I remember that I was actually demonstrating *Jo* movements at center stage at the exact same time when the founder's (O-Sensei's) son, Kisshomaru Ueshiba, came into the *dojo* (training hall) surrounded by attendants (Jp. *otomo*). He was late arriving and our eyes met even as I performed the *Jo* demonstration. It was his first public appearance since being hospitalized. I recall that he looked very frail, pale, and extremely thin, having lost much weight. He was a small man but our "connection" seemed clear and large; he was most interested in this *gaijin* (foreigner) sent by Master Tohei.

Master Tohei and Kisshomaru Ueshiba Sensei were once very closely connected through O-Sensei as well as marrying twin sisters much earlier in their lives. It was an honor to meet O-Sensei's son and, even more importantly, to represent Master Tohei at the demonstration. Master Tohei, as always, knew exactly what he was doing in sending me to represent him. I soon realized that the impact I was having was to internationalize (in a rather obvious manner) the demonstration. As a foreigner, a *gaijin*, I stood out about as much as "Eggaberth, the Mountain Goat" stood out as a non-human *uchi deshi* (live-in student). My contribution seemed to be appreciated by all, especially Kisshomaru Ueshiba Sensei who asked me to extend his warm personal greetings to Master Tohei and to extend his gratitude for demonstrating (through my participation) the worldwide appeal of *Aikido*.

Have you ever wondered what it would be like to represent something important all over the world?

Representing My Teacher in Russia

Many times I have called upon what I refer to as my "hand on the shoulder" experience with my teacher, Master Tohei (see above). In these instances, I am reminded to immediately change my state of mind when called upon to demonstrate *Ki* and *Aikido* or face unexpected important tasks in daily life. For example, in 1999 during my first trip to Russia teaching *Ki* and *Aikido* in St. Petersburg, I was told, "Between classes today you will be driven somewhere to give a brief demonstration and we hope that will be OK. There will be many photographers and videotape recorders, and you should be prepared to give an interview," said Philip, my translator. "OK, no problem," I said as Igor Ostroumov (my host, and St. Petersburg *Ki-Aikido* instructor) and Phillip swiftly moved me into a waiting Russian van.

I really was not thinking this was going to be a big deal. This was my first trip to Russia and my classes at this point were quite small with mostly St. Petersburg residents. A few people from outside St. Petersburg had come from Moscow and the city of Minsk in the Republic of Belarus. (Today, the Eastern Europe/Russia Ki-Aikido Federation is growing rapidly with students and instructors coming to our annual seminars from all over Russia, the independent Republics, and Eastern Europe). As we sped through the streets and over the canals of St. Petersburg, I could feel the tension in the car as I was told we might be late. Again I thought, "No problem, how inconvenient could this really be?" Then we pulled into the underground garage of a very large coliseum. Then I was told "this is the Olympic Center."

"Hummmm...", I thought, "This could be bigger than I expected!" We quickly changed into our *dogi* (training uniforms) and entered backstage. I could hear many people in the audience. The curtain opened just as we approached the stage and, to my astonishment, I saw over 1,000 people waiting to see my demonstration at the Olympic Center! Immediately I thought of Master Tohei and that this was a great opportunity to represent his teachings. With only that familiar thought of spreading universal *Ki* principles and internationalizing the demonstration (the *gaijin*/foreigner again), I quickly became very calm, deeply calm as though my teacher Master Tohei had once again "put his hand on my shoulder." I simply heard his reassuring voice telling me as he did before, "To relax completely and do your best."

The demonstration was a big success largely because I chose, as I always do, the *big people*. In this case, large, actually very large, Russian athletes and weight lifters who helped me demonstrate the power of *Ki* (your life force) in a variety of audience participation exercises. The 1,000 plus member audience loved the impromptu audience participation aspect of the demonstration using the enormous and powerful athletes. The thought crossed my mind that the crowd might not take kindly to an American teaching the power of *Ki* Development and a Japanese martial art at the Russian Olympic Center so soon after the Cold War had ended. But then I thought, just as Master Tohei courageously went to Hawaii to teach *Ki* and *Aikido* after World War II, I could rely upon my own Conscious Action and I, too, could extend myself and teach most positively, while practicing humility and sincerity of purpose.

If I demonstrated all the benefits of *Ki* and *Aikido* practice, then I somehow knew that even the most challenging and difficult audience could be led positively. Again, with the feeling of the Universe/*the wind at your back*, you can accomplish great things by simply trusting resources of strength that are far greater than your own private, egotistical, selfish, and ultimately disconnected, willpower. The Art of Conscious Action can be brought forth in a nanosecond just by returning to your place of deep calmness. This ability can be cultivated and developed simply by using the patience and discipline necessary to practice everyday the Dynamic Breathing and Dynamic Meditation exercises that you learned in accord with the Art of Relaxation, the fourth Art on your journey of personal transformation.

Let's look at yet another example of Conscious Action in daily life.

Have you ever wondered if you are being watched and helped by a friend or silent partner?

Representing My Father…

The third and final illustration of Conscious Action is one of a deeply personal nature. Please allow me to explain the background: My friend, Dr. Akio Urakami, was the owner (with his family) of the worldwide Ryobi Motor Products Company. The President of his company asked me to be the keynote speaker at their annual North American sales meeting at Hilton Head Island, South Carolina. Ryobi not only makes power tools under the "Ryobi" brand name, but also they have produced over the years products under the brand names of "Sears Craftsman," "Kenmore," and "Singer." By the time I was invited to speak at the Annual Sales meeting, I had already been helping the Ryobi Motor Products Corporation as a management consultant. Specifically, I assisted their initial transition to South Carolina and provided employee training and organizational development ever since they first moved pieces of the company from Japan to South Carolina.

I also had been part of an initial economic development group helping the State of South Carolina to attract companies like Ryobi, a Japanese company, to locate in the upstate region of South Carolina. For years, working with the State Economic Development Board under the direction of the late Currie Spivey, I assisted the administration of South Carolina Governor Carroll Campbell to attract investment and create jobs in South Carolina. This process began with great success under the previous administration led by Governor Richard "Dick" Riley who later became the United States Secretary of Education, serving for two full terms as a member of President Clinton's cabinet.

"My friend Dr. Akio Urakami was the owner (with his family) of the world-wide Ryobi Motor Products Company."

A fun reunion dinner in Hong Kong: Akio Urakami, PhD, Chairman and CEO, ETG Limited, Former Chairman and CEO, Ryobi North America, Inc., his son and author. Dec. 2008.

Secretary Riley is also a friend who, in 1986, was instrumental in helping me to establish my consulting business – Shaner & Associates: Performance Development Consultants. Through his efforts, I began to give seminars in Greenville, South Carolina, sponsored by his law firm, Nelson, Mullins, Riley. My first clients were companies attending these seminars endorsed by ex-Governor Riley. Dick is also a loyal alumnus of Furman University where I taught for thirty years. He has helped Furman faculty, the administration, and students his entire adult life.

I believe that all of these connections outlined above, including the initiation of my consulting practice, were created by the selfless actions of very kind people like Dick Riley who are in a position of influence and understanding. That is, when someone like Dick respects another person's sincerity and ability, then he is able to use his own influence to help make a positive difference in the lives of others and in the community at large. In my initial interactions with Dick and others, I was unconsciously projecting what I am now calling Conscious Action. By sympathizing with my sincere efforts to help others, people like Governor Riley are willing to gladly serve the call by assisting in the mission of someone (me) trying to make a positive difference in the Upstate community while building international understanding and goodwill. Governor Riley was merely matching a perceived South Carolina need (economic development, jobs, and the Ryobi transition from Japan to North America) with a trusted resource (my consulting service) for the highest good. This is a classic case of WIN/WIN. In this case, I was being supported through Governor Riley's trusted endorsement. At the same time, he also believed that the citizens of South Carolina would benefit by a successful Ryobi transition, the simultaneous creation of Ryobi jobs, supplier company jobs, and thus overall economic development.

The Hilton Head sales meeting was a major production. Senior buyers from Home Depot, one of Ryobi's largest and fastest growing trade customers, would be present for a three-day national sales meeting extravaganza. A special marketing, media, and promotions company had been hired to ensure that the three-day production would run flawlessly. As the keynote speaker for the big event, I was asked to be present one full day in advance of my speech simply to "rehearse the proper cue" of my entrance on stage complete with special strobe lights, special effects, backup sound systems, hidden microphones, the works!

This hype is not my cup of tea, but I had prepared a sincere and hopefully inspiring message that was really about maintaining positive sales growth to ensure that the jobs would remain in South Carolina. I also wanted to ensure that the very positive transformation of Ryobi's business systems (that we worked so hard to achieve in Ryobi's Research and Development, Product Development, Human Resource Development, and Manufacturing Operations Departments) could be leveraged for added expansion and thus create even more jobs. All of this seemed within reach as a result of our improved ability to design and develop quality products and services that were already yielding positive sales growth by partnering effectively with Ryobi's large trade customers (like the Sears, Home Depots, and Wal-Marts of the world).

So, now you can see that my heart was really in this. This meeting was an opportunity to take the Ryobi Motor Products Company to a new level of sales growth and development. Most importantly, Ryobi's largest trade customers would be present, and their growth meant Ryobi's long-term growth. Moreover, successful partnerships with key trade customers meant more jobs for my fellow South Carolinians. In addition to all these factors, I was personally invested in this multi-national venture being successful from the time I helped our State Government and Dr. Akio Urakami to transition his company (Ryobi) from Japan to South Carolina. After all our work together over many years, it seemed that the stars were in alignment and that this national sales partnership meeting had the potential to serve as the necessary catalyst to make all our dreams a reality.

My "investment" in this process was not of a monetary nature. My investment was one of Conscious Action that had been supported by friends who believed in me, including two South Carolina State Governors, Dick Riley and Carroll Campbell, the Chairman and Owner of Ryobi Motor Products Corporation, Dr. Akio Urakami, and all of the new South Carolina Ryobi operations employees. These fellow South Carolinians were asked (as part of our restructuring and cultural change process) to turn their factories upside down and make new products using new technology and new processes (cellular manufacturing) when the production operations were moved from Japan to the United States. I had helped to first attract the company to South Carolina and subsequently helped them to re-make the old Singer Company, which they had purchased as part of Ryobi's move to North America. In short, I felt responsible, connected to the leaders and employees of Ryobi, connected to leaders of the State Government and Economic Development Board, and I wanted them ALL to be successful!

The next big step was to take our vision of growth to the sales force so that they could understand more deeply that this was a human story of growth, development, and jobs. To be clear, my speech was not going to be some motivational "go deliver the sales numbers and get your bonus" presentation. A lot more than annual sales numbers were at stake, and I needed to be well prepared, convincing, and even inspiring. And, I was ready!

The rehearsals the day before the big event went well. I was to be: 1) on cue at exactly 10:05 a.m., 2) standing on my mark backstage, 3) have my hidden microphones and "back up" microphones checked and double checked one last time, and 4) be personally escorted on stage by the hired media director of the production (who was as nervous as a cat and praying that nothing would go wrong). He would personally give me the cue to walk out on stage at precisely 10:11 a.m. He had a headset on and was in direct communication with all the technical support people. He was a perfectionist and he wanted the spotlight operator to know exactly where my entrance mark was located, and when I would take my first step onto the darkened stage from my stage right, hold location near the side curtain. The event was so well crafted that I certainly did not want to be the one to do something off-cue, so I was there twenty minutes early at 9:45 a.m.

As I arrived backstage of the hotel's Grand Ballroom, I was given an urgent message to go to my hotel room upstairs in order to receive an emergency call from my mother! "My mother?!", I thought. "How does she even know where I am on Hilton Head Island in South Carolina?" As I learned later, she had called my best friend back home who tracked me down. I ran to the elevators and went to my room where my wife was waiting for me with tears in her eyes. She handed me the phone. "David," my mother said. "Are you there? Are you sitting down?" I sat down on the bed by the phone. "David, your father has died."

Tears are welling up now as I write this, just as they ran down my face sitting on the bed. It was 9:55 a.m., eleven minutes from "show time", and an elevator ride away from walking out on stage complete with synchronized music and spotlights. I asked my mother what had happened. My father had gone into his doctor's office for a regular check up appointment the day before. During a routine procedure having his throat examined, my father gagged, experienced a sudden heart attack, went to the hospital by ambulance, and died hours later. It had taken nearly twenty-four hours for my mother to track me down. I told my mother that I was about to go on stage and would call her in one hour when my so-called "inspiring and motivating" talk would be over.

"...my father was THE inspiring motivator..."

Charles H. Shaner, President of the Chicago Dental Society; Chairman, Harper College Dental Hygiene School; Rotary District Governor; Officer, United States Navy; Friend to all. 1968.

I honestly never questioned what I had to do. I am sure it was because my father was *the* inspiring motivator. I knew that he would want me to give the best speech that I ever gave in my entire life – and I did. Once again, I returned to the deep place of calmness that enables you to meet your challenges with the Universal *wind at your back. I did not inspire and motivate, the Universe did.* During the speech, I felt as though I was being lifted, guided, and inspired from outside myself. This time the feeling of "the hand on my shoulder" was my father's, not Master Tohei's.

During my speech, I talked about the commitment of leaders; I spoke about South Carolina jobs and the international economy; I spoke of the commitment of two South Carolina Governors and the Presidents of Ryobi, Sears, and Home Depot; I spoke about their personal lives and families and the opportunity to serve and make a difference; and, yes, I spoke of my father and dedicated the speech to his memory. There wasn't a dry eye in the ballroom.

At the very end of my talk (and reminiscent of my father), I said things like, "You know, money *and jobs* do not grow on trees! You have to work hard, use *patience and discipline* to meet your goals, and take every opportunity to serve others for the greater good." I continued my spontaneous ramblings; "There is a much bigger picture here that represents Conscious Action on the part of a large community of public servants and business leaders." And finally I said, "All this is vitally important. And, do you know why?" I asked. "Because this, that is *your life, may not be a rehearsal and you might get hit by a bus tomorrow!*"

The audience was treated to a powerful conclusion because it was sincere and heartfelt and it was my Dad speaking really. Undoubtedly, the audience scratched their heads at the very end of my speech wondering, "What's up with the 'money growing on trees,' 'no life rehearsals,' and 'getting hit by a bus' comments?!" To tell you the truth, the last comments were just for my Dad and me. He was watching, he knew, he was smiling, I felt "the hand on my shoulder," and that was good enough reason for me to introduce some of my father's (and my own) favorite maxims (even though the audience simply could not have understood them at the time). I walked off stage, pointed to heaven, felt a deep and powerful connection to my father, and returned my mother's call as soon as I was off stage. It was time to plan a funeral, grieve, and remember.

Have you ever wondered if you could live your dreams?

**The Wellspring of the Universal Mind:
Trust, Get Out of Your Own Way, and Ride Like the Wind**

The Art of Conscious Action can be practiced anytime you return to the purity and clarity of your original consciousness. Purposeful, sincere, committed Conscious Action is fueled by the pure Willpower of the Universe that, in turn, is yours to "ride like the wind" if only you give up your ego, your selfish mind. By surrendering your selfish mind (that is, the mind that is attached) to the wellspring of the Universal Mind, you can face your most difficult and critical challenges with calmness and serenity while still maintaining a high level of energy and conviction. All this is possible simply because when you embrace the Universal Mind, *you know* that the ends that you seek are based ultimately in selflessness and service to the greater good and the highest good for others.

A business mentor and close, personal friend of mine, Jack Goldsmith, (the co-founder of MARC Advertising based in Pittsburgh) told me early on that "life (and business) is really about relationships." People like Secretary Riley, Jack Goldsmith, D. Nevin Caldwell, and many others have shared their personal and professional network of relationships with me simply trusting in each person's character and ability, and not really knowing exactly *how* the new relationships would end up, or exactly *who* would get connected to whom, or *how* the relationships would all actually develop, or *where* the relations would lead once all the parties became connected. I can say, as a grateful testimony to my mentors, to those who have believed in me, and to those of you who are now reading this book – these Seven Arts, if practiced well, can move the Universe.

Over the past thirty years, I have had the honor and privilege of helping organizations, large and small, musicians, athletes, and everyday people to take their enthusiasm for life, and thus their level of performance, to higher and higher levels of excellence. The theme for the Hilton Head Ryobi national sales meeting was "Exceed Your Expectations" and that's what it is all about. By removing the negative intentions and attachments that cover your deeper, truer Self, you can step out of your self-imposed cave. By getting out of your own way, you can rid yourself of the negative self-talk that says "I can't," "I'm not good enough," "that will never work," "I'm not worthy," etc.

You are always free to *Live With The Wind At Your Back if* you simply 1) change your thinking, and 2) trust that the Universe will always support your sincere actions directed in service to others. This is simply a change *from* living your life with a selfish mind *to* living your daily life with a Universal Mind. Conscious Action is thus any action that occurs as a result of thinking (or having a "Mind") that reflects the knowledge and understanding of the interconnection of all things.

Have you ever wondered what you could achieve if only you were clear and focused?

Clarity, Visibility, Focus, and Alignment: Applying Conscious Action in the World of Business

Briefly, let me share just a few examples of Conscious Action serving the needs of even very large businesses. I have dedicated another entire book to this topic entitled **The Seven Arts of Change: Leading Business Transformation That Lasts.** Large multi-national organizations have a unique challenge. An organization is nothing more and nothing less than the collective MIND of every employee, every supplier, every customer, and every shareholder. When all these minds are aligned, you have Conscious Action with a purpose, a conviction, and a desire to serve. In an organization or business, all this can add up to a lot of energy that can move things beyond imagination. My job as a corporate consultant over the past thirty years has been to create *clarity, visibility, focus, and alignment* from the Chairman of the Board and the senior executive staff to the third shift line operator. The corporation is just one big *MIND* that is in search of common understanding, direction, and an eventual alignment of mutual interests.

I have always maintained two basic business principles that, if satisfied, will create jobs for new employees and their families who then can serve and develop their local communities for the better. That's my basic belief. The two key business principles that I always remember are as simple as it gets: *"buy low and sell high"* and *"profit is revenue less cost"* – SIMPLE. The difficulty is EXECUTION. After the two basic business principles are satisfied, then leadership, employee alignment, and execution are what it's all about – and these things are all about MIND!

The culture of any business, that is "the way we have always done things," is in people's heads. And so, the fantastic potential of aligned Conscious Action is also in the mind and behavior of every employee and every person with a stake in the business. People with minds execute and they cannot execute *consciously* if they do not understand *why* they are being asked to do things differently. Quite simply, you have to align four things –the business strategy, the operational processes, the core metrics, and the minds of the people. Often I have found that even in supposedly great companies, these basics have not been followed. The business plan of any company must include the means by which the plan will be executed. By this, I mean answering the question how the four main aspects of the business (above) will be aligned so that the plan can be delivered/executed effectively and efficiently. When you align these basics, then great performance is the result. Imagine the power of *everyone in your organization executing consciously*. More importantly, when companies experience this kind of collective success, then more jobs are created, more families prosper, and increased community service is naturally, and even universally, the result. In the next chapter, The Art of Living Naturally, I will explore this phenomenon in greater depth.

To create Conscious Action in a truly global organization, I use a time frame of three years (12 fiscal quarters) to fully execute the new strategy. The new strategy is usually formulated as a result of a new business challenge, for example, a joint venture, a merger, an acquisition, a downsizing or division sell off, Chapter 11, or even the circumstance of unexpected rapid growth that is difficult to manage. In short, I am the one asked to help *execute* the new vision. The mergers and acquisition (M & A) people "do the deal," "hire the new team," and "create the new strategy." I come into the picture only after they leave. If I like what I see in terms of the potential for clear cultural alignment (MIND) and the design of clear and focused core metrics that serve the execution of strategy, then my role is to help the company realize its dreams by simply being successful...which always means successful execution of the business plan.

Have you ever wondered what would happen if you and everyone around you improved every day?

Executing the Business Plan Means COLLECTIVE Conscious Action

Since execution should be easy to measure, I always use three basic concepts to drive collective Conscious Action in the service of the greater good – *clarity, visibility, and focus.*

Focus is all about Conscious Action. Every player on the team, even if the team is 70,000 employees worldwide, needs to know their assignment, know how they make a difference every single business day, and know how their role is related to the big picture (alignment). This is real business focus.

Clarity means the organizational and personal ability to keep score. In successful businesses, everyone must participate in creating a high performance culture characterized by the most simple and basic quality – you must "do what you say." And then, "what you promise" must be absolutely clear to you as well as those counting upon you to deliver; that is, to execute. People must hold themselves responsible and accountable for two things – *what* they do and *how* they do it. The *what* is the measurable (core metric) outcome of the effort. It is true that "what gets measured gets done." Whether it's sales growth or operational efficiency, it must be measurable and you should strive for regular intervals of measurement – preferably short ones. In manufacturing, this measurement interval might be a daily tracking metric or it might be intervals tracked by the minute or second on specific pieces of equipment. Measuring how people work also means measuring how *behaviors* mirror company values. If someone "hits their numbers" (which is the same as executing their business "deliverables") based upon "doing what they say," but they achieve those numbers by means of cheating or threatening subordinates, then you must hold such an autocratic person(s) responsible and accountable for not working with integrity.

You can also provide training for those who do not know *how to lead* effectively. If you provide training and the employee or manager still can only manage to perform using their title and position of authority as leverage to intimidate others, then you as a leader need to show them the door. If there are no real consequences for the employees who refuse to change, then the employees (who are working hard to implement the new business strategy with integrity, who are working positively to change the culture, and who are working with aligned Conscious Action) will think that senior management has lied to them about the process of meaningful change and performance improvement. Clarity for these employees means that they can see how everyone is responsible for doing their assignment and everyone is held accountable.

Visibility simply means using all forms of communication to help people stay focused upon aligned Conscious Action. In large businesses, this means displaying often the core metrics that drive the necessary performance improvement where it is needed most. This requires clear and visible metric alignment with the company's key strategic and operational priorities. It means sharing information and a lot of it.

People have every right to see the numbers. Businesses that are clear, visible, and transparent share everything with employees. This creates focus and trust. And, when you ask people to do things differently, to change the culture, to think and perform in ways that "exceed their expectations," then they have every right to share in the success when they execute.

Time and time again, my clients have adopted some type of gain-sharing plan that makes employees real owners of the company. Creative, performance-based compensation is just fair and it pays off, adding fuel to the positive growth, development, and success of the company. If you ask someone to *"think and act like an owner,"* then why don't you actually make them an owner and compensate them with some kind of pay for performance reward program? In this way, everyone is truly aligned and shares equally in the success or failure of the company. Rewarding and recognizing people who know *what* to do, know *how* to do it, and *do what they say* is key.

Over the years, I have had the pleasure of helping companies change for better by simply teaching them how to execute. I have been successful by simply creating alignment among *all* the MINDS of the company. A basic truism is that people will always act in some manner. While the mind of a person may be *"invisible"* to others, a person's behavior is always *"visible"* for all peers and subordinates (and really everyone) to see. A person's behavior always reveals what a person really believes; it reveals their mind. And action is never neutral; people always behave in some kind of manner. A person's action is either *conscious* (contributing to alignment and is *on strategy*) OR it is *unconscious*, in which case the person is thinking, acting, and behaving in ways that are not contributing to alignment; hence, it is *off strategy*. Since people can't see someone's MIND, all they can do is watch visible action and behavior.

Conscious Action in a large organization arises from understanding both the strategy and the measurement systems that must be clear, visible, and focused, thus serving to promote true organizational and operational alignment. Measuring *what you do* and *how you do it* serves the alignment of all business metrics as well as the alignment necessary to change the way people think about their job, their company, their place in the community.

I teach my clients how to measure their culture; that is, to measure how people are working together by focusing upon *visible behaviors*, not the *invisible MIND*. As the saying goes, "actions speak louder than words" and "what gets clearly and understandably measured, gets done." My clients also measure how well they pay their people. The best companies want to be among the top employers in their geographic area as measured by employee benefits and compensation as well as the percent participation of employees serving; that is, giving back to their local communities.

---

*Have you ever wondered why
people do not always do what they say they will do?*

**EXECUTION:
Take Responsibility and Do What You Say**

In short, high performance and productivity are enhanced when people participate and are involved in goal setting around the core business metrics that will evidence whether or not the strategy is being successfully executed. When people participate and are involved, they are willing to *take responsibility* for *doing what they say* as clearly and visibly depicted in the annual business plan. Clarity, Visibility, and Focus are thus the three keys to create organizational alignment for Conscious Action across an entire multinational business.

Examining the history of companies going through change management, or organizational development transformations, is not unlike examining the stages and phases that are integral to the Seven Arts of personal transformation that we have been discussing in this book. In my book, **The Seven Arts of Change: Leading Business Transformation That Lasts,** I have written in detail how these same Seven Arts can be applied to the transformation of business organizations large and small. I use business vocabulary in the aforementioned book, but the truth is companies succeed at managing change and making it sustainable when they follow the same Seven Arts (or basic steps for personal development and positive self-transformation) that we are exploring in this book.

For example, consider the Seven Arts in a business context as follows: 1) properly PREPARE the workforce for change, 2) show COMPASSION and empathy toward employees as part of the change process, 3) hold employees RESPONSIBLE and accountable so that you build trust, 4) treat employees with respect so they can RELAX and focus upon the visible behaviors that will help everyone to perform their tasks willingly to the best of their ability, 5) teach and educate employees so they understand the focus of selfless CONSCIOUS ACTION serving organizational alignment, 6) enable employees to LIVE NATURALLY by making expectations clear and understandable so that they can be shared with others, and finally, 7) SERVE employees and give back to local communities since, ultimately, employees, customers, and local communities represent the real backbone of any sustainable business/organization.

It sounds simple but these Seven Arts are difficult to execute for large organizations without sufficient patience and discipline on the part of everyone involved. Just as there is no quick fix and no skipping steps for individual transformation, there is no quick "change the culture of your business" via an Advanced Off-Site Weekend Seminar that can create sustainable and profitable change.

I say to business leaders "Do it right the first time and *invest* in your people." Give your employees access to realistic and pragmatic business change processes that lead to aligned Conscious Action. At the same time, ensure that employees reciprocate and *"do what they say"* by taking responsibility for the outcomes of their own actions and behaviors. It has been my experience for over thirty years of business consulting that this planned process for significant measurable performance improvement will always serve to create an involved, responsible, accountable, high performance, and execution-oriented business culture. The good news is that when the quality of life goes up at work, so do all the measurable performance indices, including the financials. In order to sustain the life of our communities and local charitable giving, oftentimes "net employment" in a geographic area is key. Jobs and economic development are one and the same, enabling many small towns to "Secure Their Future."

It has been my pleasure to work with businesses where their manufacturing plants are key employers in their local communities. If manufacturing jobs are lost, the entire community suffers. Unemployment goes up, stores close, social services becomes over-taxed, crime skyrockets, divorce goes up, and finally people move away. The quest to significantly improve a company's performance so that jobs continue, jobs remain local and even increase is truly a team sport. I am driven by the direct experience of the power of the Seven Arts to create positive changes in work-life and the consequent cascade of positive effects in families, communities and the larger business economy. It is my hope that others who lead organizations can learn what seems so obvious. All of these personal, family-related, organizational, and local community positive outcomes are simply the result of treating employees with dignity and respect, while pursuing a noble cause.

Have you ever wondered what it would be like to be on a successful team?

Seven Arts Business Success Stories

While teaching at Harvard University in 1985 and 1986 as an Andrew W. Mellon Faculty Fellow in the Humanities, I learned that many of my Harvard faculty peers had business, advising, consulting, or public speaking experience related to their careers as subject matter experts in their field of endeavor. Similarly, all of my consulting work has been through informal referral since 1986 stemming initially from my knowledge of Japanese culture and experience working with Japanese organizations. Consequently, for the first twenty-five years of business consulting, Shaner & Associates: Performance Development Consultants had no sales and marketing program, no advertising, and no website.

The spontaneous arising of my work as a business consultant has been simply the result of a track record of successful execution working with my client companies using the Seven Arts principles. This track record of success and simple referral is significant, especially when viewed in contrast to a 70 percent industry-wide failure rate when companies attempt to "change the culture," "re-engineer," or "re-invent" themselves in order to manage the execution of a significantly new business strategy.

Evidence of the effectiveness of the Seven Arts for managing sustainable change in a corporate environment is chronicled in my book, **The Seven Arts of Change: Leading Business Transformation That Lasts**. This companion book shares stories, details, and even a Duracell Battery Company Case Study for applying the Seven Arts to produce significant measurable performance improvement at some of the best-run companies in the world. Let's face it; the world of business is both competitive and stressful. Therefore, if you are a manager or a member of a team going through significant change in the workplace, then I encourage you to read **The Seven Arts of Change**. You will discover the tools and methods for applying the Seven Arts in the workplace. As my friend Tom Crum says, you will learn to "turn a life of work into a work of art"!

To review, the fifth Art of Conscious Action arises from *clarity* (individual clarity as well as organizational clarity). The fourth Art of Relaxation facilitates *the experience of immediate clarity* by giving you a means of returning to the center of your conscious life. From a place of deep calmness with the strength of the Universe at your back, you can focus your life selflessly through Conscious Action.

Please practice the exercises that follow and you will begin to experience both the freedom and the power of your God-given, Spirit-given, Universe-given ability to execute and fulfill all your dreams; in short, you will be *Living With the Wind at Your Back*.

**Daily Exercises
For Facilitating The Art of Conscious Action**

---

*Have you ever wondered if you could be
more calm and relaxed all the time?*

**Exercise 10:
Return to and "Presence" the World Around You**

Now you are prepared to focus upon the application of all you have learned (Exercises 1 - 9) when you need it most—in times of struggle, tension, or even crisis. When you feel tension or anxiety rising within you, you are now prepared to "return immediately" to a unified state of mindful living.

Each day strive to gain clarity about the seeds of consciousness from which Conscious Action arises. Clarity is experienced in the First Order Mode of Awareness occasioned by your Dynamic Breathing and Dynamic Meditation daily exercises (Chapter Four). When you are engaged in deep moments of calmness during your breathing and meditation practice, take a mental, physical, emotional, and spiritual "snapshot" of your total state of being. Remember this feeling. In other words, be aware that *you* were the author that brought you to this supremely calm state, since *you* have been practicing daily with patience and discipline. Know that *you can* return to this state of calmness at any time during the day.

This exercise is designed to help you apply your deep calmness in daily life. When an unexpected difficulty or challenge arises during the day, then you can rise to the occasion using the same strength and power of calmness that you first learned in meditation and breathing sessions. You can quickly re-enter these same states of consciousness to gain the clarity that you need during your daily life challenges.

At the end of each day, record in your Seven Arts Journal *your difficulties and how you have learned to move around, through, and/or beyond them by anchoring new states of being in the face of your daily life obstacles and challenges.*

The key is self-empowerment. Empowerment arises from your personal experience and deep confidence in your connection to the Universe. You have cultivated the ability to train your mind to experience deep calmness and inner peace through your Dynamic Breathing and Dynamic Meditation practice. And so, you must also realize and directly experience that you still have the ability to return to these life-giving, empowering, mental and emotional states of being at any time you need to call upon them. This is about both the freedom and the autonomy to use your own mind, body, emotion, and spirit effectively; that is, *consciously*. And so, you need not become shaken or rattled just because you encounter an unpleasant external circumstance or situation. You are both free and autonomous, enabling you to direct your Conscious Action as needed in daily life to serve others to the best of your ability.

In this exercise, you will be confidently applying the benefits of your regular practice of Dynamic Breathing and Dynamic Meditation where it counts most in your daily life. What good is deep inner calmness, peace, and joy, if you cannot bring this experience to bear in your daily life with your fellow human beings? By returning yourself to your deepest states of relaxation during the day, you will be transforming yourself and applying self-awareness and lessons learned when you need it most.

Soon your first reaction to danger, an emergency, an unexpected problem, or even just a negative person, will be to return to your real source of strength which is the calm strength of your connectedness to God, Spirit, the Universe. From this base of calmness, even in the midst of the unexpected problems and challenges of daily life, you will be prepared for Conscious Action in the positive resolution of whatever comes your way.

Have you ever wondered if you could exceed your wildest expectations?

Exercise 11:
Apply Conscious Action in Your Daily Life

Now you are prepared to apply all you have learned (Exercises 1 - 10), not just in times of crisis, but also in your daily life. You can now live intentionally in accord with your PDA 24/7 if you simply choose to; you have already developed the skills of patience and discipline to succeed.

By returning to your place of "presencing" when you face a problem or crisis in daily life, you will be able to bring clarity to the situation at hand. This is practicing Exercise 10 above. From this place of clarity, you will know intuitively which actions will serve as Conscious Actions ONLY IF you truly know, and have internalized well, your real goals in service to others. Therefore, in this exercise, you will want to begin by reviewing daily your PDA, that is your personal mission, as described in the exercises for the first Art of Preparation.

Conscious Action is the fulfillment and execution of the conscious behaviors that serve to realize your dreams. If you are steadfast and remain focused upon the services that you would like to bring to others, then you can be flexible in daily life in terms of the actual tactics and specific actions that you employ in order to execute and fulfill your dreams. Without being too attached to any specific plan of action, it is possible to be flexible and, therefore, adapt to ever-changing circumstances. Exactly *how* you carry out your PDA or personal mission may need to change from time to time. The specific plan of action at any given moment in time may need to change because you see clearly the new situation, new problem, or new challenge as it presents itself to you in a new revealing light. Any action that serves your mission, your higher calling in service to others, is Conscious Action.

This practice of reviewing daily your Personal Development Affirmation is designed to help you become clear about your goals and dreams in service to others. Each morning before your practice of "Positive Self Talk," or "Silence," or "Dynamic Breathing," or "Dynamic Meditation," or any of the previous exercises, use your Seven Arts Journal to write down and review "outcomes" that you see for yourself for the day, the week, the month, the year, and the next five to ten years. In other words, use your Seven Arts Journal to write down your personal goals as they unfold before you.

Write down and thus externalize your goals so that you can know at any moment during the day what kind of actions will contribute to the fulfillment of your dreams. This daily activity and habit will help you to raise the *visibility* of your mission, to *clarify* and internalize your mission, and to stay *focused* upon your dreams. It will help you to develop your intuitive abilities and thus you will be able to truly call upon Conscious Actions as you embrace the inevitable obstacles that arise in daily life.

When considering your life as a whole, you need to know what kinds of behaviors and actions will serve to bring about the ends consistent with your PDA - selfless service toward others. Just as a large multinational business needs to know what actions are "on" or "off" strategy, you, too, need to know what counts as Conscious Action in service to your personal mission, goals, and highest calling. Just as any business, large or small, needs to remain focused upon the goal and flexible regarding the strategies and operational processes used to attain the goal, you too need to be clear and focused on your goals and flexible regarding the specific means by which you can fulfill your dreams. Conscious Action is thus any action that enables you to fulfill your dreams and walk the Way of the Universe in service to others.

By applying both of these daily exercises as part of the fifth Art of Conscious Action, you will be able to effectively respond to any situation that comes your way. First, you will be able to return to a place of quiet, calm confidence even in an emergency. You will perceive your world with great clarity and you will be able to act consciously (Exercise 10). Second, you will be clear about your real purpose, mission, and goals because of your practice of Exercise 11. When you join and apply these two exercises in your daily life, you will know that you are practicing effectively the Art of Conscious Action. By following these exercises each day, the decisions that you make, and the actions and behaviors that you take, will certainly serve your PDA higher calling, and thus serve the greater good for all humanity. Enjoy.

6

The Art of Living Naturally

"Scientific research is based upon experimentation with the aid of specific instruments. Spiritual research relies on inner experience and meditation...The human senses can perceive the world to a certain extent, but we cannot assert that there is nothing beyond what we can access through our five senses."

Tenzin Gyatso
the XIV Dalai Lama (1935-)
Inner Peace

The Universe is in flux. It is impermanent, ever changing, dynamic, *and* it is perfectly balanced when left alone. The sixth Art, the Art of Living Naturally, means living in a harmonious manner with the Universe. It means living in accord with the principles of the Universe. It means living in a manner that preserves and protects that which is natural; natural, in turn, means following the Way of the Universe. Having cultivated and practiced the fifth Art of Conscious Action, you will know that it is possible to become One with the Universe because you are now experiencing action that is in accord with new situations just as they arise. In short, you are operating from mindful "presencing", which is synonymous with the condition we have described (in Chapter Four) as First Order Awareness.

Have you ever wondered if life is really a process of learning?

Living as a Causal Process of Awakening

Enlightenment is a verb, not a noun. Enlightenment means living naturally; that is, *living as a process* in accord with the principles of the Universe. The first such principle is that the Universe is always changing. By presenc**ing** or be**ing** with the world around you, you can operate in an harmonious manner such that peace, joy, acceptance, and abundance are yours to treasure. To treat enlightenment as static, as something to possess, as though it were a noun, merely causes you to disconnect and separate from the Universe. When this happens you are *not* living naturally for you are not operating in a harmonious manner; as a result, attachment, fear, insecurity, scarcity, pain, and suffering become yours to endure.

The Art of Living Naturally is the next level of personal transformation. It means nothing less than putting into practice *all* the Arts cultivated thus far. When this happens, the Universe gives in abundance. You will discover that God, Spirit, the Universe Itself (seen as one) is present in all things and in all activities and will speak to you and teach you (Jp. *Kaiden*) if only you are *awake*. That is, if you are truly aware and in the present moment with a mirror-like mind reflect**ing** all things and all activities clearly, then you will be receptive to the life lessons that are present all around you, and that are "preached to you" (Jp. *Hosshin seppo*) each day.

THE ART OF LIVING NATURALLY

Learning these life lessons from the Universe means learning to *listen deeply*. It means *accepting* the moment, *taking responsibility* for the moment, not blaming, not being defensive, not trying to convince others that you are right or forcing your own will or opinion; it means not judging and not criticizing. When you truly accept the moment, you are truly free to actuate your mind, your emotions, and your entire consciousness from a place of unattached abundance; you are connected to your true Self; you operate without ego; and you move through life calmly and effortlessly knowing deeply that you are already connected to the Universe. You are One with the Universe. You live your life feeling a wellspring of abundant energy (*Ki*) without end. This is the Art of Living Naturally.

When you operate from attachment, however, the opposite arises, for this also is a principle of the Universe. Attachment *causes* separation. This is manifested by your ego's craving, covetous, and dogmatic desires. This craving is an *unnatural* quest for states of permanence or a static state of being in which you desire to possess, or retain, or control people, things, or states of affairs. This manner of thinking, feeling, and behaving is like a quest for personal security in which you find it necessary to try to control the world around you. This way of being, or acting, or living is as if the Universe owes you something or is supposed to give you something in order to calm your fears and insecurity (which is the same as separation). I say this is an *unnatural* quest, not because it isn't a frequent desire for many people, but because the desire itself or the quest for permanent security goes against the *natural* Way of the Universe.

The truth is that the Universe is impermanent, in flux, and ever changing. To secure, or retain, or covet a permanent state of happiness (for example, as if you can possess it) also goes against the principles of the Universe for the same reason. When you operate from excessive attachment in the pursuit of personal happiness, you *cause* disharmony, isolation, and separation from both people and the Universe. Your energy becomes weak and depleted, you struggle, you are tired, you become ill and ungrateful, and you become negative toward those around you and the world around you.

Therefore, the Art of Living Naturally is ultimately up to you; it is *your choice*. You can choose the path of acceptance and connection to the abundant life force of the Universe and inherit its causal results, or you can choose the path of attachment and disconnection from the life force of the Universe and inherit its causal results as well. The Universe has a rhythm and a Way. Remember that causation (dependent arising) is one of the principles of the Universe described in the third Art of Responsibility. It is up to you. You are free to choose a path that goes in all directions in this life (for better or for worse). And, it is important to know deeply that you are also inevitably *responsible* for the causal outcomes of *how you choose to live your life*. I believe that you aim to be empowered, balanced, energized, confident, and filled with integrity, peace and joy. This is choosing the Art of Living Naturally.

In this chapter, I will once again rely upon personal stories and testimony to illustrate the main points summarized above. My hope is that, by this approach, you will see living examples that evidence the principles of the Universe in action. Of course, my life is but one illustration. I hope that, by sharing some of my own experiences, you will reflect upon your experience as well as your present state of being and gain some appreciation for the wonder and abundance that life has to offer.

You can never predict what lies ahead. However, if you combine preparation (using patience and discipline) with being present so that you see challenges, obstacles, and uncertainty as opportunity, then you, too, can craft your own life filled with wondrous events and unforeseen outcomes (positive and negative) that serve your transformation and deepen your understanding. When you live your life each day knowing that there are no real accidents, no real coincidences, and no secrets from the viewing place of God, Spirit, and the Universe (because there is always the causal law of dependent origination), then you will begin to "see" differently and appreciate the deep truth that the real master teacher is all around you, all the time (Jp. *Kaiden*) - - the Universe Itself.

By following the Way of the Universe, and by making the Art of Living Naturally yours, you will learn to place your life with acceptance and trust in the hands of something much greater and more powerful than your individual, isolated, separated, ego self. By sacrificing and renouncing your selfish mind (Jp. *shoga*), and then giving your life to the Universe, you will at once Consciously Act and live with a Universal Mind (Jp. *Taiga*). When this happens, *you will accomplish more and do so with greater ease than you ever thought possible.* By "doing nothing"—that is, by "doing nothing" *in particular in an attached manner*—you will discover that you are really doing everything without exhaustion, without suffering, and without excessive desire. The energy that causes positive outcomes in the form of Conscious Action is not the same as the energy that is caused by action arising from ego attachment. Rather, Conscious Action is the type of action that springs from acceptance, trust, and abundance as experienced in the present moment. Let us now begin to examine in greater detail the Art of Living Naturally, punctuated by personal events, encounters, and discoveries.

Have you ever wondered who you can believe and why?

Two Philosophical Camps: Science and Ethics

On one hand is the scientific camp. The members of this camp believe that the scientific method of careful observation and experiment is the way to answer the basic questions of life. To me, this method is certainly an effective way to answer one type of question. In the language of science, this type of question is one about predicting my sense experience: *"How can I predict what I will observe and experience?"* In more everyday language, this type of question asks *"How can I get what I want?"* or *"How can I get the material world to satisfy my wants, wishes, and desires?"* These kinds of questions are all rooted in the notion of utility.

On the other hand, distinctly different types of questions are those related to the notions of purpose, morality, and ethics. For example, *"Why am I here?"* or *"What ought I to do?"* or *"What is the purpose of my life?"* or *"What am I here for?"* If you believe that the only meaningful questions in life are those having to do with utility, and if you further believe that the only reality and the only Universe worth speaking of has a material nature (made up of things like atoms, molecules, and genes; that is, things that have mass that can be measured by length, breadth, and depth), then you might think that the scientific method is all you would ever need to learn, grow, and develop in this life. If you are a philosophical materialist and think that the only things that are real are made of physical stuff, then you could be quite happy going through life with but one means of gaining real knowledge – the scientific method.

For me, however, there is more to the Universe than matter. Not only am I *not* a philosophical materialist, I am actually what is called, in philosophical circles, a "holist." This means I consider worthwhile many different ways of gaining knowledge (epistemological methods) in addition to the scientific method. I think other methods of gaining knowledge and interpreting our experience can provide us with additional tools and windows to help us understand the entire Universe, as opposed to the scientific method, which gives us a window to the Universe defined only as one of material substance. I may as well confess that I have directly experienced many phenomena that are not publicly verifiable or repeatable as required by the demands of the scientific method. And, I am a strong advocate of good science. My point simply is that I cannot deny all that I have experienced with many different teachers over my entire lifetime. These experiences include not only learning under the tutelage of modern masters of the scientific method, but also learning from modern masters of alternative ways of knowing based upon cultivating other aspects of our *whole* being.

For example, there are ways of knowing (epistemologies) that include investigations into what the scientific community would consider paranormal phenomena. Although many of my experiences may be dismissed from a scientific point of view, I must confess that I cannot deny a lifetime of experiences that simply cannot be explained by science, yet they can be explained by other avenues, methods, processes, and dimensions that take into consideration the *whole* of human experience. In professional philosophical circles then, my position is in sympathy with the so-called "Independence Model" when it comes to explaining the relationship between, for example, science and religion. The fact that different epistemologies (means of knowing) are designed to serve different ends causes me to view these human creations and enterprises as "independent." The scientific method is one epistemology serving the end of *utility* and religious or spiritual epistemologies are serving the ends of *purpose.*

    Accordingly, there is another side to learning and it is not limited to the material world viewed through the lens of the scientific method. This line of inquiry and investigation leads us to the ethics camp. The members of this camp believe that there are ethical or spiritual questions that are fundamental to human life. The scientific method is silent in its ability to answer these types of questions. For these are not questions about *utility* ..."*How to get the material world to respond to what I want?*" ...but are related to the prior and more basic question of *purpose*: "*What should I want?*" or "*What ought I desire?*"

Have you ever wondered why lessons learned take time and why maturity and wisdom go hand in hand?

Personal Transformation is a Causal Process

Now that I have explained that some of my own experiences upon which the Seven Arts are based stand outside the purview of science, let us use this as a starting point to explain some basics about the Art of Living Naturally. I follow the historical Buddha in declaring that enlightenment is a natural, *causal* phenomenon. That the material world functions causally is also a working *assumption* operating at the core of the scientific method. That is, the scientific method does not *prove* that the world functions causally; rather, causation is a basic *assumption* that the working scientist must embrace when using the scientific method in order to gain new information and knowledge about the physical universe.

In Buddhism, however, the *entire Universe functions causally*. Anything that comes into being depends for its origin upon other things. This is the doctrine of *dependent origination* (see Chapter Three). The view that whatever exists depends causally upon other things applies to all spheres including material, mental, psychic, moral (karma), social, and spiritual phenomena.

Now consider the fact that *all people are already enlightened*, even originally enlightened; they just don't know it insofar as this reality has not become a part of their *conscious* awareness. All people, you, me, your neighbor with whom you fight, are *all* already enlightened. The *causal process* of transforming yourself in order to directly experience and realize this for yourself is consistent with taking the sequential steps to awakening as outlined in the Seven Arts. When you use patience and discipline to peel back and detach yourself from the layers of habitual intentions and attachments that arise from, and continue to feed, the ego, then you will be unveiling your original Universal Mind that can be present at all times.

The problem or challenge (as you know by now) is that the covering activity or veil of the selfish mind continues to cloud your awareness of your true Self. The selfish mind is not somehow innate but rather is formed by your own personal making, influenced by the dependent causal forces that have affected your entire life history. The Art of Living Naturally then is nothing other than living a causal process of self-discovery such that the *whole of you* (Jp. *zenshin*) that is originally and naturally connected to the Universe can be awakened and placed at the center of your conscious awareness. When this occurs, you will experience directly (perhaps for the first time) that you actually can live your life *consciously* with abundance and present awareness.

In fact, you will discover and experience that you can *live with the wind at your back* at any time because "the wind" is really the Universe Itself that has been with you all the time from the very beginning. Your job is simply to become aware of your original nature, your original gifts, and your true Self that has always been "One with the Universe." In short, your job is to make the simple transition of *trusting* the causal process enough to get out of your own way.

*Have you ever wondered why
you are doing what you are doing?*

Harvard University:
My Interdisciplinary Research and Its Causal Consequences

In 1985 and 1986, I was granted a leave from Furman University in order to teach and pursue multiple research projects at Harvard University after receiving an Andrew W. Mellon Faculty Fellowship in the Humanities. Remember, I said earlier that there are no real accidents in the Universe and that everything that occurs has a cause or, more accurately, a series of causes (dependent origination). It may appear accidental or just good fortune but my faculty office that year was in the Harvard University East Asian Library (the *Yen Ching* Library) that happens to be in very close proximity to the Museum of Comparative Zoology. My "home" department was the Department of East Asian Languages and Civilizations. My plan was to spend a lot of time with Professor Masatoshi Nagatomi, a master philologist and one of the world's most knowledgeable experts in reading Chinese, Japanese and, especially, Tibetan Buddhist texts.

"In 1985 and 1986, I was granted a leave from Furman University in order to teach and pursue multiple research projects at Harvard University after receiving an Andrew W. Mellon Faculty Fellowship in the Humanities."

However, my "adopted" department that year was the Department of Organismic and Evolutionary Biology. In fact, I spent more time in the company of the late Stephen Jay Gould, Edward O. Wilson, the late Ernst Mayr, and Richard Lewontin than in my home department. These modern "masters" of the scientific method had a proclivity for, and even a passion for, philosophy. Indeed, prior to my arrival, the Department of Organismic and Evolutionary Biology had served as host for visiting scholars who were professional philosophers specializing in Philosophy of Science and Philosophy of Biology in particular. For example, scholars Philip Kitcher and Michael Ruse preceded me and each spent a year working, writing, and conducting collaborative research at the Museum of Comparative Zoology (MCZ).

As a result of my time in association with these Harvard scholars, I founded (in 1987) a new book series with the State University of New York Press entitled *"Philosophy and*

Biology." To date, thirty-seven volumes have been published. As editor of the series, I tried to support the publication of a diversity of perspectives on many issues at the intersection of philosophy (especially epistemology and ethics) and biology (especially evolutionary biology, genetics, sociobiology, and cognitive science). In addition, that year I wrote a book entitled **Science and Comparative Philosophy** with Shigenori Nagatomo and YUASA Yasuo. It could be argued that both the book series and the **Science and Comparative Philosophy** book came into being simply because of my interest in taking advantage of my close proximity to the MCZ and the great minds of Professors Gould, Wilson, Lewontin, and Mayr.

Actually, I do believe that my friendship with these gentlemen has changed my life dramatically and I further believe that all of this was no accident. My focus upon biology was, in fact, related to my work in Comparative Philosophy. I was specifically interested in Steve Gould's ideas about *Paedomorphosis* (more commonly referred to as *neoteny*, meaning literally "holding on to youth") in relation to the evolution of *homo sapiens* as well as human cultural evolution. The concept of human *neoteny*, I thought, could have a significant bearing upon our understanding of the possibility for, and development of, the acquisition of so-called culturally dependent worldviews. In my book **Science and Comparative Philosophy**, I explore this and related phenomena more deeply.

Have you ever wondered if you are a product of nature or nurture or both?

Sociobiology Debates:
Professors Stephen Jay Gould and Edward O. Wilson

If you are familiar with the early debates between these esteemed biologists and scholars, both of whom taught at Harvard, you would know that, after the publication of Edward Wilson's **Sociobiology** in 1976, the political debate reached its climax in the early 1980s.

On one side of this debate were scientists such as Ed Wilson who believed that social behavior was like other physical traits of biological organisms, the product of an evolutionary process of natural selection. On the other side of the debate were scientists such as Steve Gould who believed that to construe social behavior (and consequently human social values) as simply a product of evolution by natural selection threatened the stability and authority of these values for society. [By the way, as a side note, Steve Gould was also a subscriber of the "independence model" that I described above. His book **Rock of Ages** illustrates the "independence model."]

In 1980, during the height of this "sociobiological debate," I was also at Harvard as a doctoral student writing my dissertation under the direction of Thomas Patrick Kasulis who was then an Andrew W. Mellon Faculty Fellow from the University of Hawaii. By the time I returned to Harvard in 1985 as a Faculty Fellow myself, relationships within the Harvard University Department of Organismic and Evolutionary Biology had deteriorated so much that you could not spend time with these famous scholars (Wilson and Gould) *together*. For example, I had lunch with Steve Gould and Ed Wilson frequently, but separately, simply because of the intensity of the very public polemics that accompanied the political debate. I do not think that department meetings in the Department of Organismic and Evolutionary Biology were much fun to attend! Ed is a charming southern gentleman who was chastised in the press for his far-reaching reductionist conclusions about the biological basis of social behavior. He was and is referred to as *"the father of sociobiology."*

Steve, though also charming, was a vocal and self confident New Yorker whose widely read monthly column in the magazine *"Nature"* became both an outlet and a bully pulpit from which he tried to dismantle what he believed was a dangerous, socially irresponsible scientific agenda. One of my favorite pastimes during this year was to spend Sunday afternoon sitting in the Harvard Square cafes with a good latte or chocolate frappé (depending on the season), and reading one of Steve's many scathing book reviews in the Sunday *New York Times* in which he pulled no punches critiquing new books sympathetic to *"the sociobiological agenda."*

To persons unschooled in understanding the scope and limitations of the scientific method, it may seem remarkable that two distinguished scientists could differ so widely on questions of empirical fact that the scientific method could not (apparently) successfully resolve or adjudicate. Over time, as I was able to know these two scientists better and was able to see how the actual practice of science was affected by the person inside the scientist "label," it became clear to me how there could be divergent opinions on the same subject within the scientific camp. The differences of opinion between Ed Wilson and Steve Gould regarding sociobiology are really related to some of the differences between their personalities and the particular ways they perceived their connection to nature. The crux of the matter has less to do with differences in understanding science as a method designed to yield useful knowledge (*utility*), and has more to do with differences of *purpose* with respect to what we as persons, who also happen to be scientists, *ought to do*. In other words, how *ought* we direct the activity of the pragmatically *useful* method we refer to as science? Let me explain further by way of personal stories once again.

Ed is a very kind soul with a giant heart and passion for the most intimate, personal, and even *felt connections* with nature. In my opinion, he is a Chinese Daoist in disguise who, as he likes to say, "never grew out of his boyhood bug phase." And, as he is the world's leading, most prolific, and most highly honored scientist in his field of Entomology, I can say that it is an honor to know him. To understand Ed, the person, I recommend reading his book **Biophilia** *(Love of Nature)* and his autobiography entitled **The Naturalist**. The type of *awareness* that Ed displays in the field (so I have heard as I have not personally accompanied him on his sojourns into tropical rainforests) and the type of enthusiasm he projects when speaking and writing about his love of nature are akin to my association with modern spiritual masters of the East Asian tradition who also speak, and write about, and even celebrate, our *felt connection* with nature and the Universe. Ed just happens to be trained as a scientist but, to me, his life work is to bring us all closer to our environment and the world around us so that we can preserve nature and, thereby, practice the Art of Living Naturally for as long as our species can survive in cohabitation with the earth's limited natural resources. In my view, Ed's work reflects a major thesis of this book; namely, that we are "One with the Universe," and causally inseparable such that we *homo sapiens* must *take responsibility* for our collective actions with each other and with the environment that sustains our life every day.

On the other end of the political spectrum were Steve Gould and Dick Lewontin. Now, you could have lunch with them together; they were academic buddies, dressed similarly in flannel shirts with white tees. Together they represented the "Marxist liberal critique" of the sociobiological agenda. Philip Kitcher is another philosopher you could throw in here as well. So, a combined lunch was theoretically possible with Steve Gould, Dick Lewontin, and Philip Kitcher because they were all in the same ideological spectrum. And just to make the polemics and discussion very human, you could have lunch with philosopher Michael Ruse and Ed Wilson at the same time as well. This was how the two factions lined up back in the mid-1980s when I returned to Harvard as a Faculty Fellow.

I chose to lunch with Steve and Ed frequently, but separately and alone; that is, one-on-one. Steve liked to walk together through Harvard Yard and dine at the cafes in Cambridge. My wife was pregnant and gave birth at the time so our eldest daughter was born in Cambridge with all the benefits of the Harvard University faculty medical plan. Back then, Steve liked to ask about my sleepless nights, discuss the evolutionary implications of breastfeeding and, of course, talk about baseball statistics! Whenever he could not attend a home Boston Red Sox game (he had two season tickets halfway up on the first base side), I managed to get the hand-me-downs during my time in Cambridge. The regular (season ticket holder) fans around that part of Fenway Park knew that these two seats were the famous Stephen Jay Gould's and so they somehow assumed that both my IQ and knowledge of baseball would be at a similarly high level. When I sat in Steve's seats, for some strange reason of association, people expected me to know a lot more than I did! Anyway, Steve was great. He inspired me to no end and it was everything I could do to fake keeping up with him in conversation. Steve was smart and he knew it. Humility was not his calling card but he sure commanded respect, so who am I to judge? I was simply honored to be in his company, and I was in awe of the breadth and depth of his keen mind.

Ed was a completely different dining companion at lunch. Incredibly charming, he just never stopped working. We would go downstairs to the sandwich truck parked in front of the Peabody Museum located between our offices. We would grab a sandwich (Ed always offered to pay) and return to his office to discuss philosophy and sociobiology amidst hundreds of thousands of ants living in glass colonies situated throughout his office and associated research laboratories.

I share these personal stories and recollections for one reason that serves an important point in this chapter on the Art of Living Naturally. I want to associate human "faces" and "personalities" with the day-to-day business and practice of science. This is because science is nothing other than the *personal practice* of a single methodology which assumes that the material Universe functions causally. The scientific method is but one means of gaining knowledge and so it must be understood as merely a tool used by human beings who possess all the biases, agendas, and attachments of ordinary people. The so-called objectivity of the scientific method is undoubtable. However, the actual business and practice of science is conducted by individual human beings who may themselves be *attached* to a particular subjective perspective and frame of reference. This frame of reference is, in turn, formed by the history of their scientific field or discipline – what the philosopher of science Thomas Kuhn calls "normal science."

Personally, I have enormous respect for all these gentlemen. And yet, throughout this scientific controversy, I saw that one group (let's call them the Gouldians) sincerely believed that the integrity of the liberal tradition was threatened by the implications of Ed Wilson's so-called "sociobiological agenda." However, I must admit that I personally never perceived any *agenda* in my interactions with Ed at all. In fact, in the beginning, Ed was quite shocked by the sociobiology controversy, as he only believed (and to this day still sincerely believes) that he (like the Gouldians) was and is simply defending the highest values and integrity of science by examining fully the potential consequences and implications of his research.

So it comes down to this. Even within the first "utility" camp (science), practicing scientists cannot help but have interests, and interests are usually related to values and frames of reference which stem from deeper, underlying philosophical questions of the second "ultimate purpose" camp (ethics). Steve Gould and Ed Wilson represented opposite ends of philosophical ideology within the political spectrum of the scientific community at the time. The history of science is filled with such examples of scientists with conflicting paradigms and ideology interpreting the same set of facts or other forms of empirical data and arriving at opposite conclusions. Steve and Ed were both operating out of, and were/are motivated by, different answers to second camp questions of the form *"Why are we here?"*, *"What are we for?"*, *"What is our purpose?"*, and *"Toward what ends ought we aspire?"*

However, the scientific method in practice addresses only questions of the first "camp" focused upon "utility." For example, "if I do such and such under this set of initial conditions, I predict we will see such and such occur." These questions are of the form *"How can I get what I want?"* or *"How can I get the natural world to give me what I seek?"* Or, more commonly, *"How can I predict my sense experience?"* in the physical/material Universe. In other words, if I have a set of initial conditions, let's say in the laboratory, and then I introduce variable X, then the scientific question being asked is *"What can I expect to occur in my sense experience?."* The expected answer is based upon the existing laws and theories of "normal science" that already have been canonized by others working in the same discipline.

Steve and Ed were both practicing science with a different set of learned values and frames of reference (second camp questions) that themselves stood outside the ability of the scientific method (designed to answer only first camp questions) to adjudicate. To deny the meaningfulness or relevance of questions and answers of the second camp (related to ethics and ultimate purpose) is to deny that which is most significant to our lives as human beings. Frankly speaking, Steve seemed to enjoy displaying his vast knowledge (intellectual ego) while Ed was driven by a kind of endless energy focused upon the selfless activity of *making connections* whether it was between people (like myself, a young philosophy Faculty Fellow at Harvard) or in the realm of ideas (as in cross-disciplinary connections between philosophy and biology). Yet, in the "trial by the media," Steve was portrayed as a liberal, soulful person with a selfless heart, while Ed was portrayed as a heartless, neo-nazi who was blind to the fact, or just didn't want to understand, that his work could be used to support radical ideology in the defense, potentially, of even genocide. This was the publicity side of the "Sociobiology Debates"!

The media view and my view were opposite. I was friends with and respected both Steve and Ed. I could respect their individual philosophical convictions and I certainly could understand how the media misrepresented both of these great naturalists. Steve's eyes and Ed's eyes *in the field* were completely in tune with nature when observing specimens in their areas of expertise. The very human, romantic, *"felt" connection with nature* (the Universe) was as alive with both of these gentleman as was the *"felt" connection with nature* experienced in my walks with Shingon Buddhist monks at Mt. Kyosan near Osaka, Japan, or with Soto (Zen)

Buddhist monks at the Daitokuji monastery in Kyoto, Japan, or with my own teacher, Master Tohei, residing in Tochigi Prefecture near the city of Utsunomiya, Japan. At this point, I would like to turn our attention toward this *"felt"* connection to nature. This feeling is integral to the Art of Living Naturally.

I believe that the Art of Living Naturally is possible for *all* human beings because no matter who you are, what you do, or how you are trained to see the world, when you open yourself to discovery, when you free your mind to see and hear and observe nature in a manner that *invites nature to do the teaching*, only then are you capable of *learning directly from the Universe Itself*. The famous founder of Harvard's Museum of Comparative Zoology, Louis Agassiz, used to tell his students "read nature, not books." Agassiz would even lock his students inside MCZ laboratories with no books and nothing but tortoise shells, for example, and then expect them to discover the law-like principles of morphology. Again, *Nature itself can teach you (Jp. kaiden) as long as you prepare yourself to presence and witness the lessons that unfold before you.* This learning process also happens to be consistent with the deeper meaning of the Japanese philosophical concept of *kaiden*—the Universe Itself is teaching us all the time if only we prepare ourselves to see deeply, hear deeply, listen deeply, feel deeply, and witness deeply.

Let us take this discussion of Steve and Ed, two of the most famous personalities in the history of science, and continue to weave another closely related thread in creating this tapestry called the Art of Living Naturally.

THE ART OF LIVING NATURALLY

Have you ever wondered what it would be like to spend a day with royalty?

**An Audience with
the Emperor of Japan, His Majesty Emperor Akihito**

I experienced the honor of having a personal audience with the Emperor of Japan, His Majesty Emperor Akihito. I received the Crown Prince Akihito Foundation Award given each year to a person, or persons, who are scholars of some aspect of Japanese culture and sometimes are practitioners (usually at some high level of proficiency) of a uniquely Japanese art or discipline. In my case, the scholarship was related to Japanese Buddhist philosophy and the practice was related to my study of *Ki* Development and *Aikido* under Master Tohei.

We were escorted by three limousines (bearing the flags of Japan and the United States of America) from the Keidanren government office building to the Akasaka Palace. In addition to coordinating international business economic activity, the Keidanren works closely with the Imperial Household Agency (*Kunaicho*) that manages all the affairs of the Imperial family. Upon arriving at the Palace, we were taken through the personal living quarters of the Royal Family and into a special meeting room for guests. The room was designed specifically to help foster intimate conversation and connection. I learned that this connection was to include a deep, intimate, and personal connection *between* not only His Majesty and his privileged guests but also *between* his guests and *nature itself.*

As we approached the special meeting room, an Imperial Household attendant opened the door. Standing before me was His Majesty dressed in a gray suit made of shiny silk. Immediately, I bowed respectfully and deeply. Unbeknownst to me (because my head was lowered) and at the exact same time, His Majesty extended his right hand for a proper western-style handshake as his formal opening courtesy. An Imperial Household staff photographer was already positioned inside the room and was prepared to capture on film the very first moment of our formal introduction and meeting. The humorous photograph that he captured was His Majesty standing elegantly in an upright posture extending his right hand pointed to the very tip of my bowed head. I guess we were not yet properly "connected"!

After we corrected the awkward (but funny and "ice breaking") situation with multiple Japanese bows coupled with western-style handshakes, I turned and noticed the beauty of this special room. As I admired its beauty, the Keidanren staff and Imperial Household attendants departed. Only the award recipients and His Majesty's personal aide, The Grand Chamberlain, remained in the beautiful room with His Majesty.

One entire wall, floor to ceiling, was made of glass; it was a Sea World type aquarium with rare species of primitive-looking fish (the kind that live at great oceanic depths).

His Majesty's father, Emperor Hirohito, was a highly trained ichthyologist who even published articles in peer review scientific journals. The wall opposite the aquarium was floor to ceiling glass, only this time the glass revealed the outdoors; specifically, it was the "personal" garden of the Royal Family - the most beautiful and highly manicured Japanese garden that I had ever seen. The room was nearly empty—two *ikebana* (floral arrangements) sat on small tables

THE ART OF LIVING NATURALLY

The Emperor of Japan, His Majesty Akihito (right), shakes author's hand during a personal audience at Akasaka Palace, Japan. In the middle is a representative of the Keidanren. 1989.

near the two other opposing walls. The only furniture in the room was a small sitting couch for His Majesty's guests and two chairs, one for His Majesty and one for The Grand Chamberlain. A small coffee table sat between us with beautiful pastries crafted in the shape of exotic birds. The impression was magnificent. *There you are under the deep sea and in a beautiful Japanese garden all at the same time!* Inside the room there was nothing "busy," "cluttered," or "cumbersome" that would take your mind away from the "intimacy" (Jp. *mitsu*) to be experienced *between* new friends fully exposed both to each other and to nature. If there were ever an environment especially created to *connect* two human beings and humans with nature, then this room, this setting, was the place.

At the time of our afternoon together, my research was focused upon environmental ethics and so I started the conversation by simply admiring the setting. I described to His Majesty the splendor of the room, the *"feeling"* of intimacy, and that this *"felt" connection to nature and each other* was marvelously occasioned by the design of this beautiful room. His Majesty smiled knowingly and immediately shared his interest in environmental protection.

We struck up an enlightening conversation about the social/moral/political concept of rights as entitlements. The interesting aspect of the dialogue was our discussion of the concept of a right as something that can not only serve as an entitlement for human beings, but also serve as an entitlement for things existing in nature. In the western philosophical tradition, human beings are deemed to have inalienable rights as, for example, life, liberty, and the pursuit of happiness. I asked His Majesty if he believed that the concept of "rights" as an inalienable entitlement could be "extended" to include non-human entities – animals, plants, mountains – and, if so, might this serve as a basis for environmental protection?

His Majesty's response was wonderful. While he argued that the Japanese tradition espoused a nature-centered (ecocentric) worldview, as opposed to a human-centered (homocentric or egocentric) worldview or a monotheistic, god-centered (theocentric) worldview, His Majesty added that he did not believe you could simply "extend" to nature, to the external world, or to anything non-human, the western notion of "human" entitlements that serves as the principled core of "rights-based ethics." "*It is not as simple,*" His Majesty said, "*as thinking that this man is deserving of moral entitlements and so does this precious tree* (pointing outside) *or this rare species of fish* (pointing to the aquarium)." Then His Majesty looked at the two of us (gesturing to himself and then to me), "*We, on the other hand, have to cultivate* (Jp. *shugyō*) *within us a connection* (Jp. *rei*)*, a relationship of intimacy* (Jp. *mitsu*)*, a relationship of between-ness* (Jp. *aidagara*)*, so that we can feel that we are all One in this Universe together.*" This, I thought, was marvelous; the Art of Living Naturally is the same as cultivating yourself *(Jp. shugyō)*, and transforming yourself, so that you realize experientially your capacity to *be with* and even be *instructed by* nature simultaneously. This is the essence of learning from the Universe Itself (Jp. *Kaiden*).

Have you ever wondered how dreams come true?

The Place of Peace:
Ecocentrism, Sustainability, and Bodymind Education at Furman University

Like the special Imperial meeting room at Akasaka Palace that promotes the sense of intimacy and connection between persons and nature (that I was able to experience during my audience with His Majesty Emperor Akihito), I am now able to experience a second very special space that promotes connection every single day! This special place called "*Hei-Sei-Ji*: The Place of Peace" is a training/educational space that truly is a dream come true.

Hei-Sei-Ji, The Place of Peace, 2008. Photo by Jeremy Fleming.

How dreams come true is easy to explain. The causal process (dependent origination) that we described in Chapter Three (The Art of Responsibility) explains how everything comes into being, including our dreams. As famously stated in the Pali **Nikayas** (the earliest Buddhist texts), "On the arising of this, that arises; upon the cessation of that, that ceases." In other words, all things come into being as the result of a myriad of causal processes all coming together to produce a singular event/result. The causes are not merely physical or material causes, but are the result of the totality of mental, emotional, psychic, historical, social, and spiritual causal forces. Accordingly, even a one-of-a-kind, never-been-done-before project (like The Place of Peace story) is the causal result of the totality of personal relationships, intentionality, and, ultimately, connection of all those involved.

As stated in **The Chronicle of Higher Education Review** (August 15, 2008), *"This reconstruction of a Buddhist temple—*

which was disassembled into 2,400 pieces in Japan, shipped in four containers across the Pacific Ocean and through the Panama Canal, and reassembled in South Carolina – is a unique undertaking, especially for a Southern college once closely associated with the Baptist church.... The temple once belonged to the Tsuzuki family, which owned and operated a textile company in the Carolinas....The Tsuzuki family also owned a plot of land in Japan upon which sat the family's handcrafted temple, built by some of the best artisans in Japan from the finest materials....The matriarch of the family, Chigusa Tsuzuki, had long ties to Furman. Twenty-six years ago, she began taking courses in Japanese philosophy with David Shaner, professor of philosophy and Asian studies here. Shaner is one of the world's leading aikido instructors, and later she became one of his students – and a friend."

In short, I had no idea that, decades after I moved from the University of Hawaii to Furman University (in order to teach Asian philosophy), an authentic Buddhist temple would be moved piece by piece from Japan to my University. It was my high honor and pleasure to officiate the blessing and dedication at the official opening of The Place of Peace on September 5, 2008. The Place of Peace now serves as an engaged learning space serving to educate Furman students and the general public about the oneness of all things, which can be experienced in the present moment. Our connection to the environment (sustainability), each other (social justice), and especially ourselves (bodymind) can all be experienced in this very special place.

It was truly an honor to meet His Majesty Emperor Akihito and experience the special meeting room at Akasaka Palace that serves to promote connection between people and between people and nature. And, it is also the case that I feel truly honored every single day when I can experience the joy of teaching how to unify mind and body (bodymind) [as described in this book] in the very special Place of Peace. This was a dream come true due to the many causal sacrifices of all those committed to bringing this project into reality.

"*The Place of Peace cannot technically be called a temple anymore,*" the **Chronicle** continued, "*the butsudon, or shrine, once encased at the center of the temple, has been removed and is in the family's possession. But the building will not merely be an artifact or museum piece, either. Shaner plans to use The Place of Peace as a lesson not only in Asian studies but also in sustainability, another strategic focus at Furman. The construction of The Place of Peace itself reflects a mind-set immersed in sustainability. For example, the original wood joinery was designed to be taken apart, so that craftsmen might repair pieces of the building as they wore out, rather than tear down and replace the whole thing.... Where the butsudan once sat Shaner may hang a poem in calligraphy (penned by his teacher Master Koichi Tohei): 'Shinpo uchurei kanno soku genjo', or 'Blessed universal spirit, immediately we feel your presence'.... The Place of Peace, including the nearby Asia garden and surrounding grove, should be for meditation and reflection. Pay attention to your surroundings. Close your eyes. Listen to the running water, the wind in the trees, your own breath. 'The place is an opportunity for each person to connect with nature', Mr. Shaner says, 'but maybe with themselves first'.*"

A dream of mine was to create a learning space in which to learn and experience the principles of bodymind unification as discussed herein. Before we can experience our connection to nature, all things, and the Universe, we must first learn to experience connection with ourselves – our whole self – mind, body, and spirit. The Place of Peace on the campus of Furman University is such a place and there is nothing like it anywhere in the world. Never before has an authentic Buddhist temple ever been deconstructed piece-by-piece and reconstructed by Japanese artisans outside Japan. The Place of Peace has come a long way from Nagoya to Greenville and everyone is invited to come and experience calm meditation that gives rise to personal clarity.

In addition to practicing Breathing and Meditation with Furman students enrolled in the Philosophy 202 "Realizing Bodymind" (Jp. *Shinshin Toitsudo*) course, other faculty members and students also use The Place of Peace as a site for experiential learning. Creative faculty have developed all kinds of innovative pedagogical strategies to take advantage of this icon for international education at Furman University. At Furman this kind of "engaged learning" was championed by the Furman administration and Furman faculty working in partnership. In particular, faculty representing multiple academic disciplines (including history, art, creative writing, language, philosophy, religion, and anthropology) have successfully utilized this one-of-a-kind educational "space" (Jp. *basho*).

Hei-Sei-Ji, The Place of Peace, 2008. Photo by Jeremy Fleming.

The worldview espoused in Buddhist philosophy, Daoist philosophy, and some schools of Indian philosophy are all consistent with monism. In contrast to the world view espoused in monotheistic traditions (for example, Christianity, Judaism, and Islam) where the divine is considered to be *transcendent*, all knowing, unchanging, perfect, and eternal, in monistic traditions the divine is considered to be *immanent* in all things (nature) and in a constant state of change. Specifically, in a monistic framework, nature itself is the divine ultimate reality as is everything and everyone. The implications of cultivating an experience of deep connection with nature (*biophilia*) have important ramifications for supporting the aims of sustainability, environmental stewardship, and personal/spiritual development.

In sum, The Place of Peace serves as a paradigmatic example of a living space that promotes (through its design, orientation, and building materials) the experience of intimate connection with nature (*biophilia*) consistent with the aims of sustainability and environmental stewardship. It is based upon this intersection of a nature-centered worldview that I now share the common theme of ecocentrism that brings together my Harvard biology mentors (Ernst Mayr, Ed Wilson and Stephen Jay Gould) with my several Japanese teachers, especially Master Tohei. Indeed, The Art of Living Naturally crosses both disciplinary and cultural boundaries.

Have you ever wondered what it would be like
to make an important discovery?

Pure Experience and Rare Book Libraries: A Cross-Cultural Insight

Permit me now to go full circle with all that I have shared with you thus far in this chapter. While at Harvard, I was also working on an article revealing a most interesting connection between the famous Harvard psychologist and philosopher William James (1842-1910) and the famous Japanese Zen Buddhist philosopher, NISHIDA Kitarō (1870-1945). In Nishida's famous work entitled **A Study of Good *(Zen no Kenkyu)*,** he developed a concept he calls "pure experience" (Jp. *junsui keiken*). "Pure experience" is like a First Order Mode of Awareness that occurs without any intentionality. I know that you are familiar with this concept at this point in our journey through the Seven Arts. I am sure you are thinking that "pure experience" sounds like a Buddhist concept as well. Well, the interesting connection is that, in the first pages of his book entitled, **A Study of Good**, Nishida credits the American philosopher William James with first introducing him to the notion of "pure experience" in James' two volume **Principles of Psychology.** I think Nishida was purposefully reaching out to some western individuals and occidental views in order to demonstrate the *cross-cultural* relevance of his work, as well as provide a *trans-cultural* platform for his central thesis that focused upon a rich development of the notion of "pure experience." Comparative Philosopher David Dilworth has done extensive and interesting work exposing the connections between James and Nishida.

    I also found this connection between psychologist/philosopher William James and Zen Buddhist philosopher NISHIDA Kitarō fascinating and so I used part of my time at Harvard to play detective and investigate where and how James first discovered, and then further developed, his own idea of "pure experience." The Harvard University rare book and manuscript collection library, the Houghton Library, houses James' personal book collection as well as an extensive collection of his personal correspondence. Here is what I discovered.

By examining the notes James had written to himself in the margins (*marginalia*) of his personal books as well as his personal correspondence, I discovered an incredible link to Professor Louis Agassiz, the original nineteenth century collector and curator of Harvard's Museum of Comparative Zoology. Professor Agassiz taught Natural History to James when James was an undergraduate student at Harvard. In fact, I discovered that Agassiz also took James under his wing and mentored him. He even took the twenty-three year old James, who was then a graduate student, with him during his 1865-66 Thayer expedition up the Amazon. James absolutely idolized Agassiz, as evidenced in particular by his letters to his parents. On August 25, 1865, James wrote, *"Agassiz found forty-six new species of fish in four days!"* Agassiz was a brilliant field naturalist and was famous for his impatience with metaphysical rhetoric. When James asked him probing philosophical questions, Agassiz would quip his famous line, "Read *nature* to understand God's mind and works, not *books*!"

In another letter dated only "Christmas day", James describes Agassiz's method of instruction as one that taught his students to become naturalists by developing a *feel* for their subject matter in the same way that artists learn to *feel* their way into a new medium. This was a particularly appropriate comparison for James to make because he had studied painting before going to Harvard. Agassiz preferred new students who were wholly uninstructed. He wanted his students to come to him as if they were blank tablets (Lt. *tabulae rasae*). James writes that Agassiz would then mold the student's skills by not letting them "look into a book for a long while," forcing them to "learn for themselves, and be *master* of it all." James goes on to say, "He makes naturalists of them [the students], he does not merely cram them...He must be a great teacher."

Agassiz was one who was truly "intimate" with nature. This characterization is perfectly consistent with His Majesty Emperor Akihito who suggested the need to truly become "intimate" (Jp. *mitsu*) *with* nature, as opposed to the mere intellectual exercise of "extending" the concept of inalienable rights *to* nature. Agassiz passed on to James (and then James to Japanese philosopher NISHIDA Kitarō) the intimacy-related concept of "Pure Experience." For James (through Agassiz's influence), exploring the notion of "pure experience" was not an intellectual exercise at all. Rather, this concept spoke to a much deeper feeling of experiential intimacy with the world around us (Jp. *kaiden*).

Later in James' life when he turned his attention away from psychology and to philosophy, the concept of pure experience took on even religious significance. In this context, it is interesting to remember that Agassiz was a vocal critic of Darwin within the intellectual circles of Cambridge. Agassiz was sympathetic to the Nineteenth Century School of "Natural Theology." For Agassiz, his passion for field collecting was really about understanding God by understanding the majesty and wonder of God's creation. Agassiz believed his work had theological significance insofar as field collecting demonstrated greater "natural" diversity and, thereby, added greater glory to God, the creator. The religious sensitivity of a great field naturalist like Agassiz was characterized by James as the *"felt"* condition of intimacy that could only be cultivated (like Japanese monastic training - *shugyō*) through extensive field training over time.

Have you ever wondered why you feel spiritual in nature?

Biophilia as Intimacy with Nature

The late Harvard Professor Emeritus Ernst Mayr, nestor of evolutionary biology, similarly emphasized to me that mastering the techniques of a skilled cladistics systematist required developing a *feeling* for one's subject matter. Like the European guild system of training or monastic training, true professionalism and competence in the discipline of phyletic classification requires a long developmental time period in order to nurture "the sensitivity" required to collect and properly classify flora and fauna. Similarly, Steve Gould liked to discuss "developing an eye for detail" in order to properly and "sensitively" excavate fossil remains, especially the most difficult remains as in the case of "soft bodied" organisms. Likewise, Ed Wilson uses his monocular vision to great advantage when classifying ants; he can detect, without a magnification aid, subtle morphological differences, even hairs, in individual specimens.

In Ed's own field journal, the entry that became the basis for his book **Biophilia: The Human Bond with Other Species** refers to the same *felt intimacy with nature* that is common to these great naturalists:

"On March 21, 1961, I stood in the Awawak village of Bernardsdorp and looked across the white-sand coastal forest of Surinam. For reasons that were to take me twenty years to understand, that moment was fixed with uncommon urgency in my memory. The emotions I *felt* were to grow more poignant at each remembrance.... The object of reflection can be summarized by a single word, *biophilia,* which I will be so bold as to define as the innate tendency to focus on life and lifelike processes." [Emphasis mine.]

The Art of Living Naturally combines all of the above – his Majesty Emperor Akihito's notion of *intimacy;* Louis Agassiz's, Ernst Mayr's, Steve Gould's, and Ed Wilson's special *felt connection* with the natural world, William James' notion of *pure experience,* and NISHIDA Kitarō's efforts to further develop *pure experience* (Jp. *junsui keiken*) as the basis of *all* human experience in order to make a cross-cultural (East-West) philosophical *connection.* In combination, these closely related concepts suggest that the Buddhist concept of intimacy with nature is not unique to the East Asian philosophical and religious tradition. The bottom line is that we are all One and we are all causally unified and connected to the Universe *except* when we allow conscious attachments (like Agassiz's distain for metaphysical theories) to interfere with our experience of deep intimate connection with others and the natural world around us. It was, for example, Agassiz's disdain for metaphysical theories that colored his perceptions of nature. Since the attachments of all our levels of consciousness serve to disconnect us from our original connection to others and to nature, let us explore the role of attachment a little further.

Have you ever wondered why you keep getting in your own way again and again in the same way?

Attachment and Dis-connection

To begin, allow me to cite yet another **Ki Saying** *(Shokushu)* written by my teacher, Master Koichi Tohei.

> **The Principle of Non-Dissension**
>
> There is no conflict in the Absolute Universe, but there is conflict in the relative world. If we unify our mind and body, become One with the Universe, and practice its principles, others will follow us gladly.
>
> Do not say that this is a world where we must struggle to live each day. The true way to success is exactly one and the same as the principle of non-dissension, and that is the way to peace.
>
> —Koichi Tohei

In the introduction of the Art of Living Naturally, I discussed the importance of acceptance. This means presencing your true Self as *being with* the world to which you are intimately and originally connected. *Acceptance causes you to feel connected;* it is just letting be, seeing, listening, observing, allowing yourself to be instructed by nature (Jp. *kaiden*) and allowing yourself to witness the conditions of human interaction. In much the same way that acceptance leads to connection, attachment leads to dis-connection. Attachment causes you to feel dis-connected because of your own mental and emotional formation projections. Projections include: 1) seeing people as you *wish* to see them, 2) assuming you know *what* people are thinking, 3) assuming you know *how* people will react toward you if you do such and such, or 4) holding on to things, persons, money, or even happy states of being that you *wish* to remain permanent.

There are two problems with these four types of projections. First, subconscious projections cloud your ability to be in the present moment and thus cloud your ability to witness the world as it truly is. As a result, projections cause your awareness to be covered over or filtered as a result of your attachments and preconceptions. Second, subconscious projections and deep unconscious attachments cause you to desire things or states of being that you want to control, or possess. or hold fixed, or remain permanent. In fact, however, the opposite is true – the Universe is impermanent and in a constant state of flux. Human dis-satisfaction or suffering (Sk. *dukkha*) of one form or another is thus caused by attachments, projections, or any of these unnatural ways of being.

Remember our definition from the Art of Living Naturally; what is natural is in accord with the Universe. It is, therefore, unnatural to live with the expectation of holding, fixing, controlling, or possessing things, persons, affairs, or states of being in a Universe that is, in reality, in a state of constant change. The Art of Living Naturally requires that you presence your dynamic world in what we have called First Order Awareness and that you understand and consciously operate in harmony with a Universe that is ultimately impermanent. Acceptance and non-attachment are thus natural and are the conditions of being connected in a manner that is in harmony with the Way of the Universe. Attachment is unnatural and the condition of being disconnected with the Universe.

Have you ever wondered why you think you know what someone else is thinking or will say?

Two Attachments:
What Happens When You Know What Others Will Think and Your Stuff Goes Up in Smoke

I can share two examples of attachments that certainly clouded *my* thinking.

Interestingly, both were related to interactions with my own teacher, Master Tohei. While I was living as an *uchi deshi* with my teacher in 1979, my dissertation chairman, Tom Kasulis, confided in me that, while he was spending the academic year teaching at Harvard University on leave from the University of Hawaii, he would be actively looking for a new teaching position on the mainland. Tom had graduated from Yale, his wife Ellen was from Connecticut, and they were both eager to get back to a climate with four distinct seasons and rear their young boys in the Northeast or Midwest. This was shocking news for me living in Japan because of the specialized nature of my doctoral project. Tom was the only faculty member qualified to supervise my doctoral dissertation focused upon understanding the relationship between the mind and body. This study used Edmund Husserl's phenomenological method to examine the writings of Dogen Kigen (1200-1253), founder of the Japanese Soto Zen School, and Kobo Daishi Kukai (774-835), founder of the Japanese Shingon School. Tom was the only person at the University of Hawaii with knowledge of all these thinkers.

The problem that Tom's moving plans presented for me was as follows: I was already his graduate student, I had already passed all my field examinations and comprehensives; my dissertation topic, annotated bibliography, and thesis abstract had already been approved by my doctoral committee. I was already living in Japan conducting research, and I was already steeped in my work pursuing this course of study with Professor Hajime Nakamura at the Eastern Institute (Tokyo) as well as living with my personal teacher, Master Koichi Tohei (also in Tokyo). Moreover, living as an *uchi deshi* was an extremely rare experience for a *gaijin* (foreigner), and my living with Master Tohei was 100 percent focused upon mind-body unification training that *was* the subject of my doctoral dissertation. If I had to change topics and select a new dissertation chairman due to Tom's impending move from Hawaii to the mainland, then my graduate school life would have to be completely changed and surely extended for many years. This was a real problem!

I agonized and agonized silently about my options while serving my teacher, Master Tohei. While serving as his *otomo (special assistant),* and thus having special access to him, I would ask questions constantly. My endless questions would amuse my teacher, but Master Tohei was more than patient with me as we spent a lot of time discussing the connection between *Ki* Development (as he taught it) and all the other Indian, Chinese, and Japanese traditions about which he was well read and familiar. Each night I would return to the single room that housed all six *deshi* at our headquarters. I would write extensively in my journal recording all the precious words of wisdom that my Master openly shared with his eager young student. Master Tohei often told me that I wrote down too much and that, as a budding academic and practitioner of Ki Development, I was too attached to my journaling notebooks.

To be truthful, I had many, many notebooks filled with detailed recordings of our conversations. And, yes, I was attached to them AND, yes, I even felt justified in this attachment to my extensive journals because they were both personal treasures and incredibly valuable research material that I believed would take a lifetime for me to unravel their true meaning and significance. Master Tohei was often critical of academics who "think too much" preferring instead to teach presencing as in the Zen Buddhist tradition. I knew, therefore, that all my note taking and journaling was not consistent with his preference for focusing upon direct experience and personal awakening.

So let's review. Here are the two attachments that I possessed at the time. First, I was attached to, and afraid of, the implications of Tom Kasulis' imminent move to the mainland from Hawaii. Tom was a young leader and "All-Star" in the field of Japanese Philosophy and I knew that he would have no problem securing a position at another university on the mainland. Tom told me "you have two choices: 1) Come with me to Harvard as soon as possible (early January 1980) and write your dissertation. Then, you must finish and successfully defend your dissertation back in Honolulu by the end of June 1980 when I will be officially leaving the University of Hawaii, OR, 2) Stay in Japan living as an *uchi deshi* while I am at Harvard...then start over, change dissertation topics, and eventually find a new chair to oversee your work." "Great choice!", I thought sarcastically. Neither of these options suited me.

I was in *angst* "big time" for one reason – if I left for Harvard at the end of December 1979, I would be leaving my teacher earlier than *I* wanted and earlier than *we both* expected. "What would he think of me?", I thought. My emotional and mental projections were in high gear and I thought Master Tohei would just think I was ... "a terrible student and a terrible person," I would "lose face" (Japanese style), and I thought X, Y, and Z (all negative things) that would reflect poorly on behalf of all *gaijin* (foreigners) that would never get the experience of serving as Master Tohei's *otomo* and live-in *uchi deshi* student in the future. In short, all my projections about "what Master Tohei would think" were terrible.

The second attachment that I had was simply related to Master Tohei's view that I journaled too much and that I was too attached to recording all of our detailed conversations whether it was for: 1) personal development to digest over time, or 2) research purposes relevant to my doctoral dissertation and eventual book – **The Bodymind Experience in Japanese Buddhism.**

Now here is what I decided to do. I really did not want to start my doctoral program all over again with a new topic and new dissertation chairperson. The topic of mind and body unification was of a deep, personal interest to me. (As you can see, I am still writing about it over thirty years later!) I simply did not want to start the graduate school process over from scratch creating a new dissertation topic, forming a new doctoral committee with a new chair who would replace Tom, and losing years of work already completed. As was the case when I left high school early to start college, I was now eager to get the dissertation out of the way, secure my Ph.D. "in hand," as they say, and get on with the next phase in my life.

So, I was going to tell Master Tohei of my decision to leave Japan early. I would inform him of my departure to go to Harvard and write my entire dissertation in five months under Professor Kasulis' direction. I thought that I did have one positive thing going for me. I thought that my difficult conversation with Master Tohei might be made easier simply because I had previously introduced Tom Kasulis to him the year before in Honolulu. For Master Tohei to be able to match Tom's face with my move to Cambridge somehow made the painful conversation about leaving Japan more palatable. The fact that I had previously brought Tom to one of Master Tohei's four-day evening seminars at Iolani High School in Honolulu made the three-way connection to Tom more personal and real. Accordingly, I would not have to explain the relation and the importance of this *other* teacher in the scheme of my doctoral program. Master Tohei already knew Tom as my dissertation director and, more importantly, he knew that Tom supported my training and learning under Master Tohei's personal direction.

Once I made my decision in early December 1979, I chose a time to speak with Master Tohei. I would have the "dreaded" and "feared" conversation just *after* changing clothes (it is an *otomo's* duty to assist Master Tohei dressing out of and into street clothes before and after early morning *Aikido* class) and *before* his first meeting that was not scheduled until 9 a.m. on that particular day. As I planned it, we would have *ocha* (green tea) after class and "talk-story," as they say in Hawaii, until the person with the 9:00 appointment came to headquarters. I knew Master Tohei liked this "talk-story" phrase of Hawaiian pigeon-English and I could use it to break the ice thus preparing him for my difficult conversation.

After I had served tea, which was part of our training, my teacher could see that I was squirming trying to start my "story," and so he basically said in Japanese, "Come on boy, spit it out" (*Ima Haiyaku!*). After I explained all the details, all my options, all my anxieties, and my preparation for the terrible wrath that I had "projected" on to my teacher, Master Tohei looked me in the eye and simply *put his hand on my shoulder once again* (as usual, it had the same calming affect), and then he basically laughed hysterically. He thought this was funny! *"Dochira?"* (Why?), I immediately asked, "is this so funny?" I thought to myself, "I am dying over here and you are laughing – why?"

Master Tohei explained that I had indeed made a "great decision and that it was time for me to go maybe one month ago"! *"Honto?"* (Really?), I asked. Then he calmly explained that deep, deep learning takes time. He said, as a compliment to me, that I was a "human sponge," that I had absorbed so much in such a short time that already "my cup was full" and that nothing more could "get in" until I returned home to America and teach others so that all that I had learned in "my head" could be absorbed by "my body." He then immediately concluded our conversation *with his hand on my shoulder* (as usual) by looking deeply into my eyes saying, "*Shinjin Ichinyo*" (Oneness of Mind and Body) and he just smiled at me. The message was "take what is in your 'full' head at present, and make it part of your whole self—mind, body, emotion and spirit."

"The night before I left, just before Christmas 1979, he took me out alone in the typical Samurai tradition...to drink sake!"

So, my "projections" were just that. I was totally wrong about what "I thought" Master Tohei would think (and say) and so it remains today for me a powerful lesson not to judge and not to be attached to what *you think someone else will do or say.* For the rest of the month of December, my last month as an *uchi deshi* live-in student, Master Tohei treated me like a king. The night before I left, just before Christmas 1979, he took me out alone in the typical Samurai tradition...to drink *sake*! It was a great night of wonderful memories and picture taking, just my teacher and me, and he made me feel like a king on top of the world.

My second attachment, you recall, was feeling the need to journal and thus record for my personal development and doctoral research our many conversations about comparative philosophy, *Ki,* spiritual matters, and the lessons learned from Master Tohei's own teachers—Morihei Ueshiba, Tempu Nakamura, and Tetsuji Ogura. Years later Master Tohei laughed at me one more time. Once again he had his *hand on my shoulder* looking at me knowingly. This was the occasion when I told him how my notebooks had been destroyed in a fire. When I told him the story of the fire and of my destroyed notes, he said, "You see, the Universe knows and is taking care of you." This "taking care of me" was the complete destruction of all my material possessions in a fire, including my precious personal notes and research notes. At times when it seems like and feels like the Universe has delivered to you a crushing, heart-wrenching blow, it may well be the precise fuel or catalyst that the Universe has "gifted" to you in order to propel you to the next level of your spiritual development journey. Let me explain.

I had just come back from a Fulbright research project in India and was preparing to move all my personal belongings to Greenville, South Carolina, where I was to begin teaching at Furman University. Due to my extensive travels for many years, my material possessions were in storage at my parents' home in Chicago. Since they were planning on retiring soon to Florida and downsizing to a smaller home, they added onto the United Van Lines tractor-trailer not only my personal possessions kept in our family's basement storage area, but also all the possessions that they wanted to "will" to me. My parents wanted to surprise me with the family heirlooms (more "possessions") that they had planned to give to me eventually. My parents used both my move to Greenville and their retirement move to Florida as an opportunity to surprise me with numerous family treasures including furniture, paintings, medals, certificates, etc.

Well, the moving van trailer caught fire north of Asheville, North Carolina, about sixty miles north of Greenville. Another family's possessions (that were also on the huge eighteen-wheel moving van) had included paint thinner and other garage-related flammables which caught fire due to the extreme heat building up in the trailer moving down the interstate in the hot August summer heat. Everything I owned, including my precious notes of conversations with Master Tohei, was destroyed. When I told my teacher what had happened in the moving van fire, he said "The Universe was providing an opening for me to learn about my attachment to my notes." Referring to our memorable conversation in Japan years earlier he added, "That which you have 'internalized' through real *shinjin ichinyo* (mind and body oneness) is what is important now, the rest can 'go up in smoke.'"

Actually, since I had just returned from the Fulbright project in India, I really was detached completely from all my material possessions. I had just been living in a part of the world where most people had no possessions. I actually felt empowered and full of abundance just to start my new job teaching philosophy at Furman University. "I was loaded with blessings," I thought. I had a job and I was paid $17,000 a year. I was thinking that I was rich. "How great is this?" I thought. "I am actually being paid just to think, teach philosophy, write, and hopefully grow more wise."

> *Have you ever wondered,*
> *"how the hell did that just happen"?*

A Treat From the Universe:
Be Positive and Grateful

One more treat from the Universe before we close this chapter. There was literally only one thing that survived the fire, not blackened and charred. Tightly sandwiched between lots of paper artifacts that my parents were "willing" to me early in their lives before their move to Florida was a painting that my mother had done. She was an artist, a painter. Most of her artistic work was done using the medium of watercolors. Her subject matter was typically landscapes, mid-western farmhouses, and wildlife paintings usually depicting waterfowl, which my father enjoyed. When using the medium of oil-based paints, which was rare, she usually created still life paintings – a fruit basket, a violin, books in a study, pipe and glasses on a desk, etc. To my knowledge, there was only one "abstract-style" painting that my mother ever did. It was a painting of me - ski racing!

My mother apparently had created the painting working from a photograph taken of me at a ski race. In the painting, she wanted to capture the speed of ski racing ever present in the photo. She used the "abstract" genre to create an image of flying hair, raw speed and power! This one painting I discovered standing in the smoldering trailer and fire ruins off the interstate near Asheville, North Carolina. By "peeling back layers" (pun intended) of ash and charred paper composed of the precious family heirloom items "willed" to me, including rare certificates, special letters, honors, awards, and military documents, I discovered miraculously my mother's painting.

"This one painting I discovered standing in the smoldering trailer..."

This painting, this one gift from my mother AND the Universe, was completely unharmed remaining in perfect condition! It is now hanging in my home where I can see it everyday. Each day the painting reminds me of other lessons in the Art of Living Naturally: 1) accept things as they are, 2) do not become attached, and 3) be both positive and grateful for the Universe is teaching us all the time if only you prepare yourself to receive the lessons taught (Jp. *kaiden*) by the Universe Itself.

The Art of Living Naturally is yours to embrace. Please practice daily the following exercises to remind yourself of the main themes of this Sixth Art on your journey of personal transformation for positive spiritual, interpersonal, and overall well-being.

**Daily Exercises
To Facilitate The Art of Living Naturally**

Have you ever wondered if you could feel your heart beat, your skin breathe, or the earth rotate?

**Exercise 12:
Be In and With Nature**

Now you are prepared to extend your ability to "notice" in new and profound ways. Your "going deeper" now means reflecting all things much more clearly without the interference of your mental chatter. Presencing the universe around you is transformational because you are now "witnessing" the teaching (jp kaiden) that is available to you at all times. You are not alone.

Each day, connect to the greater world around you. *Be in and with nature* and allow yourself to *feel* the life and abundance of the Universe that surrounds you. Your mind must be very calm to feel the various rhythms of the Universe. My teacher has developed *Aikido* arts *(taigis)* and a Oneness Rhythm Exercise to help people experience the natural rhythm of the Universe. This can be learned by practicing *Ki-Aikido* (see Chapter Seven). However, even without these more elaborate training exercises, you can use the deep calmness that you have reached through Dynamic Breathing and Dynamic Meditation (daily exercises for the fourth Art of Relaxation) to "connect" to your surroundings in a most intimate manner. By living your life through Conscious Action, based in a First Order Mode of Awareness, you will naturally be present in the world and you will experience abundance and much positive energy.

Nature and the Universe have lessons to teach. Can you be calm enough, very deeply calm to feel the rotation of the earth? It is possible to do this. You can practice this by calming yourself enough to feel the movement of shadows at sunrise or sunset. However, the fact is the sun neither rises nor sets! That which you can feel with conscious practice is the rhythm of the "morning earth turn" and the "evening earth turn." Plan to quietly observe the "morning earth turn" and "evening earth turn." Remember that the earth is what is moving. Practice this on a regular basis until you feel the earth turning. Place yourself *in and with nature* and you will know that you are the Universe and the Universe is you. This practice can be done daily by merely presencing nature anywhere and at any time. The Universe can and does teach at every moment (Jp. *kaiden*) if only you prepare yourself to feel the intimacy of your original connection.

Have you ever wondered if something deep inside you is causing you to act in self-destructive ways?

Exercise 13:
Be In and With All Your Emotions

Now you are prepared to "go deeper" still and build upon your self-honesty practice (Exercises 3 and 6). This practice enables you to tap not merely your conscious mind and behavioral habits, but now the depth of your cultivated calmness enables you to surface the subconscious and unconscious "seeds" that powerfully influence your behavior and choices in daily life. Understanding these causal seeds is the final step to your true liberation and transformation journey.

Earlier in Exercise 6 entitled "Take a Deep Breath and Introspect Before You Act" (at the conclusion of the third chapter - - Art of Responsibility), I asked you to journal about your "you know" feelings and desires. As part of Chapter Six, at this later point on your journey of positive self-transformation, I am asking you to now go deeper in your quest toward self-discovery. By "going deeper" I mean revealing your truest Self with additional self-honesty through more detailed, more aware, more self-conscious introspection. Now that you have learned to relax deeply, relax completely, and access greater depths of calmness [occasioned by the disciplined daily practice of Dynamic Breathing and Dynamic Meditation (as part of the fourth Art of Relaxation)], you are now prepared to enter a *deeper stage of self-understanding*—as Socrates would say *"know thyself,"* your true Self.

This process of going deeper and deeper will reveal for you a true Self that is really a no-self, an empty self where there is no separation, no independence, no dis-connection.

Remember, your true Self is a self already connected with the entire Universe. The sixth Art of Living Naturally will require you NOW to access your deepest truths, your subconscious, and heretofore unconscious, mental formations created by the causally related experiences of your entire lifetime. For this reason, you can interpret this Exercise 13 as the natural extension (The Art of Living Naturally) of the work you began in Exercise 6 (The Art of Responsibility) in which you were encouraged to ponder and journal about the seeds of your "you know" feelings. These are the feelings that arise from deep within you.

Now that you have practiced Dynamic Breathing and Dynamic Meditation and are much further along on your journey of positive self-transformation, these deep feelings and mental formations are now accessible to you. You have learned methods for deep relaxation enabling you to experience for yourself deep mental and emotional calmness.

The linkage here is to understand that these "you know" feelings (discussed as part of the Art of Responsibility) are the same seeds that cause a perceived "dis-connection" occasioned by your attachments, projections, suppressions, and repressions, all of which *cause* separation. These mental and emotional formations *cover over* (Sk. *samvrti*) your true Self, your real Self that is already (originally) connected to something much greater—the Universe Itself. Remember, your true Self has no separate existence; it is empty of independence. As long as your deep-seated attachments remain unidentified and undiscovered, they will continue to affect and distort your awareness. Your progress will be impeded unless you go deeper as if you were peeling an onion which represents the layers of your consciousness, mental/emotional formations, and corresponding attachments that *cause* you to remain separated from your highest connected Self.

In this chapter, I have shared two examples of my own deep-seated attachments. The opposite of acceptance (that promotes connection) is attachment (that creates separation and thus "dis-connection"). But how do you know the things or people or states of affairs toward which you are excessively attached? Attachment stems from insecurity and fear. Therefore, make a new list in your Seven Arts Journal that builds upon your practice of, and experience with, Exercise 6. List those things, people, or states of affairs that make you feel insecure or afraid. Remember, it is important to be *in and with all your emotions* and then "externalize" them by recording them *daily* in your Seven Arts Journal. In this way, you can learn to grow by acknowledging and being present with your deep emotions and mental formations. In time, you will come to both feel and understand your true Self at an even deeper, more penetrating, more authentic level of self-honesty and self-expression.

Your excessive projections and attachments cause you to be dis-connected from the Universe. Consequently, you are losing power, energy, creativity, and health each day as compared to experiencing directly your full potential. Suffering or dis-satisfaction (Sk. *dukkha*), experienced as your negative emotions, continues on and on and remains unaddressed as long as your excessive projections and attachments cause you to remain separated from your Original Self and the Universe. By summarizing "themes" that arise as a result of rereading and reflecting upon your daily Seven Arts journaling, you will be able to make a monthly list of attachment and projection "categories" often related to fear and insecurity that give rise to blinding mental formations that cover true Self-awareness as well as your awareness of the needs of others.

By sitting quietly and contemplating the seeds of your attachments and projections, you will learn to become not only aware of their power over you, but also you will become aware of the process of true liberation and forgiveness of Self as well as others. Liberation and forgiveness cannot occur, however, until you delve honestly and deeply into the seeds of desire within you. If you do not accept these dark "shadows" as part of your whole being, then you will suffer the consequences of unconscious, subconscious, and even conscious "suppression" and "compartmentalization." That is, you will simply develop the survival skill to either ignore or suppress deeply those same things that could actually fuel your real growth and development and help you actualize your full potential (in accord with your PDA) if only you could bring them to conscious awareness and then "take responsibility" for them.

When you acknowledge basic emotions, especially the negative ones, then you are embracing and accepting as yours *all the things* (not just the "good things") that will make you whole. When this happens, you will be practicing the holistic Art of Living Naturally. Attachments stem from desire and desire stems from your ego, your selfish mind. To embrace the Universal Mind, you must first embrace your Whole Self, including your negative emotions and the dark, mental formations/shadow aspects of your life. The brighter the light (the "good things"), the darker the shadow (the "hidden things")...your whole connected Self includes both.

Awareness of Self will lead to awareness of others by uncovering the layers of mental formations and attachments acquired over a lifetime. With this kind of liberation, you will be prepared to truly empathize and sympathize with others (compassion) by truly "putting yourself in the place of others." In other words, in order to truly practice the Golden Rule and experience the world from another's viewing place, you first must uncover the causal seeds of your separate, isolated, independent self. When you move beyond your separate self and you can truly experience your connected, true Self, then you can transform your relationships in a most responsible (The Art of Responsibility) and compassionate (The Art of Compassion) manner.

To help you formulate your personal list of emotions for deep contemplation and honest reflection upon the causal seeds of your excessive desires, projections, and attachments, consider the following relationships relevant to five typical emotions:

Have you ever wondered if there is something hidden inside you causing you to be very sad but you just don't know exactly what it might be?

Are You Sad?

Sadness is normal, but excessive, energy-consuming (attached) sadness can lead to depression, a loss of energy, ill health, and the desire for things (drugs/alcohol) or states of affairs that cover over (Sk. *samvrti*), suppress, or compartmentalize your deep seated sad emotions. However, honestly contemplating the *seeds* of your sadness, as well as your sadness-related coping mechanism(s), that may be injuring yourself and perhaps others, will help you to become whole. *This is because if you cut yourself off from your own sadness, then you also simultaneously cut yourself off from your ability to feel empathy and sympathy for others.* Therefore, to practice mindfully the Art of Compassion, you must be able to feel your whole, true Self. Try to "uncover" and record your feeling(s) of sadness in your Seven Arts Journal and explore, in writing, what the seed(s) of your sadness might be.

Accordingly, in order to practice mindfully the Art of Living Naturally, you must be connected not only to your true, higher, Original Self, but also to the Universe that sustains your life at every moment.

Have you ever wondered if there is something hidden inside you causing you to be really mad but you cannot put your finger on it?

Are You Angry?

Being angry is normal, but excessive, energy-consuming (attached) anger can lead to depression, a loss of energy, ill heath, and the desire for things (drugs/alcohol), or states of affairs that cover over (Sk. *samvrti)*, suppress, compartmentalize, or even repress your deep seated angry emotions. However, honestly contemplating the seeds of your anger, as well as your anger-related coping mechanism(s), injuring yourself and perhaps others, will help you to become whole. *This is because if you cut yourself off from your anger, then you also cut yourself off from your positive life force and the wellspring of universal energy, connection, and compassion that enables you to meet each day with enthusiasm, vitality, creativity and the feeling of "the wind at your back."* Anger is a most depleting, wasteful, and debilitating emotion. Try to "uncover" and record your feeling(s) of anger in your Seven Arts Journal and explore, in writing, what the seed(s) of your anger might be.

To practice mindfully the Art of Living Naturally is to feel the abundance of energy that comes from positively embracing the Universe. In order to do this, you must first become whole, including understanding and addressing the seeds of your excessive anger. Daily practice of: 1) forgiveness, 2) not being defensive, 3) not blaming others, 4) not judging others, 5) not criticizing others, 6) taking responsibility for your negative emotions, and 7) accepting that your deepest fears, insecurities, and desires (shadows) are an important (not to be ignored) part of you, is all part of the larger process of becoming truly whole.

In order to practice mindfully the Art of Living Naturally, you must be connected to not only your true, higher, Original Self, but also the Universe Itself that sustains you at every moment.

Have you ever wondered if there is something hidden inside you causing you to 'hold back,' or have fear, or be insecure, but you cannot understand why these feelings sometimes arise?

Are You Afraid?

Being scared is normal, but excessive, energy-consuming, attached fear can lead to depression, a loss of energy, ill health, and the desire for things (drugs/alcohol) or states of affairs that cover over (Sk. *samvrti*), suppress, compartmentalize, or even repress your deep seated fears and insecurities. However, honestly contemplating the seeds of your fear as well as your fear-related coping mechanism(s), injuring yourself and perhaps others will help you to become whole. *This is because if you cut yourself off from your fear, then you also cut yourself from your internal "protector"; that is, you cut yourself off from your ability to be SAFE.* If you have cut yourself off from the seeds of deep-seated fear because they are masked deep within you, then you can do yourself serious harm. Try to "uncover" and record your feeling(s) of fear in your Seven Arts Journal and explore, in writing, what the seed(s) of your fear(s) might be. Talk to your fears, make friends with your fears, and please, above all, do not negatively judge your fears. Know that you are only truly solid and whole when your fears and insecurities are fully owned and embraced by bringing them to the light of day.

To practice mindfully the third Art of Responsibility, you must have the strength, patience, and discipline to confront your fear(s), your "you know(s)", while believing and trusting deeply that the Universe will protect you. In order to "take responsibility" for your own actions, you must first feel safe and powerful, and not afraid, scared, and weak. Therefore, to practice mindfully the Art of Responsibility, you must first be able to be at peace with your whole, true Self. Accordingly, first identify the causal seeds of your fear, then talk to and make friends with your fears. Finally, you must accept, embrace and, ultimately, own your fears by taking responsibility for them as well as the entire process of self-transformation.

Thus, in order to practice mindfully the Art of Living Naturally, you must be connected to not only your true, higher, Original Self, but also the Universe that gives you the internal power and strength to face your fear(s) as well as sustain you at every moment of your life.

Have you ever wondered if there is something hidden inside you causing you to remain blocked, causing you to repeat the same mistakes, and causing you to be unable or unwilling to move beyond past errors and correct your moral compass?

Do You Only Feel Shame and Guilt? Or, Can You Feel Sorry?

Are you sorry? Feeling sorry and having true remorse for your actions are vital to help you transform your life for the better. Can you embrace yourself with compassion and forgiveness? If you have acted selfishly and injured others in the process, then you must take responsibility and embrace true feelings of remorse. Honestly contemplating the seeds of your actions that caused you to be blind, as well as the causal seeds of your guilt-related coping mechanism(s) injuring yourself and perhaps others, will help you to become whole. *This is because if you cut yourself off from your feelings of remorse and instead only experience feelings of guilt and shame, then you are likely to repeat the same behavior again causing further pain and suffering. The emotions of feeling sorry, regret, and remorse (not shame and guilt) serve as your moral compass for corrective action.* Try to "uncover" and record your feeling(s) of sorrow in your Seven Arts Journal and explore, in writing, what the seed(s) of your regret(s) might be.

To practice mindfully the Art of Conscious Action you must be able to be at peace with, and sincerely believe in, the aim of your actions directed toward bringing about greater goodness to those around you. The Art of Conscious Action stems from selflessness; it is *action serving others*. If you know deep down that the causal seeds of your actions are selfish and cause harm to others, then you cannot be *whole* with the Universe. Accordingly, you must feel remorse and contemplate deeply both the seeds of your selfish desire(s) as well as the corrective action(s) to return you to wholeness. If you only feel shame or guilt, then you may continue to be on a self-destructive path because your moral compass has been covered over (Sk. *samvrti*). Selflessness and Conscious Action, however, arise from being awake, present, aware, and connected. In order to *do unto others as you would have them do unto you*, you must place yourself in the position of those persons that you might otherwise harm due to your blindness and dis-connection. Therefore, in order to truly practice and really *do unto others as you would have them do unto you* in daily life, you must *first* have compassion and forgiveness for yourself and then extend that love to your neighbor. This is the meaning of "Love thy neighbor *as thyself.*"

In order to practice mindfully the Art of Living Naturally, you must be connected to not only your true, higher, Original Self, but also to the Universe Itself so that you see that you and others are the same being.

Have you ever wondered if there is something hidden inside you causing you to not be truly happy?

Are You Happy?

Feelings of love and happiness are vital to fuel your positive transformation of growth and development. However, sometimes people cut themselves off from feelings of love and happiness, preferring instead to feel unworthy, unlovable, and undeserving. Honestly contemplating the seeds of genuine happiness within you will help you to be whole by reinforcing a positive self-image. Similarly, honestly contemplating the causal seeds of your feelings of unhappiness or unworthiness, as well as your self-loathing or the self-defeating coping mechanism(s) injuring yourself and perhaps others, will also help you to become whole. The key is practicing self-honesty by integrating and balancing these true (positive and negative) aspects of ourselves. Personal equanimity is the causal result of embracing all these aspects. Thus, wholeness, connection, and happiness are the result of embracing deeply *all* aspects of your true Self including both positive and negative aspects, the good as well as the bad, and even our potential for sin as well as sainthood. *This is because if you cut yourself off from your ability to see yourself positively and bright, then you also cut yourself off from the ability of others to see you positively and as someone worthy, deserving, desirable, and lovable.*

And, *if you cut yourself off from your ability to see yourself as dark with negative aspects (a "holier than thou" attitude), then you also cut yourself off from your ability to see others positively and worthy of your love and respect.* In other words, without embracing the hidden, perhaps negative, aspects of yourself, you cannot have compassion for others, you cannot forgive their sins against you and, ultimately, you cannot release yourself from the self-imposed bonds of anger, resentment, and judgment that you unconsciously project onto the world. By simply embracing the seeds of darkness within you, you can experience the joy of acceptance of your whole Self, which is connected to all aspects of yourself, others, and the Universe. Try to "uncover" and record your feeling(s) of happiness and joy as well as unhappiness and unworthiness in your Seven Arts Journal and explore, in writing, what the seed(s) of genuine happiness might be.

In order to practice mindfully the Art of Living Naturally, you must first learn to experience your original connection to not only your true, higher, Original Self, but also the Universe that loves and protects you, others, and all of creation at every moment.

Please practice the Chapter Six Exercises 12 and 13 as part of your Seven Arts journey to become whole. Use the awareness and self-discovery occasioned by your practice of all these exercises in order to reshape and positively transform yourself consistent with your PDA as the expression of your "highest good." *By practicing daily all of the exercises associated with each of the Seven Arts, your life will become transformed and you will experience the joy and abundance of spiritual, interpersonal, and overall well being.*

7

The Art of Service

"The fruit of love is service."
Mother Teresa (1910-1997)
The Simple Path

Have you ever wondered if you could practice what you preach?

Know Thyself Deeply…Your Whole Self, and then, Love Thy Neighbor As Thyself

Jesus said, *"Love thy neighbor as thyself."* That about sums it up. The Art of Service is nothing more than putting into daily practice all that you have learned on this journey of positive self-transformation. The transformation process is never ending; it is never complete as long as you are alive in this world. Perfection is not of this world, which is characterized by change and impermanence. You and I can, however, evolve further as spiritual beings through Conscious Action directed toward serving others. For us to act, we need energy.

To have boundless energy, we must be connected and, to be connected, we must learn to give up our selfish mind (Jp. *shoga*) and adopt instead a Universal Mind (Jp. *Taiga*). In order to serve others and put into daily practice all that you have gained in the process of your spiritual journey, you must learn to first know and then operate from the original *seeds* that characterize your whole self, your divine Self.

You will bring to light and become more aware of the various causal seeds and formations residing deep within you by practicing daily the exercises associated with the Art of Responsibility as well as practicing Exercise 13 just completed in the Art of Living Naturally ("Being In and With All Your Emotions"). These combined daily practices of true Self discovery are critical to the real work of "Knowing Thyself," your whole Self, including facing the seeds of your darker shadows, mental formations, and attachments along with the seeds of your original, connected Self. Only when you become whole can you know your divine Self and thus put into practice true selfless service twenty-four hours a day. The Art of Service is nothing more than practicing selflessness in daily life.

This last point is critical. Consider that you have the opportunity to practice Conscious Action twenty-four hours a day. If you only practice Conscious Action in service to others one hour a day, then you are possibly living with a selfish mind twenty-three hours a day. Remember that real personal transformation requires taking responsibility for not only your conscious mind but also your subconscious mind and unconscious mind. In order to truly change yourself deeply, you must practice deeply. The opportunity afforded you by the Art of Service is to practice deeply twenty-four hours a day. In this way, you will, over time, begin to transform your subconscious mind and even your deep, unconscious mind. Again, there are no short cuts. Whatever you put in to your conscious mind becomes your deeper self over time. If your intentional practice is but one hour a day, then you only get one hour of transformation against a potential twenty-three hours of bad habits.

Consider that your whole Self, your entire consciousness, is like a bathtub full of water. If your unwanted attachments and unconscious desires are significant, then let that be represented by muddy (impure) water. Every time you intentionally practice daily exercises, and every time you practice Conscious Action in service to others, you add small drops of clear water into the bath of your consciousness. To truly affect and cleanse the darkness of the muddy bath water, you first must put into your consciousness many, many drops of clear, pure water. In this manner, drop-by-drop, pure water is placed into your consciousness. If you have a lifetime of thinking and acting out of selfish desire(s) and excessive attachments, then you have very muddy water in your tub and much work to do to clarify it and truly transform your deep consciousness. There is much cleansing to do, many drops of pure water are needed, and so your Conscious Action can be your tool for deep personal transformation twenty-four hours a day. Practicing only Dynamic Breathing or Dynamic Meditation for even two or three hours per day is still not enough to truly transform yourself.

The real gift of the Art of Service is to begin to practice Conscious Action all the time twenty-four hours a day. When you sustain your intentional focus in this way, then you are practicing causally, drop-by-drop, the Art of Living Naturally. And, when you are living naturally, then you will discover (causally) that you are actually accomplishing more with less effort. And, when this happens, you will tap (causally) the infinite life force that will bring you health, energy, joy, and a positive spirit that is capable of serving others in abundance. The Universe will support you (causally) in this mission precisely because you will be living in accord with the principles of the Universe. You are One with the Universe.

Have you ever wondered if you are truly accountable in this life or beyond?

> Intoku
> Good Done in Secret
>
> Just as the number one can never be reduced to zero, once we act or speak, our action or speech is never completely erased.
>
> An old Oriental saying tells us, "Sow good, and the harvest will be good. Sow evil, and reap evil." We must understand that everything we do comes back to ourselves.
>
> Therefore, before wishing for our own happiness and welfare and that of our children, we must do good in secret. To do good in secret means to act without seeking attention and praise, to act without any hope of reward. This is called Intoku.
>
> Among the various ways of performing Intoku, to walk the Way of the Universe, and to lead others along this way is best.
>
> —Koichi Tohei

**The Universe Has No Secrets:
Doing Good in Secret Twenty-four Hours A Day**

My teacher, Master Tohei, describes this kind of living as *Intoku*, which means "Doing Good in Secret." It means serving others twenty-four hours a day by following the principles of the Universe.

As we have seen, real training means cultivation (Jp. *shugyō*). Cultivation means committing yourself twenty-four hours a day. Partial training means only practice (Jp. *keiko*). Practice is both productive and positive but, ultimately, the Conscious Action that springs from your deeper, calmer, connected Self must become your habit more often than not. When my teacher discusses *Intoku*, he describes it as a "way of life." This means applying the principle all day, every day. "Doing Good in Secret" must be done all the time so that it becomes your causal habit, not just an anomaly done whenever it is convenient.

The *otomo* training that I described in earlier chapters is designed to help *Ki-Aikido* students, and *uchi deshi* in particular, to instill the habit of serving others twenty-four hours a day. Habits require repetition. Both positive and negative habits are always (inescapably) being created depending upon your conscious effort or lack thereof. Therefore, you must practice mindfully in order to create and develop pure intentions. Pure intentions are the causal seeds of positive deeds, Conscious Action and, ultimately, causally dependent "service habits" of the heart and mind. Over time, your practice of the Art of Service will require less conscious intention because the positive "service habits" that you create and develop will succeed in changing causally (drop-by-drop) your subconscious mind and unconscious mind. In short, your total consciousness will become characterized by

"The otomo training that I described in earlier chapters is designed to help Ki-Aikido students, and uchi deshi in particular, to begin the habit of serving others twenty-four hours a day."

Author during Ki-Aikido Seminar in
Saint-Petersburg, Russia, 2010.

habitual connection. When this happens (causally), your life will become completely dedicated to the service of your greater mission. Your greater mission will become actualized by your Conscious Actions that, in turn, will always (by definition) be directed toward serving others for the greater good.

My teacher has developed other means, besides monastic-like *otomo* training, to help people practice continuously in daily life. As in the previous chapters, I will rely upon personal stories to illustrate my points. Indeed, the specific events that I am sharing with you helped me to develop and crystallize in my own mind the Seven Arts and twenty-one phases of positive personal transformation.

Have you ever wondered if you could teach people well what you know how to do well?

**Individual Exercises *(Hitori Waza)*,
Two Person Exercises *(Kumi Waza)*, and
Continuation Exercises for Daily Life *(Tsuzuki Waza)***

In 1953, my teacher, Master Koichi Tohei, first brought the art of *Aikido* outside of Japan by teaching in Hawaii. He came each year and would teach for many months before returning to Japan. He responded to requests from students to develop exercises that they could practice by themselves when not attending *Ki-Aikido* classes at the *dojo* (training hall). From this request, Master Tohei developed what are called *"hitori waza"* which are techniques/exercises that can be done alone in order to practice the basic movements that are integral to both *Ki* Development and the martial, self-defense arts of *Aikido*. The exercises should be performed continuously, that is, one after the other, so that you do not break your concentration and the natural flow of your rhythm.

Even today many *Ki* and *Aikido* practitioners misunderstand the importance of the continuous flow that can occur by linking the exercises together as an on-going, relaxed series of continuous movements with your mind and body unified. Understanding the importance of maintaining this connection *between* (Jp. *aidagara*) the different exercises reflects Master Tohei's emphasis upon practicing for daily life. It may be easy to maintain your concentration for a matter of seconds in the martial arts but, more often that not, students find it difficult to maintain and experience deeply their continuing connection to the *Ki* (life force) of the Universe. Practicing well even during the connection and spaces between the individual exercises provides the practitioner with a taste of maintaining their calmness in daily life.

In the 1950s, *Aikido* students in Hawaii would practice diligently until the return of Master Tohei each year. More student requests were made in successive years to standardize all of the thousands of possible *Aikido* techniques. Again, Master Tohei obliged and developed *"kumi waza"* which are techniques/exercises that are done with two people – the attacker (Jp. *uke*) and the defender (Jp. *nage)*. During black belt examinations, students had to perform five different defense arts (in rapid succession) from each of the standard strikes, punches, grabs, and attacks. This included front punches, strikes to the side of the head, strikes to the front of the head, kicks, chokes, and grabs of all kinds from the front, the back, one hand, two hands, etc.

During these examinations, Master Tohei recognized (again) that the student's energy *(Ki)* would be calm, poised, and *connected* with the attacker *during* each technique. However, again and again, *between* (Jp. *aidagara*) the arts, the *nage* (defender) might "slacken" their *Ki* (energy) and become *dis-connected* from their *uke* (attacker) so very easily. Master Tohei observed that students would *"gear up"* for the attack but would not maintain their awareness and connection between the five different arts that they were expected to perform for each attack during the black belt examinations.

To remedy this problem, Master Tohei developed and taught the principle of *"tsuzuki waza"* which means "continuation exercises." Continuation is all about applying your learning in daily life. The Art of Service requires that you continue your practice twenty-four hours a day. If you develop deep calmness during your early morning breathing and meditation sessions, then you must continue to extend this deeply experienced calmness into your daily life. In this way, you will learn to not only connect your personal Self with the Universe, but also you will learn to connect *interpersonally* in the *dojo* while practicing the *kumi waza* or two-person exercises and the *tsuzuki waza* or continuation exercises. This practice would extend further to your interpersonal connections in daily life.

But how can you help people to maintain their awareness of this interpersonal connection? How can you help people to maintain this fluid, energetic, and harmonious connection beyond the brief second or two required to perform an effective *Aikido* self-defense art?

Have you ever wondered if you could truly be in control of yourself?

Taigi Arts: First Control Yourself, and Then You Can Lead Others Well in Daily Life

Again, Master Tohei is a *Master Teacher.* To help remedy the problem of maintaining connection, he developed (over a period of years in the 1970s) thirty one different series of interconnected arts to be performed with Ki extending in a continuously connected manner. Master Tohei called this series of thirty different categories/groupings of interconnected *Ki-Aikido* arts (with *Ki* extending continuously) *"taigi."* The most important point about *Taigi Arts* is that they prepare you for daily life; that is, you must learn to *first control yourself,* maintain unification of mind and body with a Universal Mind, and only then can you expect to *lead others well.* In addition, by training in the *Taigi Arts,* students would learn to imitate Master Tohei's continuous rhythm when he performed an entire series of six to ten *Aikido* arts (performed on the left side and then on the right side). The entire *taigi* series, depending upon the attack and the pinning techniques, may take up to two minutes to complete. When defending against weapons and then performing the pinning techniques, the times can be slightly longer.

This training process ensures that students continuously maintain their calmness and connection to the Universe and each other over an extended period of time, the prescribed time for each *taigi* series. These times include the time for the performance of the entire series of techniques on both left side and right side. The *Taigi Arts* are performed in succession like pairs figure skating. Each participant, both attacker and defender, must remain completely connected throughout the exercise. The complete series of techniques defending against a knife (Jp. *tanto*), *Taigi* #21 for example, lasts for over two minutes—a total of 131 seconds. This time includes the time required to bow to your partner from the *seiza* (kneeling) position through the continuous performance to the time required to bow to each other at the conclusion of the arts. Thus, Taigi #21 (arts in defense of a knife attack) require sustained concentration and complete unification of mind and body for over two minutes.

I said that, in the beginning of the creation of *Taigi Arts*, Master Tohei was trying to help us understand the importance of self control first, and then how to lead others well by maintaining connection *(tsuzuki waza)* and learning to *feel*, by imitation, Master Tohei's own rhythm. His rhythm truly tapped into the rhythm of the Universe itself. Therefore, in order to help us imitate his movement *exactly*, his idea was to use a stopwatch in order to time *exactly* (for example, 131 seconds for *Taigi* #21) the time it took for Master Tohei himself to perform each of the *Taigi Art* series. This was truly teaching by example.

*Have you ever wondered, "Oh now I get it."
Why did that take so long?*

Ki ga Tsuku:
You Must Experience and Realize Deeply…For Yourself

When I was living at headquarters as a *uchi deshi* in 1979, we had an Instructor's Class every Friday morning followed by a shared Instructor's Class lunch. This was *the* big class of the week because: a) Master Tohei himself taught the class, b) all the senior professional instructors not living at headquarters would attend this special class, and c) the exact times of the *taigi* series were still being adjusted according to Master Tohei's own rhythm/opinion.

Let me explain that this last reason sometimes made for a most humorous and tiring class! You must remember that the Master is "king" and so there were really only two classes of citizens in this "closed" instructor's class – one class was Master Tohei "by himself" and the other class was "the rest of us." "The rest of us" would form a monastic-like brotherhood trying to help each other perform to the very best of our ability so as to avoid Master Tohei's critical eye and sometimes severe criticism. He called these critiques "scoldings out of love" because, as he said, he cared deeply that we "catch" and "grasp deeply for ourselves" (Jp. *ki ga tsuku*) his real teaching. He even taught us how to positively receive these severe, tough love scoldings as if they were directed from father to son.

Master Tohei would tell us (enthusiastically) that if we, the privileged few with access to him, did not "catch" deeply for ourselves *(ki ga tsuku)* his real teaching, then who would? He believed that we had a real responsibility to learn the true depth of his teaching so that, as instructors, we could pass this on to future generations. Suffice to say, Master Tohei has always been a very serious, sincere, and strict teacher. He was always kind to the masses (general *Ki-Aikido* students), but he was always very strict with us in Instructor's Class and in daily life. This meant that our monastic bond at the headquarters *dojo* during Instructor's Class was even more pronounced and important as we shared the pleasure of training together under Master Tohei's watchful eye.

Master Tohei would create new ways for each of us to have those "eye-opening," "gee whiz," "now I understand" learning experiences. He referred to these learning experiences by using the common Japanese expression *"ki ga tsuku."* This meant that, as privileged senior instructors with an enormous future responsibility, Master Tohei believed that we must *notice for ourselves experientially* the real depth of his teaching to become One with the Universe. The phrase *ki ga tsuku* can mean many things in Japanese depending upon the context, but Master Tohei always used it to refer to the fact that both our minds and our bodies must "catch" his teaching in a deep way so that each one of us could experience the essence of each point he taught us. By realizing deeply and experientially the *universal essence* of any principle he taught, Master Tohei believed that we then would be able to *apply* the principle in a great variety of *particular* circumstances or situations. He would "test" our knowledge by creating new particular training situations (attacks or holds) where we must apply the universal principle that he believed we had deeply "noticed" and "captured" as our own experience – *ki ga tsuku.*

*Have you ever wondered if you could
get away with something?*

**The Monastic Bond of Mutual Protection (or)
"Why Can't We Get Away With Anything?"**

Below is an example of how we used our unspoken monastic bond to "protect each other" during our intense Instructor's Classes at the old *Ki-Aikido* Haramachi headquarters in Tokyo. I should add that we were usually unsuccessful in these "mutual protection" schemes because Master Tohei (being the Master) saw through everything! He knew *what* we were up to, *when* we were up to something, and he knew if we truly experienced his teaching or not. During the special Friday Instructor's Class, we would be asked to regularly perform *tsuzuki waza* (continuation exercises) through the practice of *Taigi Arts.*

Master Tohei typically would call two of us up to the front of the class and ask us to demonstrate for him whatever *taigi* happened to come into his mind at the time. Remember that there are thirty *taigi* series with six to ten arts to be performed on both the left and right sides. Of course, we never knew which *taigi* would come to him (nor why) and so we needed to be able to perform at a moment's notice any *taigi* as either the attacker *(uke)* or the defender *(nage).*

Master Tohei would ask his assigned *otomo* for that day to hold a stopwatch and sit next to him. As soon as the two demonstrators, sitting opposite one another, moved the tip of their heads in the initial act of bowing to each other from the *seiza* (kneeling) position, the stopwatch must start. The stopwatch runs continuously throughout the performance of all the arts including left and right sides. For example, *Taigi* #21 mentioned previously includes self-defense arts performed against attacks with a knife and the sequence lasts exactly 131 seconds. The timekeeper stops the watch as soon as the *uke* and *nage's* head returns to the upright position after the closing bow. The attacker *(uke)* and defender *(nage)* must also be aware of their relative position on the *dojo* mat throughout the performance of the *taigi* so that they bow from the exact same position on the mat (at the end of the *Taigi Arts*) as when they started.

Now here is the clincher. You must perform the *Taigi Arts* for Master Tohei within two seconds plus or minus of the 131-second goal. So, if your time is between 129 and 133 seconds, you and your partner are OK, at least on Master Tohei's time criteria. Your performance time might be fine but you could still receive a "scolding" from Master Tohei if the *Taigi Arts* themselves were not performed well. If you needed instruction (and we all did), then inevitably you would be asked to return to the front of the class to perform the *taigi* again and again until Master Tohei was satisfied. If the execution of your *taigi* performance was outside the acceptable two-second range, then you would be asked immediately to repeat the *taigi* and correct the time required to execute the series of arts in whatever direction you needed – slower or faster.

You have to understand that the *uke* (the attacker) is the one being thrown all over the place for a total of, for example, 131 seconds (*Taigi* #21). As the *uke*, you attack with a knife, get clobbered by the *nage* (defender), you are then disabled and pinned on the mat, then you have the knife taken away by the *nage,* and then the *nage* defender politely returns the knife to you. Immediately, as *uke,* you strike again from the other side only to experience the same result again and again and again. Basically, if you are the attacker *(uke)* doing *Taigi*

#21, you strike the defender *(nage)* with the knife ten different ways (front, side, slash, overhead, etc.) and you are thrown, disabled, pinned, and have the knife returned to you twenty times (right and left side) in 131 seconds, including the time required for the initial and concluding bow. The attacker is usually totally out of breath after 131 seconds of continuous pounding.

Some people are clearly in better shape than others and Master Tohei preferred that we be in good shape. It was common, therefore, to be asked to repeat the entire *taigi* series again and again if your time was too slow in comparison to the previously established "target" time. The problem is that, with each repetition of an entire *taigi* series, the attacker *(uke)* is "sucking air" (as we used to say) in a big way, and then (unfortunately) the *uke* tends to slow down even more which, of course, makes the total elapsed time even slower! Thus you become subject to Master Tohei's persistent requests to repeat the *taigi* again and again in spite of your condition. At the conclusion of the *taigi*, Master Tohei would simply look at the *otomo* holding the stopwatch and the *otomo* was expected to call out the recorded *taigi* time to Master Tohei. If your *taigi* time was too slow, then Master Tohei would simply look at you and your partner and say, *"moichido kudasai"* (one more time, please). If he was frustrated with you, he was known to drop the polite *"kudasai"* (please) and just look out the window saying, *"moichido"* (once more)!

The monastic bond and our mutual protection for each other would surface in the following form. Let's say two people are demonstrating the *taigi* in front of the class and they have been too slow as deemed by the *otomo* timekeeper. The *otomo* timekeeper had to live with his fellow *uchi deshi* and so there was good reason to help each other out! So, suppose that you see that your fellow *deshi* brothers are repeating *taigis* again and again; they are dying right in front of our teacher, Master Tohei. They are "sucking air" and they are being pummeled time and time again only to end up with slower and slower times due to mental and physical exhaustion. Remember, each time this would happen, Master Tohei asked that the *taigi* be repeated "until we got it right."

Occasionally, any one of us being asked to sit next to Master Tohei and keep time as *otomo* would feel particularly empathetic toward our suffering *uke* friend and fellow *deshi nage* who were being asked to repeat the *taigi* and thus throw and be thrown again and again and again. Let's say it's the third time a pair has performed the entire *taigi* (possibly sixty successive arts), and the stopwatch still says that they are too slow by a mere three seconds. Remember also that two seconds off the "target time" is considered an acceptable time. If you are the *otomo* and tell this three-second slow time to Master Tohei, then you know that the pair will have to repeat the *taigi* a fourth time! So, what do you do? The answer is – you lie about the time - you cheat – you try to save your monastic brothers, your comrades, from another *taigi* series! And so, you look at Master Tohei *very positively* (but not in the eye) *and smile*. Then you fudge the numbers and call out loud in a very extended voice, "a perfect 131 seconds" (even though you know full well that the watch in your hand says 134 seconds, three seconds off)!

We got away with this kind of helping each other only a few times. I remember one particular time that this deception was attempted, and Master Tohei could just *feel* that the reported time was not right. When the false time was reported to him, he wrinkled his forehead and said, "*Honto?*" (Really?). "Still too slow," he stated. This time when the false number was empathetically reported to Master Tohei, he surprised us by asking to actually *see the watch!* "Bummer!" we all thought.

Let's just say that at this point the room turned dead quiet because we knew that the *otomo* was ready for death, ritual suicide (Jp. *hara-kiri*) for falsely reporting the actual time! The *otomo* had no choice but to immediately make up some lame excuse like, "Ahh...I was squinting with...ahh sweat in my eye...and ahh...I guess I could not see the stopwatch correctly." Or, something like this that was also an obvious lame excuse, "I started the watch too early at the first bow and so I made a quick mental adjustment of two seconds when I reported the time." Master Tohei never bought any of our quickly made up, lame excuses. He knew that we were supporting each other with our monastic bond mentality, and he knew to trust his own instincts rather than count upon our management of the stopwatch.

We did learn, however, a new trick. Now this one took guts! OK, let's say you just lied about the time again to cover for your ailing *deshi* roommate, the attacker *(uke)* in the *taigi*. And, let's also say that Master Tohei did not believe you (again) and so rather than showing Master Tohei the evidence (the actual stopwatch), you hand it to him and ACCIDENTALLY hit the reset button in the hand-over so that Master Tohei only sees "0:00" (a cleared time of zero minutes and zero seconds). Of course, this accident may save you, the *otomo* timekeeper, from being "caught" covering for your fellow *deshi*, but still the *taigi* would have to be repeated. Clearly, Master Tohei believed that imitating his *exact rhythm* would help our minds and bodies to *feel the rhythm* of the Universe as he did during the *taigi*. Master Tohei believed that this kind of training enabled us to follow deeply the Way of the Universe and to experience the natural universal rhythm that is always present.

*Have you ever wondered
what it would be like to be vindicated?*

"You Are All Too Slow!" ...Well, Not Really

One time Master Tohei actually changed the *taigi* series time right before us. What happened was that a *deshi* pair executed a series of continuous *taigi* performances that were all "too slow" when compared to the standard target time previously established. Master Tohei himself always established the standard times. Master Tohei would perform the *taigi*, we would time him and, "bingo", his recorded time would become the precise time for the rest of us to achieve henceforth.

On this particular Friday, I was asked to start the demonstration of *taigi* as *uke* (attacker) for another *uchi deshi* who served as the *nage* (defender). I think Osaki sensei (who is now a professional instructor and senior *taigi* judge in Japan) was my partner. We were slow, slow, slow each time. Eventually, after four successive attempts at the correct *taigi* time, even Master Tohei saw that the *uke* (in this case me) was "dead to the world" and so out of breath that I could never speed up enough to make the correct *taigi* time without a moment to catch my breath. In this case, and this is really a bad "lose face" sort of a thing, Master Tohei would simply shake his head in disappointment, and then look around the room for a new pair. He would demand that a "new" (always higher ranking), pair replace the previous pair (Osaki sensei and I) in order to get "fresh meat," as it were, for Master Tohei to critique. Of course, now the pressure to perform correctly is really on the "new" more senior pair of substitute performers.

On this particular day, Otsuka sensei ("Sensei," remember, is an honorific term that simply means "teacher" or, literally, "one-step ahead") and Kataoka sensei were asked to perform the same *taigi* that Osaki sensei and I had never managed to get quite right. On this occasion, Otsuka sensei and Kataoka sensei were once again too slow. In fact, their times were slow repeatedly, as they performed the same *taigi* to the same point of exhaustion that I had just experienced.

Otsuka sensei was in charge of us lower-ranking *deshi*, so we clearly had incentive to change Otsuka sensei's stopwatch time, if at all possible. Let's just say you did not want to get on Otsuka sensei's bad side. Master Tohei, however, was completely aware of our covering for each other with our stopwatch tricks. Our efforts to help our *dojo* "boss", Otsuka sensei, failed miserably. So, Otsuka sensei and Kataoka sensei experienced the same "loss of face" that Osaki sensei and I did. We were all too exhausted to improve the *taigi* time consistent with Master Tohei's previously established standard. The net result was that this second pair needed to be replaced.

At this point in the class, two *taigi* demonstration pairs had succeeded in making Master Tohei slightly perturbed, to put it mildly. Remember, we were the "treasured few" who needed to understand deeply and correctly. If our performance evidenced neither—well, you can probably use your imagination. Think of the most charismatic, powerful person you know becoming more than a little disappointed in your performance. He was so disappointed that now he was going to ask for an even more senior pair to "show us the right way."

This time he called for "Tamura-san" and looked at the most senior instructor living outside headquarters—Iwao Tamura sensei. Tamura sensei was the Chief Instructor of the

Kanagawa Branch, the largest Ki Society in Japan. Tamura sensei commuted each Friday to attend Instructor's Class and then stayed for our group lunch and organizational meeting. Tamura sensei chose an *uke* to perform the same *taigi* yet again. However, again and again the same result occurred —"too slow!" Finally, Tohei sensei said "Maru-san" and pointed to Koretoshi Maruyama sensei. Master Tohei had affectionate nicknames for all of us and this was his name for Maruyama sensei who was then the most senior instructor living at headquarters. As did Tamura sensei before him, Maruyama sensei chose his *uke* and the same "too slow" result occurred, not once but three times. With the most senior *taigi* pairs before us, the pressure was on "big time"! And, yet again, the times were too slow when even Maruyama sensei and Tamura sensei performed. Even the "big dogs" were *not* getting it right—repeatedly! I must admit that I was feeling a little vindicated since this entire situation began with the slow times recorded by Osaki sensei and me, the first pair. So far in this particular Friday Instructor's Class, four pairs—eight people—were not achieving Master Tohei's standard for this *taigi*.

At this point, Master Tohei just looked down at the mat and shook his head in disgust. He had sat in the *seiza* position (on his knees) and had been watching all of this now without moving an inch for over forty-five minutes. He said "All right!" and then proceeded to stand up and approached center stage at the front of the *dojo*. Now it seemed the Master was going to have to demonstrate the *taigi* himself! He pensively looked at everyone in the room, eyeing each person, slowly, one at a time. We all knew that he was thinking and deciding whom he would choose as HIS *uke* for the "correct" demonstration. I was thinking only this—"I do not want to be the one with the stopwatch just in case the time is off! No way am I going to tell my teacher that he is 'off' or 'too slow' as measured against the standard of his own time!"

Now, on this particular Friday, I was Master Tohei's *otomo*. Normally, as *otomo* I would serve as his teaching *uke* (attacker), his *taigi* partner, and his demonstration partner for the entire day no matter when or where Master Tohei would teach. I was the logical choice as Master Tohei's *uke* and, more importantly in my humble opinion, "no way did I want to be the one recording his time with this stopwatch." So, when Master Tohei's eyes hit mine as he scanned the room, I overtly placed the stopwatch to my side on the mat next to Otsuka sensei, raised myself slightly from my *seiza* position (as if to stand up), and I gave Master Tohei my best "puppy-dog eyes" to communicate "choose me, Master, please choose me as your uke." The combination of my body language and hopeful expression did the trick! By 1) making eye contact with Master Tohei, then 2) divorcing myself from the stopwatch, then 3) giving him my best "choose me," "puppy-dog eyes," and then, 4) slightly raising myself up from my *seiza* kneeling position as if to get up and join him for the demonstration in front of the class, Master Tohei finally did in fact nod his head to me indicating that I should rise to the occasion and serve as his *uke!*

As I stood up to join Master Tohei at the front of the class, I thought to myself for the first time that "actually being the uke for this demonstration would be no picnic either – maybe I should have kept the stopwatch!" I had had plenty of time to rest since my first excursion with Osaki sensei when we were the first slow *taigi* pair at the beginning of class. Well, now Otsuka sensei had the stopwatch, and I was in front of the class, sitting *seiza,* and facing Master Tohei. Our *Ki* was connected and we were ready to bow to each other signaling the start of our *taigi* (and the stopwatch!).

We performed and I got slammed repeatedly and joyously with all the zip and energy I could muster. And, the time? You could hear a pin drop after we bowed to each other signaling the conclusion of our *taigi* demonstration. All faces turned to Otsuka sensei, the man of the moment with the stopwatch. As all eyes stared at Otsuka sensei, I felt that I had made a good decision dumping the stopwatch. Now I was "protected" by Master Tohei as his demonstration partner. After all, *taigi* performance is all about the *connection* between the *nage* (Master Tohei) and the *uke* (me). The lead and, therefore, the overall pace of the *taigi* performance time comes as a result the *nage's Ki* movement. (Remember, the purpose of the *Taigi Arts* is first "control yourself," and then "lead others well.") Since the *nage* was Master Tohei himself, I felt both at peace and scared to death for Otsuka sensei who kept staring at the watch, squinting, turning it sideways, and so on as if the watch was broken. *We all knew he was stalling!*

Now, the only reason for stalling would be that the time was off – too fast or too slow. Otsuka sensei was speechless (this, by the way, is the only time I had ever seen him speechless). Apparently, Otsuka sensei's tongue didn't work and he just kept adjusting his *seiza* position again and again, first to the left and then to the right – this would be squirming Japanese style. Finally, he said, "*Sumimasen sensei,*" which simply means "Excuse me Master...," or "I am sorry Master...," but no more words would come out of Otsuka sensei's tongue-tied mouth. Finally, Master Tohei walked over and simply took the stopwatch out of Otsuka sensei's hand. He looked at the time and, in the most calm, nonchalant manner, said *"Oh, 106 seconds, OK, change."*

That's it—that's all that was said. Master Tohei's time on this particular taigi was the same "slower" time that all the rest of us had performed for the last forty-five minutes! But, because Master Tohei himself performed it, it now became the new, standardized, correct time for the rest of the world. When he said, "OK, change," we all dutifully went to our notepads (which we always brought to class in order to record Master Tohei's teaching for the day) and we recorded the newly authorized *taigi* time. We officially noted that the new time for this particular *taigi* would be adjusted from 103 seconds to the new, rhythmically slower, 106 seconds. To this day, the time for *Taigi #22 (Tachidori* – arts in defense of the sword) is 106 seconds!

---

*Have you ever wondered if
the people you are talking to actually get it?*

Are They Learning and Discovering For Themselves?

I invested a lot of time to share this story for three reasons. First, the concept of *tsuzuki waza* (continuation practice) is vitally important. Master Tohei is *very* particular about detail, time, and rhythm because he wants to teach his senior instructors well. "Continuation" is all about *Ki in daily life*. If you cannot even perform well with correct rhythm for an exacting 106 seconds, then how can you remain connected in daily life twenty-four hours a day?

Second, I wanted to give you a taste of my teacher's caring mind. His teaching was selfless, as he desired that others truly "capture for themselves" (*ki ga tsuku*) the depth of his knowledge, experience, and understanding. He wanted students to understand deeply as a result of their own personal experience. He wanted us to consult our own personal experience instead of believing in things just because someone else "says so" (including Master Tohei), or because "it is written in a book."

Third, I wanted to illustrate my teacher's patience and deep concern that others truly learn the Way of the Universe. It is one thing to experience Oneness with the Universe in daily life, but it is quite another to receive a gift from the Universe that enables you to serve as a "Master Teacher" and help others discover and walk the Way of the Universe *for themselves*.

Even if you experience something *for yourself*, it is still quite another skill to be able to understand the topic so well and so clearly that you are able to transmit the principles of the Universe *to others*. To this end, Master Tohei used many vehicles to teach people to become One with the Universe in daily life – *hitori waza* (individual exercises), *kumi waza* (two-person *Aikido* exercises), *tsuzuki waza* (continuation exercises), *randori waza* (*Aikido* arts with multiple attackers), healing arts (Jp. *Kiatsu Ryoho*), breathing arts (Jp. *Ki no kokyuho*), meditation arts (Jp. *Ki no Ishiho*), and bell meditation arts (Jp. *Sokushin no Gyo*). Time and space does not allow for a complete explanation of all these topics in this volume, but perhaps future books can be dedicated to revealing the depth of these other development "arts."

By 1996, Master Tohei believed that he had taught *taigi arts* widely enough, and that he had taught instructors "to see" the *Ki* movement in the arts well enough, to have the first international competition in the performance of *taigi*. Senior instructors who had been taught *"to see"* were trained as *taigi* judges using three main criteria – rhythm (to evidence relaxation), balance (to evidence maintaining your center), and largeness (evidencing extension of *Ki*). Correct timing, correct spacing *(maai)*, proper bowing, etc., were also used as additional criteria for the first international competition. *Taigi* pairs (remember this is "pairs" competing against other "pairs") came from all over the world.

The competition included many different categories including basic compulsory *taigi arts* called *kitei taigi*, selective hand-to-hand *taigi arts* called *sentaku taigi*, *taigi arts* with weapons (wooden staff, sword, and knife), as well as *taigi arts* with weapons done as a *kata*; that is, both persons perform a series of movements with the wooden staff or sword moving seamlessly in a synchronized manner. Gold, silver, and bronze medals would be awarded for *each* of the aforementioned categories of competition. One overall winner of the *Taigi* World Cup would be the pair whose results were judged to be the highest overall by combining the results of all the categories of the competition. Of course, the pair must enter all of the categories of competition in order to be eligible for the overall World Cup.

At the conclusion of the 1996 First International *Taigi* Competition held at the new Ki Society headquarters in Tochigi, Japan, all of the judges went into an isolated room where the results would first be shown to Master Tohei himself. Before anyone could speak, Master Tohei proceeded to scold judges because he believed that, based upon his observations of all the events over two full days of *taigi* competition, the Japanese judges were being too critical of the foreign competitors who came from all over the world. Iwao Tamura sensei, the Chief Taigi Judge, had to politely inform Master Tohei that, "actually, a *gaijin* (foreign) pair had earned the highest combined score!" "A non-Japanese pair would become the very first overall World Cup winners," he said. "What?" said Master Tohei smiling, "The actual winners of the First International *Taigi* Competition would not be Japanese?" Tamura Sensei later told me that Master Tohei's surprised reaction went on and on, "*Honto* (Really?), *Dochira* (Who?)", he asked.

The World Cup winners were two of my students from South Carolina. Eric Harrell *(nage)* and his partner, Ileana

Shaner *(uke)* won the World Cup at the 1996 First International *Taigi* Competition. Master Tohei was very pleased grinning from ear to ear. He said that since Ileana was a musician (she is a pianist), she must have had very good timing and rhythm. And, he added, Eric was very calm as the *nage*. Finally he said, "Both looked very 'large' (extending *ki*), 'balanced' (keeping one point), and

Eric Harrell (nage) and Ileana Shaner (uke) won the World Cup at the 1996 First International Taigi Competition.
Eric Harrell (left), Koichi Tohei (center), Ileana Shaner (right), and author (back) in the new HQ in Tochigi, Japan, 1996.

'rhythmic' (relaxing completely)." Again, the main *taigi* judging criteria are always balance, rhythm, and largeness of movement (extension of *Ki*).

Since Master Tohei was the first to bring *Ki* and *Aikido* training outside Japan in 1953, he also said it was fitting that in 1996 the Universe gave him non-Japanese winners of the First International Competition. Master Tohei said that this clearly demonstrates that the teachings are, in fact, *universal* and not restricted to any *particular* people, culture, or spiritual tradition.

I must say (selfishly) that the real reason I was so pleased was because only days earlier I had received one of Master Tohei's severe, father-to-son scoldings (with love, of course) that he reserves for a select few of us who have personally trained with him the longest. A few days before the *taigi* competition, we were training in the main *Tenshinkan dojo* and he was frustrated that I was not doing what he wanted me to do when he spoke to me in Japanese. The problem is that, at that point, my Japanese language ability was nothing like what it was when I lived in Japan with Master Tohei. Yet, my teacher still preferred to speak to me in Japanese most of the time. When I failed to demonstrate what he was asking (because I didn't understand him), he went into the lecture that goes like this – "if you don't get this, then how are all those that you teach in the next generation going to learn correctly!"

"Ouch!", I thought. These scoldings are always instructive but not much fun. I tell my students in a smiling way "Remember, it is always a pleasure to be corrected! If you are not corrected, how can you learn?" So, when Master Tohei once again *put his hand on my shoulder* (this time in 1996) and thanked me for teaching my students well enough to win the First International World Cup, I felt "vindicated" (a second time) from the scolding that had occurred only days earlier. "It's all a process," I thought. And so, I said to myself, "The Universe is teaching us all the time, even when (or especially when) you least expect it."

Have you ever wondered why you always have to take one step at a time?

Kaizen: Improvement is a Continuous Process in All Spheres of Development – Personal, Spiritual, and Business

The key is to appreciate that real committed training (and training in daily life, Jp. *Shugyō*) is an ongoing, continuous improvement and awakening process (Jp. *kaizen*). By practicing in this way, it is possible to engrain rhythms and connection so deeply that your subconscious mind and unconscious mind can become transformed. Whether it's personal development, business development, organizational development, or spiritual development, improvement is always a gradual, drop-by-drop, sequential process of transformation.

In the last twenty years, Master Tohei has made other pedagogical inventions to help people with *tsuzuki waza* (continuation practice) for daily life. We have, for example, a "Oneness Rhythm Exercise" performed to music in order to help people not only *feel* rhythm, but also move with rhythm from your "one point"; that is, from your physiological center. Again, in this form of "continuation" *(tsuzuki)*, the Oneness Rhythm Exercise takes over six minutes to perform, not just seconds, as in *Aikido* techniques for self-defense. It is all about *continuing the practice of universal principles (already experienced and learned through Ki Development and Aikido) in order to apply the universal principles to our daily lives.* When this occurs, you are really practicing the Art of Service in your daily life twenty-four hours a day.

Have you ever wondered what it would be like to focus all your energy when you need it most?

Managing Life's Obstacles in the Improvement Process

Everyone knows that in daily life "stuff happens." The Universe does not just give you goodness and ease because one day you say you wish to become One with the Universe and learn to live harmoniously in accord with its principles. Real development, in any sphere, means real work and real sacrifice. When Master Tohei scolds us and corrects us, he truly does so lovingly as a father to a son. However, his *Ki* (energy) is so strong that it can penetrate you. Therefore, Master Tohei has actually taught us how to properly receive his strong *Ki* and "corrections" so that we do not just completely fall apart.

For those of us who have actually been instructed in how to properly receive Master Tohei's instruction, it represents another type of continuation exercise *(tsuzuki waza)*. This is very useful in daily life when it seems that some "lightning bolt" of energy wants to become an obstacle to your life and your Conscious Actions. It is even possible to demonstrate how to receive (or not receive) a lot of energy or power coming in your direction. These things are easy to demonstrate and help to show others the power of operating in accord with the principles of the Universe.

The key to receiving Master Tohei's strong, corrective energy is actually to not receive it where it can literally knock you over mentally, physically, emotionally and spiritually. Allow me to explain. You learned the practice of Dynamic Meditation in Chapter Four as part of the Art of Relaxation.

Remember, the "one point" (Jp. *itten*) at your physiological center can be reduced by half infinitely. Therefore, in the improvement process, it is possible to learn how to receive any of life's obstacles, or any force, power, or energy, even Master Tohei's sharp words, and allow it/them to dissolve infinitely into your center. Master Tohei sometimes calls your physiological center the "magic pot" because you can throw anything into it (infinitely) and not let it upset you.

In daily life, the Art of Service means practicing acceptance and remaining detached from the exact outcome of any step on your journey. Remember that the Art of Conscious Action asks you to remain steadfast in your mission to serve others, but not attached to any specific path on your journey of personal transformation. In daily life, you want to remain flexible. If you are stuck and attached and receive negative energy or power from others, then you become weak and feel overpowered by your naysayers. However, when you face new and challenging obstacles, you want your mind and body to be free and light. You want to be unstuck and detached, as it were, so that you can engage the world with the mind of clarity. A clear and present mind allows you to see new paths and new options in the face of adversity. For example, in the actual practice of *Aikido*, it is this clarity of mind that enables you to be flexible in order to lead your attacker in whatever direction harmonizes with the force and direction of the attack.

Let me explain in greater detail this practice of managing life's obstacles in the improvement process of personal transformation. Receiving or not receiving power, energy, or even sharp words can illustrate this kind of practice in daily life. One year I was demonstrating this very point at a Sports Psychology Conference in Miami, Florida. I was a speaker along with many others including National Football League (NFL) Head Coach George Allen. The theme was Peak

Performance. On the first day, I gave a presentation to a group of about 50 people, most of whom were active players and coaches in the National Hockey League (NHL). At the end of the session, I was demonstrating how it was possible not to receive a hockey player's "body check" by maintaining your unification of mind and body. Now professional hockey players see themselves as "tough guys" and do not take kindly to some "small guy" philosophy professor (me) telling them how to "hit" or "check" opposing players or how to be "hit" by opposing players on ice skates.

I have performed these *Ki* Development demonstrations enough to know that I can feel it when the people in the audience (the skeptics) want to challenge me. More specifically, I can feel it when the people in the room simply do not believe me nor do they want to believe in the power of *Ki* energy. However, *Ki* energy is available to all of us through the practice of deep relaxation in which we can experience directly the power and original unity of mind and body. In these situations, I have learned that audience participation demonstrations using the skeptics are most helpful indeed.

I calmly sat *seiza* (kneeling) in my street clothes and asked five big strong NHL players to line up behind one another and push me over. I sat on my knees with my upper body upright. I let the first person that stood opposite me place his large hands squarely on my shoulders in order to push me backwards with all his power. The second, third, fourth, and fifth hockey player stood behind the first person, one after the other, in a straight row, such that all five NHL "tough guys" were trying to push me over using the combined power of their bulging legs, thick backs, and strong arms.

I normally do not like doing these "showy" kinds of demonstrations. However, sometimes in order to truly serve new students (in this case, the skeptical, "tough guy," NHL players) who do not yet believe in this power, you need to grab their attention in some dramatic manner. By actually giving all five of them a simultaneous personal experience of my *not receiving* their tremendous power, I could gain not only their attention and respect, but also the attention and respect of all the other NHL players and coaches observing the demonstration in the audience. In this demonstration with the five NHL players, I really just let all their power pass into my center and let it dissipate there infinitely (half, half, half ... Master Tohei's "Magic Pot") as though I were practicing Dynamic Meditation. In this way, the entire audience observing the demonstration immediately began to learn from me with a completely different attitude. I knew this approach would work and I was happy to oblige.

"One of the very few women in the place was my mother..."

Author with his mother Janis M. Shaner, 1993.

The demonstration worked so well that the hotel guests were buzzing all night about how this little martial arts, philosophy guy had done all kinds of different powerful demonstrations with a whole bunch of big, strong, NHL players. The actual players that I used during the four or five different demonstrations gave further testimony (at the hotel bar, I think) telling everyone who would listen how amazing all this was.

By the next morning, the conference organizers asked if I would do a "repeat performance" and give a second, and greatly expanded, session that afternoon. The organizers said that they wanted to open the hotel's grand ballroom to accommodate everyone who wanted to attend my presentation and demonstration on the topic of *Ki and Peak Performance*. I said "No problem" and by early afternoon the grand ballroom was packed. This was a "*macho*" – type crowd of about 300 people affiliated with professional sports (NHL and NFL), collegiate athletics, and sport psychological organizations. I think one of the very few women in the place was my mother who accompanied my father also in attendance. My Dad drove down to Miami from Venice, Florida, because he wanted me to introduce him to Washington Redskins Head Football Coach, George Allen. Coach Allen was a celebrity in my father's eyes – my Dad had a real affinity for the "over the hill gang" for those of you who can remember that era of Redskins football glory.

My teacher, Master Tohei, frequently used the phrase "satisfy the feeling." That is, when someone wants a piece of you, they want to attack you, destroy you, put you down, then by all means "let them come," "satisfy their need to attack you"! Master Tohei says, "If you like to fall, then please attack; otherwise, please be nice." Well, given the rumor mill at the hotel, I knew that the large crowd on the second day was there for one reason only. Therefore, I decided that rather than giving my presentation on *"Ki and Peak Performance"* first, and then provide demonstrations at the end of the session (as I did the day before), this second time I would just give them what they wanted and I would "satisfy the feeling" right up front at the start of the presentation.

I knew that once I conducted the audience participation demonstrations (that they would once again think were "amazing"), then I would be able to really explain and "demystify" what I had done in order to truly teach them well. I thought that *if* I followed this course of action, *then* the audience and actual demonstration participants would have a chance to see and personally experience the power of *Ki for themselves (ki ga tsuku)*, and then they would become true believers, and only then would they be ready to really learn something of value that they could immediately apply to their sport. The key is that I wanted to first educate them and then give them something of value long term. To do this effectively, I had to "satisfy the feeling" and give them what they wanted at the onset of the presentation. In this way, I would be preparing them for their own experience *(ki ga tsuku)* of *Ki* and unification of mind and body during the bulk of my seminar session.

So, I began by asking ten strong men (doubling the number from the previous day) to please join me on stage. Ten of the strongest NHL defensemen and football linebacker types showed up on stage and I lined them all up in front of me just as I had done the day before. To be honest, it does not matter how many men are trying to push me over. I know that if I do not receive the power of the first person pushing my shoulders, then I do not receive all the force of the other nine men pushing as well – one person or twenty, it makes no difference *in my mind*. All the power of ten strong men goes into my infinite center (half, half, half...the "magic pot") and so I remained unmoved by them. The lesson is that managing this force is achieved with the same *mindset* as *managing life's obstacles* in daily life. If you do not receive problems as negative and disabling, then you can use your mind and body together to change unexpected problems or obstacles into opportunities for creativity and conflict management.

This demonstration, by the way, is much, much easier than receiving (that is, *not receiving*) one of Master Tohei's scoldings! Give me ten professional football or hockey players any day compared to one Master Tohei who will succeed in making his point stick to you! After all, as an *uchi deshi,* I was practiced in: 1) receiving Master Tohei's "scoldings," 2) serving as his *otomo* twenty-four hours a day, and 3) enduring very long and strenuous bell meditation *(misogi)* sessions. Accordingly, this kind of public demonstration of Ki is very easy in comparison! It's like my downhill Coach Phillipe Mollard preparing us for "scary" high-speed downhill competition by asking us to practice doing "scarier" things in comparison!

In this particular demonstration though, one little problem developed right when I was holding, actually redirecting and not receiving, all the power of the ten strong men on stage. I was wearing my street clothes rather than a martial arts uniform, and my pants (instead of my "infinite center" or "magic pot") apparently decided to *receive* the power and force of these men. While my mind and body did not move, from the front zipper-down through the crotch and up my backside all the way to my belt loops, *my pants exploded!* I mean the seams burst and made a loud popping noise. I now stood in front of "a standing room only" crowd in the grand ballroom at the very start of my presentation with a gaping hole in my pants from front to back.

People were amazed but one woman in the center aisle was laughing hysterically – *my mother!* She thought this was hilarious. This was not exactly my opinion since I had just started a lengthy morning program in the grand ballroom with everyone watching me at center stage. So, while I succeeded in the first of my many demonstrations on stage, the embarrassing problem at hand was that my pants were falling off! Someone handed me a towel that I wrapped around my waist (locker-room style) and so I just continued my teaching with the towel (and ripped pants below) for the remainder of the session. If they didn't mind, I didn't mind.

The lesson here relevant to the Art of Service is simply for you to know the tremendous power of your unified mind and body when you learn to be calm and relaxed in the midst of any situation or when facing any obstacle.

Have you ever wondered if you could be a gracious host when your guest is acting like a jerk?

Security and the *Art of Service* at Caesar's Palace and the Mirage Casino

For years, I trained all the security people at Caesar's Palace and the Mirage Casino and Resort Hotels in Las Vegas, Nevada. In a gambling environment, the security challenge is enormous. Every night "bad guys" frequent the big casinos. Some "bad guys" are so bad that they bring their own personal bodyguards. Some bad guys get high or drunk or both and then, on top of all this, they get mad and hostile because they lose a lot of money! At the same time, the Las Vegas gambling environment has been reshaped and reinvented over the last two decades to transform the desert area into a destination vacation resort for *families*.

Therefore, the security challenge is to meet unexpected bad-guy "occurrences" with professionally trained security personnel who can quickly, politely, and calmly render the bad guys helpless using *Aikido* techniques while, at the same time, *serving* to create and preserve a positive and nice *customer service* environment for families and all the other hotel and casino guests. This security work with the bad guys must be tactful, inconspicuous, and must be performed amidst a crowded casino full of nice people (guests) trying to enjoy their vacation experience. Sometimes we could use the extensive surveillance equipment to spot bad guy situations before they get out of hand, but usually fights would break out unexpectedly, especially when drugs and alcohol and explosive tempers were involved.

I have witnessed how the personal lives of these security professionals can become totally transformed simply because they come to truly understand the universal principle of non-dissension. When security professionals learn new ways to manage conflict, they immediately learn how these same principles can be used in their personal lives. Law enforcement and security professionals can learn to apply the Art of Service not only in their professional lives as *service providers* but also in their lives at home *serving their spouse, children, or anyone else they encounter in daily life*. When you learn how to not receive an obstacle, how to not receive another person's physical power, or how to not receive another's negative words or energy, then you can apply this ability in countless situations at work or in your personal life.

Have you ever wondered how some people learn things so quickly?

"Master... When Do you Practice?"

The key to the Art of Service is simply taking all the benefits of the first six Arts and putting them into practice even, or especially, when you face adversity. You are transforming yourself and building inner confidence everyday when you operate from the power of your calm, connected Self. Since I always saw Master Tohei *teach,* I once asked my teacher when he *practiced.* He responded "Twenty-four hours a day." In other words, Master Tohei's practice was his *life in service to others.* He practiced the Art of Service by teaching people all over the world how to live a healthy, happy, empowered life.

Once, while serving as *otomo* and riding in the back seat of a car with Master Tohei, I watched him move his head and body ever so slightly while his eyes were closed. I politely just watched trying to figure out what he was doing. After watching for a few minutes, I could see by his rhythmic movement that he was *practicing taigi* arts "in his head." More precisely, as evidenced by watching the almost imperceptible rhythmic motions of his body sitting in the back seat of the car, he was practicing in his head (mind) and his body while we were being driven across town to teach another class. I observed this event only one day after I had asked Master Tohei when he practiced, and he answered "Twenty-four hours a day." Accordingly, I somewhat jokingly leaned over to my teacher as we sat together in the back of the car and softly asked *"keiko desu ka?"* ("Are you practicing?"). He simply responded with a "yes" nodding motion so as not to interrupt the *taigi* he was performing with his mind and body in the back seat of the car!

My teacher's *feel* for the *taigi* series times were so accurate, I learned, because he practiced in his mind and body all the time, twenty-four hours a day...continuation, continuation, continuation *(tsuzuki waza).* When you practice the correct universal rhythm even *in your mind,* you develop an awareness and sensitivity that goes along with the actual physical performance of the *taigi*. This includes performing the *taigi* yourself (after practicing in your mind) as well as teaching others to perform the *taigi* correctly; that is, in accord with the principles and rhythm of the Universe.

You also can practice in your mind all the time. Exercising the patience and discipline necessary to apply the Seven Arts into your daily life will create situations where you will be constantly learning and deepening your understanding of all Seven Arts at the same time. Many of the exercises you have learned at the end of each chapter can be applied almost anytime. The more conscious effort you put into your journey of positive self transformation, including practicing in your mind throughout the day, the more you will reap the benefits for not only your life, but also the lives of your loved ones.

Have you ever wondered why learning sticks when you "do it"?

Engaged Learning and Service Learning

I am most grateful for the support of Furman University faculty and administrators who have created occasions for me to deepen my own understanding of the Seven Arts over the last thirty years. Administrative support enabling faculty to "practice what they preach" is an example of why Furman University has become a national leader in the practice of "Engaged Learning" and "Service Learning." Engaged Learning and Service Learning simply mean teaching and working in all disciplines across the curriculum in ways that facilitate discovering innovative ways to help students apply their learning and experience education in daily life.

The Art of Service can begin at a very young age. In my field of philosophy, for example, I piloted a Service Learning program with the help of the Urban League in which some of our Furman University philosophy majors would tutor the parents of at risk children. These at risk children had been identified (in grades 1 through 3) by the elementary school faculty and administrators. "At risk" simply means that behavioral problems already had been documented, learning challenges had been identified, and both occurrences had been determined to be, at least in part, related to problems at home. Usually, one or both parents were absent from the home, or the parents were physically present at home but they were not at all interested in supporting learning and education. The child's schoolwork was not completed at home partly due to the fact that, in the parent's own lives, they did not achieve in school.

The program we piloted used philosophy majors who volunteered to share thought-provoking readings and discussions with the parents one night a week at the children's elementary school. The goal was simply to try to connect with and encourage the parents to become interested in learning once again. The theory was that, if the parents could get re-connected with the school and become excited about ideas and education, then they might share their newly discovered enthusiasm with their children by getting involved with school activities.

Another example of Engaged Learning at Furman University occured when my Japanese Philosophy students were supported through the Furman *Ki-Aikido* Club to travel to Japan and learned by "engaging" the Art of Service in a uniquely Japanese context. Furman students can serve as *otomos* for a full week of special training at *Ki no Kenkyukai* Headquarters as they attend to the needs of others twenty-four hours a day. For example, when our South Carolina students won the overall World Cup in 1996, three Furman University undergraduate students traveled with us to Japan and were able to participate in everyone's success by mindfully attending to the competitor's needs so that they were free to focus upon their performance of all the *taigi*. While this kind of engaged learning experience is exhausting twenty-four hours a day, how else can a student reading about Japanese Philosophy actually get a chance to experience for themselves *(ki ga tsuku)* the real Art of *Otomo* Service?

I am truly grateful for Furman University's support for this kind of unique educational experience. In subsequent International *Taigi* Competitions held in Japan in 2000, and again in 2004, Furman University students and faculty have won Gold, Silver, and Bronze medals. The important part of this is not the international competition itself but in the acts of preparation and service that lead up to the event in Japan. Today, Furman University graduates are now senior *Ki-Aikido* instructors in not only South Carolina, but also in New York, New Jersey, Minnesota, Colorado and Hawaii.

In both of these examples of Engaged Learning and Service Learning, Furman University is supporting students to learn *how to serve others while they are learning the basics themselves.*

Our students may choose not to become elementary school teachers, social workers, or martial arts professionals, but they are learning something valuable about the process of education as well as the lifelong Art of Service.

My father was a Rotarian, a little league coach, a school board member, and a dentist (among many other things). In all these capacities, he was a general service provider in daily life. In my office at home stands a plaque that was given to him in 1968. It reads:

> BARRINGTON PUBLIC SCHOOLS
> TO
> CHARLES H. SHANER
> IN GRATEFUL APPRECIATION FOR YOUR
> UNSELFISH INTERESTS IN THE EDUCATION
> OF THE YOUTH OF BARRINGTON.

This plaque is so valuable to me because it serves as a daily reminder of the importance of the Art of Service as both the linchpin and the culmination of the Seven Arts.

Have you ever wondered when you will start applying yourself as you know you can?

How Will You Apply the Seven Arts?

As you step back and consider how you will apply The Seven Arts in your personal life, consider all those who have served you in your life. Parents, teachers, coaches, religious leaders, friends, relatives, the neighbor across the street - all these people attempted to give you something positive even if they were not perfect or were misguided in how they would "give" and you would "receive" their offerings. Your responsibility is to focus upon their best efforts and repay them by extending positive services that make the lives of others better.

When seen in this light, the positive transformation development journey that may have begun out of the recognition of a personal need to improve yourself actually ends up where it should be... with a focus upon something other than your personal needs. That is, the focus now is how you can help others. Your private, personal transformation journey is important only in the broader sense that it will give you the strength and stability to serve others more deeply, more truthfully, and with a calm, serene spirit.

By developing an experiential understanding of your true connection to the Universe, the Universe gives you the responsibility to share this insight and positive energy with others. This positive transformation moves you from a *selfish mind* (Jp. *shoga*) focused on personal needs to a *Universal Mind* (Jp. *Taiga*) focused upon *serving others* through the power of the Universe. Ultimately, serving others well is not achieved by your own willpower; it is accomplished through the power of the Universe Itself. In Japanese, this is called *"tariki"* meaning "other power" or the "power of the Universe." *Tariki* is contrasted with working only through your own "personal power" or "self effort" called *"jiriki."* When you begin your journey, you develop your own power *(jiriki)* by cultivating patience and discipline. However, as you develop yourself through The Seven Arts, you eventually will come to a place where you accomplish more with less personal effort *(jiriki)* by simply trusting the power of the Universe *(Tariki)* to guide your Conscious Action in daily life.

Remember that your mind, your deep inner consciousness, is never, ever, static. Accordingly, you cannot escape the fact that you are influencing your own mind positively or negatively at every given moment. This influence, positive or negative, is truly inescapable; hence, you must take responsibility for the whole of your consciousness at all levels. You must surround yourself with the people, the books, the media choices, and all the influences and conditions that will truly make possible a successful journey of positive self-transformation.

The Universe is causal and so you must begin by exercising personal discipline (*jiriki*) in order to make daily choices that will have the positive affect of putting into your consciousness all the ingredients necessary to make yourself whole, make your dreams come alive, and finally make your dreams a reality by executing Conscious Action in service to others. The more unselfish the dream, the more it is in harmony with the Way of the Universe, and you will be supported in your efforts by the power of the Universe Itself *(Tariki)*. You simply do not have the choice not to create conditions (positive or negative) for your consciousness moment to moment on a daily basis. You are One with the Universe, and so you cannot escape either the freedom or the responsibility to craft causally your life as you intend it.

Your mind has a culture – it is a culture of your own making. Your mental culture is the sum total of all that you have chosen to receive and not receive. Throughout your entire life, what you put into your consciousness or allow into your consciousness and spirit is your responsibility. If you desire to change the culture of your deepest Self, then you must not skip steps but must recognize that there are no shortcuts to true spiritual, personal, and interpersonal development. The culture of your mind is either growing in the direction of selflessness toward a Universal Mind (*Taiga*) or in the direction of selfishness toward a selfish mind (*shoga*).

Have you ever wondered about starting "now"?

Considerations About Time and Personal Development

Ultimately, the questions are: "How do you choose to live your life?", "What kind of influence are you contributing to this world?", "When will you honor your highest Self?", and "When are you going to affirm that you will become all that you can be in service to others?" In other words, "When will you decide to train yourself deeply in The Seven Arts of true personal transformation?"

"When" is an interesting word if you examine it carefully. If used in the above context, it is unconsciously assumed that you have options regarding "when." For example, you can start "tomorrow," "next week," "next New Year's resolution," "next Lent," "after your vacation," "when the current project is over," etc. However, the only time we really have is the present moment. Only by the grace of God, Spirit, the Universe Itself do you breathe each day. Yet, people act erroneously as if they will live this life forever, never feeling a sense of urgency to get on with their dreams starting now, in the present moment.

As I sit now summarizing this book, I can see three pictures of people, all now deceased, positioned around me in my home office. Each person gave me so much, and yet they are no longer here for me to learn from, and to ask questions of, when I need their advice and support. Nevertheless, I can still treasure my relationship with these three people. I see a picture of my father first. My father, about whom I have shared much in this book, was the one that instilled patience, discipline, and a sense of urgency. Remember he would say, "You might get hit by a bus tomorrow."

Second, I see a picture of an *Aikido* teacher and very close personal friend who for twenty-five years invited me into his home in Kajigaya, Japan, to share and discuss more deeply not only the teaching of Master Koichi Tohei, but also other matters of deep spiritual connection. His name is Iwao Tamura, 9th degree black belt and the most senior Ki Society *Aikido* instructor serving under Master Tohei until his untimely death on April 4, 2003, at the early age of 65. I am deeply grateful to Tamura sensei who, like a big brother, unselfishly gave himself to me and to the world so that we might understand more deeply the principles of the Universe.

As a symbol of our deep personal connection, on the occasion of Tamura sensei's funeral, Mrs. Tamura presented me with Tamura sensei's *dogi* and *hakama* (training uniform). Two years later, on the occasion of the second anniversary of Tamura sensei's death, I accompanied Mrs. Tamura and Hideo Ohara sensei to Sendai, Japan, in order to visit Tamura sensei's gravesite. On this trip to Japan, Mrs. Tamura honored me further by presenting me with Tamura sensei's formal *kimono* worn on the occasion of his 9th *dan* celebration awarded by Master Tohei.

As I write, in this very moment, these personal treasures lay on the shelf above me as a daily reminder of all the love and teaching Tamura sensei bestowed upon me for twenty-five years.

Finally, the third photo is of young Philip (not my ski coach) standing in his *Aikido* uniform at the *dojo* in St. Petersburg, Russia. You can see a picture of my teacher, Master Tohei, visibly behind Philip in the 1999 photo. Philip was my translator during my first trip teaching *Ki* and *Aikido* in Russia. Philip was only 27 years old and had just received his Ph.D. in the physics of crystals. He spoke seven languages. He knew the history and literature of Russia backwards and forwards, and he even served as my guide in St. Petersburg, commenting as an expert on the architectural splendor of that marvelous city. Philip was the smartest man I ever knew (right there alongside Steve Gould).

"The third photo is of young Philip (not my ski coach) standing in his Aikido uniform at the dojo in St. Petersburg, Russia."

One week after my return from Russia in December 1999, Philip was murdered, being shot in the mouth by a gangster in the back streets of St. Petersburg. Philip was murdered for nothing more than a few *rubles* in his pocket. Such senseless acts of violence that take away a life full of hope, promise, sincerity, and ability can be stopped only when we understand the root cause of such actions. His assailant must have been suffering deeply. His assailant was thoroughly disconnected from the Universe, from other people, and from himself. To treat life so callously is to underscore the despair, the sickness of consciousness, that still typifies the true state of the collective human consciousness.

WHEN will humanity begin to become *awake?* WHEN will we begin the process of change whereby each individual, one-by-one, chooses to take responsibility by intentionally sowing the seeds of consciousness transformation? *It is my dream for you to practice* The Seven Arts *and thereby help transform the state of global consciousness for all human beings.* I am deeply grateful for not only these three men whose memory is occasioned by photos and remembrances in my home office, but also I am grateful to all my teachers to whom I have dedicated this book.

There is much suffering, much pain, and much despair in the world. The seeds of this suffering are all in the mental, emotional, and spiritual *culture* of each individual consciousness that is dis-connected from God, Spirit, and the Universe. Senseless acts of violence are just one piece of evidence that demonstrates how much our global consciousness can change for the better *if* each individual, one at a time (drop-by-drop), heeds the call and perceives the need for deeper personal, interpersonal, and spiritual transformation.

Have you ever wondered if you could make a difference in this world?

Follow Your Dreams – Enjoy!

I am sure that you have a dream or dreams that will help you to fulfill your true mission in service to others. There are many kinds of Conscious Action that I have had the pleasure of experiencing in athletics, law enforcement, business consulting, state economic development (and the creation of jobs), college teaching, writing books, editing a book series, serving as a *Ki-Aikido* student, teaching *Ki-Aikido* students, being a son, grandson, brother, husband, parent, friend, student, mentor, and so on. In all of our activities and relationships, we all have the opportunity to view our efforts with a higher calling in mind.

Everyone can make a difference in this world by simply getting to *Know Thyself* at a deeper level of introspection and connection. Your true, connected Self already contains the seeds of your higher calling. Please use all that has been shared in this book to uncover your true gifts, your mission, your real work, and your unrealized dreams. That which you learn in your journey through The Seven Arts change process will certainly be of value to some other person as well. Others may learn to "Ride Like the Wind" through your positive example of self-transformation. My teacher always said "What you learn today, you can teach another the next day."

Please share your journey through The Seven Arts with friends, form support groups, and surround yourself with positive people to help you realize your most positive life affirmations. *Be all that you can be for yourself as well as others.* Enjoy!

> *Setsudo*
> Teaching the Way of the Universe
>
> *Selfish people have never understood and traveled the Way of the Universe. Therefore, if you have realized the principles and Way of the Universe, then the Universe gives you the responsibility and duty to spread this understanding to all the people of the world.*
>
> *Do not think that you are not ready or able to help others. What you learn today, you can teach another the next day. The world is full of people who have lost the Way of the Universe. Let us do our best to explain the correct principles of the Universe to them.*
>
> —Koichi Tohei

Daily Exercises
To Facilitate The Art of Service

Have you ever wondered...?

Exercise 14:
Serve Others in Daily Life

The final step is to put into action a life of service. By noticing and connecting with others, you have cultivated the ability to put service ahead of all other daily life activities. By focusing upon helping others, you are truly living with the wind at your back.

Please simply make an extra effort to *believe in yourself* and stick to the positive journey of your personal transformation. To discover and fulfill your higher calling, your true mission in service to others, is the reason that the breath of life is within you. If you are reading this NOW, then *the breath of life is strong within you*. Do not doubt and do not despair, practice *daily* the exercises for Arts One through Six and *apply them* (the Seventh Art) in your daily life twenty-four hours a day. In this way, you will turn the monastery of your "life-in-the-making" into a life that is consistent with your desired *legacy,* your *PDA,* and your *highest good performed in service to others.*

Continue writing in your Seven Arts Journal. It is now your Life Journal. Continue observing, exploring, and externalizing the events of your life as they unfold before you.

Peace be with you on your journey of positive transformation.

GLOSSARY

Japanese = (jp); Chinese = (ch); Sanskrit = (sk); Pali = (pa)

aidagara (jp):	between-ness, relation between
Aikido (jp):	Way to Union with Ki
anātman (sk):	no self, selflessness
ātman (sk):	Self, soul
basho (jp)	space, place, an area, a point
bhakti (sk):	devotion, love
bokken (jp):	wooden sword (used in Aikido training)
Bráhman (sk):	Universal One (as in monism)
chí (ch):	life force, Universe Itself
chikara (jp):	power
Dao (ch):	the Universal Way, energy of the Universe
datsuraku (jp):	to cast off, molt, shed, get rid of, let go
deshi (jp):	special student, monastic student
dogi (jp):	training uniform
dojo (jp):	training hall
dukkha (pa):	dissatisfaction, unsatisfactoriness, suffering

fu (ch):	returning, balancing energies
gaijin (jp):	outside person, foreigner
genjō (jp):	to be present (in the moment)
hakama (jp):	pleated pants, men's formal wear (also used in martial arts training)
hitori waza (jp):	individual exercise or technique
ichinyo (jp):	oneness
ikebana (jp):	the art of flower arrangement
ima (jp):	now, immediately, right now, the present moment
intoku (jp):	to do good in secret, stealth-like, concealment
itten (jp):	one point
jiriki (jp):	self power or self effort (through patience and discipline)
jnāna (sk):	knowledge, intuition, insight
jo (jp):	wooden staff (used in Aikido training)
junsui keiken (jp):	pure experience
kaiden (jp):	learning from the Universe Itself; initiation to the mysteries or secrets (of an art).
kaizen (jp):	continuous improvement

kanji (jp):	a Chinese character (ideograph) used in the modern Japanese writing system
kanno (jp):	feeling, reply
kanzen ni nuku (jp):	to remove or draw out completely, to let go completely
karma (sk):	action, causal consequence of ethical/moral action, destiny
kata (jp):	model, pattern (of movement)
keiko (jp):	practice
ki (jp):	life force, Universe Itself
ki ga tsuku (jp):	to experience or realize for oneself
Ki no Ishiho (jp):	*Ki* Meditation
Ki no Kenkyukai (jp):	*Ki* Society
Ki no Kokyuho (jp):	*Ki* Breathing
ki o dasu (jp):	*ki* extending, *ki* is extending, extend *ki*
Ki-Aikido (jp):	*Aikido* with Mind and Body Unified
Kiatsu Ryōhō (jp):	*Ki* therapy, *Ki* healing arts/treatment
kimono (jp):	traditional Japanese apparel for men and women
kitei (jp):	compulsory, required
kokoro (jp):	mind/heart (interpreted as one)
kumi waza (jp):	two person exercise or technique

Kunaichō (jp):	Imperial Household Agency
maai (jp):	space between, spatial relation
mandala (sk):	visual diagram (used for meditation)
mantra (sk):	continuous sound (used for meditation)
misogi (jp):	purification, cleansing practices
mitsu (jp):	intimacy, intimate, close
mudra (sk):	continuous hand postures (used for meditation)
nage (jp):	defender (person leading) performing *Aikido* Arts
nen (jp):	the condition of a present mind/heart
nen no chikara (jp):	the power of a present mind/heart
otomo (jp):	service attendant
paticcasamuppada (pa):	causality, dependent origination
paticcasamuppanna dhamma (pa):	causally conditioned phenomena
prajña (sk):	knowledge, insight, mentality, intelligence
prana (sk):	lifeforce, breath
samvrti (pa):	something that covers or conceals (our true nature), conventional thinking/concepts

sankharas (pa):	dispositions, causally-conditioned tendencies
sankyo (jp):	*Aikido* wrist technique, third technique
seiza (jp):	kneeling position
sentaku (jp):	selection, choice, option
setsudo (jp):	Teaching the Way of the Universe
shinpo (jp):	blessed, respectful, sacred treasure
shinjin ichinyo (jp):	oneness of bodymind
shinshin (shinjin) (jp):	bodymind (oneness)
shizen ni (jp):	naturally
shodan (jp):	First level (black belt)
shōga (jp):	selfish mind, small self
Shokushu (jp):	***Ki* Sayings** (book)
shugyō (jp):	cultivation of self (as in monastic training)
soku (jp):	mutual interpenetration (as in "A soku B" where A and B become One)
sokushin no gyō (jp):	bell meditation practice/discipline
tachidori (jp):	arts in defense of the long sword
Taiga (jp):	Universal Mind, Greater Self
taigi (jp):	ceremony (of *Aikido* Arts with *Ki*)

tanto (jp):	wooden knife (used in *Aikido* training)
Tariki (jp):	other power (as in the Universe Itself)
toitsu (jp):	realization
tsuzuki waza (jp):	continuation exercises or techniques
uchi deshi (jp):	live-in student, special student, monastic life
uchurei (jp):	universal spirit
uke (jp):	attacker (person being lead) performing *Aikido* Arts
ukemi (jp):	to fall, being acted upon
waza (jp):	exercise, technique, or art form
yajña (sk):	sacrifice (the fruits of action)
yang (ch):	energy associated with active production, asserting oneself
yin (ch):	energy associated with giving life, restoring oneself
zenshin (jp):	Whole self

Exercises Summary

Exercise 1: Positive Self-Talk   pg. 76
Personal Development Affirmation (PDA)

This is setting the foundation for intentional living and the transformation process; it serves as the beacon, the compass, the true north as you progress. At this first stage you are defining the goals and purpose of your life.

- Develop a positive PDA that will provide a foundation for establishing who you are, where you are, and what direction you want to go.
- Take your time—at least a day, a week, or even a month of introspection to establish a meaningful course for your journey.
- In developing your PDA, ask yourself the following questions:
    1. When all is said and done, what will be my *legacy* in this world?
    2. When I am at the end of my life, what kind of person will I have been?
    3. How do I wish to treat others?
    4. How should I treat myself differently than I am currently treating myself?
    5. What quality do I admire most in others?
    6. What quality do I admire most in myself?
    7. What meaning and purpose do I wish to fulfill and bring to this world?
- Each night before you fall asleep and when you first awake in the morning recite a personal development affirmation.
- Write your own positive affirmation message and keep it with you each day to repeat as often as you can.

Exercise 2: Make Silence Your Friend   pg. 79

This is the first and most basic daily exercise. Here you simply practice reducing the "noise" of your busy mind. Let your critical, judging mind take a rest. Your aim is to learn how to be calm and still even for just a short time.

- Recite your positive affirmation, then immediately take five minutes three times a day to just sit quietly, making serenity and silence your source of strength.
- During these quiet periods, just do nothing and think about nothing in particular.
- As thoughts and ideas arise, let them melt softly away.
- Just sit, be still, and *be present*.
- After your quiet time, record in your journal your specific observations and physiological responses to this practice, recording the positive effects that doing these activities has had upon you throughout the day.

Exercise 3: Practice Self Honesty   pg. 81

Now you move to the next stage, focusing upon "awareness of self." This exercise is setting a most basic foundation piece for cultivating self-honesty down the road. Think of it as a college course entitled "Self-Honesty 101."

- Throughout each day and as often as you can, using self-discipline and overall awareness, think deeply before you speak.
- Thoughtful speech is essential in daily life.
- If faced with conflict and interpersonal struggle, do not just REACT but practice sincerely and deeply, just taking a breath and reflecting before you speak.
- By reflecting wisely, your words will gradually have new meaning, new sincerity, new credibility, and new power, thus positively affecting and connecting with those around you.
- Learn to "Know thyself."

- Record in your journal the observations you make, noting such things as different reactions from people you encounter, anything different about yourself or others, if the ultimate purpose of your conversation came to fruition?

Exercise 4:   pg. 120
Can You Feel the Energy of the Universe?

Now you expand upon Exercise 3 and move to the next stage, focusing on "awareness of others." Here you are cultivating another foundation piece to be built upon as the transformation process continues. You are learning to "notice in detail" all things around you. You are setting the stage for later development by learning to extend your mind without judgment.

- Each day, practice observing the dynamic changes of energy between two or more people.
- Observe how different people react differently to the same thing during the course of the exchange.
- Be mindful of the interactions of others and *consciously* become more aware of your own reactions to others.
- Focus on *cultivating your awareness* of individuals as well as the overall context of human interactions/relationships.
- Focus on your own inner states of consciousness as well as ways of acting and being with others.
- Notice how people sometimes treat complete strangers with more respect than their own family members.
- Learn to create the highest sensitivity within yourself, promoting *love and compassion for all living things.*
- *Practice simple awareness without conscious projection.*
- Be more aware of your own patterns of interpersonal interaction in your daily life.

- Become *aware* of negative intentional patterns in your conscious life.

Exercise 5:   pg. 124
Practice Compassion Through Mindful Attention

Now you are prepared to go deeper. This practice focuses on "noticing 100%." You are practicing in daily life how to give your "full attention to others."

- Be mindful in the present moment.
- Treat everyone that you encounter as a joyous and unique gift.
- Practice giving your undivided and sincere attention to others.
- Look at people when you speak and listen.
- Avoid "multi-tasking" when engaging people.
- Do not "ignore," "discount," or prematurely "judge" others.
- In your journal, explore the reaction that you receive from people when you give them your undivided attention and mindfulness. What was their response?
- How did you feel about them as you encountered each person? What did you learn from your encounters?

Exercise 6:   pg. 184
Take a Deep Breath: Introspect Before You Act

This is the second stage of self-honesty; you are building upon Exercise 3. You already "notice" where you are at all times and so now is the time to begin "acting with purpose"; that is, not simply re-acting or acting mindlessly. Here the practice is to act with purpose in accord with your PDA.

- Take a deep breath and "introspect", acknowledging the existence of all of your feelings.

- Have a dialogue, make friends, make peace with all of your feelings, *confronting them with honesty.*
- Acknowledge deeply and make peace with unwanted desires, emotions, and actions and take responsibility for them.
- Confront them, take a breath, and talk to them, acknowledging that all these thoughts, feelings, and motivations are in fact a part of you.
- Acknowledge not only your thoughts and feelings but their causal conditions as well.
- Exercise *patience and discipline* to manage the transformation process.
- Redirect the energy behind these aspects of your consciousness to new and positive ends.
- Remember that the true process for deep transformation must start with self-honesty.
- Recognize that you are not only responsible for you, but also that all of your actions are causally linked to those around you.
- Act so that your loved ones, co-workers, friends, and relatives will be proud of you.
- In your journal, externalize the desires that emerge, listing them one by one and explain why you think they are not constructive, the ramifications of these actions, and *why* you believe you have these desires. Record ideas about alternative and healthy approaches to transform and reshape your deepest desires.

Exercise 7: pg. 169
Be an Otomo: Empty Yourself and Serve Others Selflessly

This exercise combines, and builds upon, your prior practice of "awareness/noticing" (Exercises 2, 3, 4, and 5) and "intentional action" (Exercise 6) in daily life.

- Practice each day emptying yourself of your own agenda.
- Focus on serving others so that you will not only create positive influences in this world but also will be intentionally transforming your "selfish mind."
- Exercise patience and discipline to do this intentionally with a present, purposeful, and "awake" conscious mind.
- Perform actions of service to others without effort and, by serving others, you will extend your energy away from yourself and will find that, the more you give to others, the more the Universe gives back to you.
- Give to others without expectation of reward. To give in this fashion is the true meaning of selflessness.
- Give to each person you meet each day your attention, your kindness, and your love while also selflessly serving those in your direct sphere of influence.
- Serve others as you wish to be treated and you truly will be cultivating the Golden Rule, the Silver Rule, and the Art of Responsibility.
- Enter in your journal any observations, feelings, and reactions resulting from carrying out this exercise.

Exercise 8: Dynamic Breathing pg. 225

Now you are prepared to "go deeper." In Exercise 2, you were first introduced to the simple experience of stillness and calmness. At this point on your journey, your practice (Exercises 1 – 7) has prepared you for longer periods of silence and stillness. The breathing exercise will enable you to calm the waves of your mind much more deeply. This is mindfulness practice for mindful living.

- Each day choose a quiet place without distraction.
- Sit in a chair with an upright posture, knees at right angles, and the bottoms of your feet squarely on the floor.

- Relax and draw your shoulders first up and then roll them gently backwards, opening your chest fully, and arching (taking the "slack" out of) the small of your lower back so that you feel long, stretched, and floating upright in the chair.
- Feel large, positive, and full of energy, allowing the weight of every part of your body to fall naturally to its most "underside," completely relaxed position.
- Soften your face and relax your mouth and jaw.
- Inhale slowly through your nose and exhale calmly through your mouth making the sound of AHHH.
- After your lungs have expelled almost all the air, bend very slightly forward at the waist (only an inch or so while keeping your back straight and shoulders square) until the air is exhaled completely.
- After all the air is expelled, softly close your lips and begin to slowly inhale through your nose.
- As your lungs expand and become almost full of air, gradually and calmly return to your upright position as the air is inhaled completely.
- Repeat for each breath.
- As you begin, merely watch, observe, and become aware of your natural breathing process of inhalation (expansion) and exhalation (contraction).
- As you practice, naturally allow yourself to gradually increase the duration of *each* inhale and exhale. Do not attempt "to force" prolonged breaths as this will merely make you tense and undermine your progress.
- Your goal is *calmness and complete mental, emotional, and physical relaxation.*
- Mindful of your natural breathing rhythm, allow your respiration cycle to lengthen naturally without attempting

- to slow your cadence to longer time spans until you can remain deeply calm in the process.
- Perform Dynamic Breathing for ten minutes *each* day to begin and, as you gradually learn the pleasure and benefits of longer sitting, work up to one-hour sessions while remaining calm and relaxed.
- The best time for longer, uninterrupted breathing sessions is early in the morning when all is quiet and calm.
- Practice each day until the physical breathing action and rhythm are comfortable. Once you no longer need to consciously and intentionally think about the mechanics of the process, simply feel your *"connection"* to the Universe around you.
- Breathe out imagining that your breath travels infinitely to the ends of the Universe. Breathe in imagining that your breath comes from the ends of the Universe into your deepest, truest Self. Be at peace with the *dynamic rhythm* of the breathing process.
- Annotate your progress in relaxation and connection in your journal as your practice continues.

Exercise 9: Dynamic Meditation pg. 230

Now you are prepared to "go deeper" still. By learning to empty your mind of needless clutter, you will begin to experience the pure stage upon which your intentional life has been cast. This experience of First Order Bodymind Awareness will serve as the foundation for "conscious action" in daily life.

- Each day choose a quiet place without distraction.
- Sit in a chair with an upright posture, knees at right angles, and the bottoms of your feet squarely on the floor.
- Relax and draw your shoulders first up and then roll them gently backwards, opening your chest fully, and arching (taking the "slack" out of) the small of your lower back so

that you feel long, stretched, and floating upright in the chair.
- Feel large, positive, and full of energy, allowing the weight of every part of your body to fall naturally to its most "underside," completely relaxed position.
- Observe and become aware of your own breath, your own heartbeat, your own state of being and gradually relax yourself to the point of breathing without "observing," without "noticing," or having "intention."
- Begin by feeling your positive *Ki*, energy/life force, extending outward naturally and expanding sequentially in all directions. Feel your physical self first and then expand your energy all around you until it fills the room, your home, your town, your state, your country, the globe, etc.
- Continue this process of expansion eventually including the earth, the solar system, the Milky Way, other galaxies, and beyond. Continue until you cannot consciously think of any particular *thing* that is bigger. Allow the feeling of outward energy expansion to continue infinitely.
- After you have reached the outer limits of your conscious, intentional mind, reverse the process. Instead of **expansion,** you are now practicing **contraction** beginning with the outer galaxies and again reducing by halves all the way back to yourself, continuing by condensing your energy to the physiological center of your body located about four inches below your navel. From this single one point, continue your concentration by halves to even smaller categories, further reducing/contracting your *one* center point and continuing your concentration to the size of a pinhead, a molecule, an atom, an electron, a quark, and so on until you can no longer "conceptualize" anything smaller.

- At this point, you will realize that your experience of infinite expansion and infinite concentration or contraction is the exact same and you will realize that the experience of "no thing" or "nothing in particular" is the same as the experience of "everything."

- With time and continuous practice, you will not even need the "sustaining focus" pedagogical tool of moving through the expansion and contraction "half, half, half" imagery. Instead, you will quickly be able to simply go to the place where *nothing in particular is the same as everything*, the Universe Itself.

- As always, annotate your experiences in your journal as you continue to progress.

Exercise 10: pg. 283
Return to and *Presence* the World Around You

Now you are prepared to focus upon the application of all you have learned (Exercises 1 - 9) when you need it most—in times of struggle, tension, or even crisis. When you feel tension or anxiety rising within you, you are now prepared to "return immediately" to a unified state of mindful living.

- Each day strive to gain clarity about the seeds of consciousness from which Conscious Action arises.

- When engaged in deep moments of calmness during your breathing and meditation practice, take a mental, physical, emotional, and spiritual "snapshot" of your total state of being and remember this feeling.

- Be aware that YOU are the author that brought you to this supremely calm state, since YOU have been practicing daily with *patience* and *discipline* and know that YOU CAN return to this state of calmness at any time during the day.

- When an unexpected difficulty or challenge arises during the day, rise to the occasion using the same strength and power of calmness that you learned in meditation and

- breathing sessions and quickly re-enter these same states of consciousness to gain the clarity that you need during your daily life challenges.
- At the end of each day, record in your journal your difficulties and how you have learned to move around, through, and/or beyond them by anchoring new states of being in the face of daily life obstacles and challenges.
- Apply the benefits of your regular practice of Dynamic Breathing and Dynamic Meditation where it counts most —in your daily life.

Exercise 11: pg. 285
Apply *Conscious Action* in Your Daily Life

Now you are prepared to apply all you have learned (Exercises 1 - 10), not just in times of crisis, but also in your daily life. You can now live intentionally in accord with your PDA 24/7 if you simply choose to; you have already developed the skills of patience and discipline to succeed.

- Review your PDA each morning to help you become *clear* about your goals and dreams *in the service of others*, reminding yourself of the "outcomes" that you see for yourself for the day, the week, the month, the year, and the next five to ten years as your personal goals unfold before you.
- Consider your life as a WHOLE, with an awareness of what kinds of behaviors and actions will serve to bring about the ends consistent with your PDA—selfless service toward others.
- Adapt to ever-changing circumstances; you may need to change how you carry out your PDA or personal mission from time to time.
- Remain steadfast and focused on the services that you would like to bring others, and be flexible in daily life as to how you might execute and fulfill your dreams.

- Write down and externalize your goals so that you can know at any moment during the day what actions will contribute to the fulfillment of your dreams, thereby helping you to raise the visibility of your mission and to stay focused upon your dreams as you embrace the inevitable obstacles that arise in daily life.

- Follow these exercises *each day* and the decisions that you make and the actions and behaviors that you take will certainly serve your PDA higher calling, and thus serve the greater good for all humanity.

Exercise 12: Be In and With Nature   pg. 341

Now you are prepared to extend your ability to "notice" in new and profound ways. Your "going deeper" now means reflecting all things much more clearly without the interference of your mental chatter. Presencing the universe around you is transformational because you are now "witnessing" the teaching (Jp. kaiden) that is available to you at all times. You are not alone.

- Each day connect to the greater world around you.
- Be in and with nature and feel the life and abundance of the Universe that surrounds you.
- Calm your mind and feel the various rhythms of the Universe.
- Practice this on a regular basis until you feel the earth turning.
- Place yourself in and with nature and you will know that you are the Universe and the Universe is YOU.
- Practice this daily by merely presencing nature anywhere and at any time.

Exercise 13: Be In and With All Your Emotions   pg. 342

Now you are prepared to "go deeper" still and build upon your self-honesty practice (Exercises 3 and 6). This practice enables you to tap not merely your conscious mind and behavioral habits, but now the depth of your cultivated calmness enables you to surface the subconscious and unconscious "seeds" that powerfully influence your behavior and choices in daily life. Understanding these causal seeds is the final step to your true liberation and transformation journey.

- Now go deeper in your quest toward self-discovery by revealing your truest Self with additional self-honesty through more detailed, more aware, more self-conscious introspection.
- Access your deepest truths, your subconscious and heretofore unconscious, mental formations created by the causally related experiences of your entire lifetime.
- Understand that these feelings are the same seeds that cause a perceived "dis-connection" occasioned by your attachments, projections, suppressions, and repressions, all of which cause separation.
- Remember your true Self has no separate existence; it is empty of independence.
- Make a new list in your journal that builds upon your practice of, and experience with, Exercise 6, listing those things, people, or states of affairs that make you feel insecure or afraid.
- Learn to grow from acknowledging and being present with your deep emotions and mental formations.
- Summarize "themes" that arise as a result of rereading and reflecting on your daily Seven Arts journaling and make a monthly list of attachment and projection "categories" often related to fear and insecurity.
- Sit quietly and contemplate the seeds of your attachments and projections; become not only aware of their power over you but also of the process of true liberation and forgiveness of self as well as others.
- Delve honestly and deeply into the seeds of desire within you and acknowledge basic emotions, especially negative

ones. Consider, for example: Are sad, angry, afraid, shameful, guilty, sorrowful, happy, etc.
- Try to "uncover" and record your feelings of happiness and joy as well as unhappiness and unworthiness in your Seven Arts Journal and explore, in writing, what the seeds of genuine WHOLE happiness might be.
- Practice daily all of the exercises associated with each of the Seven Arts and your life will become transformed and you will experience the joy and abundance of spiritual, interpersonal, and overall well-being.

Exercise 14: Serve Others in Daily Life   pg. 409

The final step is to put into action a life of service. By noticing and connecting with others, you have cultivated the ability to put service ahead of all other daily life activities. By focusing upon helping others, you are truly living with the wind at your back.

- Make an extra effort to *believe in yourself* and stick to the positive journey of your personal transformation.
- Discover and fulfill your higher calling, understanding that your true mission is in the service of others and that is the reason that the breath of life is within you.
- Do not doubt and do not despair.
- Practice *daily* the exercises for Arts One through Six and *apply them* (the Seventh Art) in your daily life, twenty-four hours a day.
- Turn the monastery of your "life-in-the-making" into a life that is consistent with your legacy, your PDA, and your highest good performed in service to others.
- Continue writing in your Seven Arts Journal—it is now your Life Journal—and continue observing, exploring, and externalizing the events of your life as they unfold before you.
- **Peace be with you on your journey of positive transformation!**

Seven Arts Testimonials

"Yes, David Shaner is a distinguished philosophy professor and high ranking *Ki* and *Aikido sensei*, so he certainly knows what he is talking about in **Living with The Wind at Your Back: Seven Arts to Positively Transform Your Life**. But far more important is the fact that he lives what he is talking about. He eats, sleeps and breathes it. I know this because I have known David for over thirty years. I have skied with him, taught *Aikido* with him, laughed with him, and watched him never stop growing and learning. If you want to understand how *Ki* and *Aikido* principles can help you live a healthier and happier life, then read this book. And then, as David does, practice the teachings daily."

Thomas Crum
Author **Three Deep Breaths**, **Journey to Center**, and **The Magic of Conflict**; and Founder and President, Aiki Works Inc.

"**Living with The Wind at Your Back** is about realizing your full potential through personal and spiritual development. Dr. David Shaner addresses those who sincerely wish to find fulfillment in life with a quality of life that comes only through a commitment to real training and development.

While he is an accomplished communicator and scholar of cross-cultural philosophy, Shaner *Sensei* is first and foremost an accomplished practitioner and teacher of the Way. With this *rare* combination of being both an academic theoretician and a practitioner of the Way, this book spells out **Seven Arts** in concrete detail in order to help others achieve a positive personal and spiritual transformation. As graduate school classmates together at the University of Hawaii, Department of Philosophy over thirty years ago, I personally witnessed David's deep commitment to training as well as emanating to others positive energy he absorbs through training. David has lived through the creation of these Arts as he describes personal stories revealing both the breadth and depth of his discoveries studying under Master Koichi Tohei. Master Tohei is one of the world's greatest spiritual masters past and present and Dr. Shaner has studied at his feet from even before I first met him. As Shaner *Sensei* has been a source of inspiration and admiration for all those who have had the pleasure of knowing him, I am, therefore, delighted to see my friend finally focus his talent and gifts into a vehicle for communicating to a wide audience. **Living with The Wind at Your Back** communicates a Seven Arts approach and process that *speaks to everyone*. And so it is my wish that this Seven Arts book is read throughout the world [East and West] and inspires others to also walk the Way of the Universe."

> **Shigenori Nagatomo**
> Professor, Department of Religion, Temple University and author of **Attunement Through the Body; Miki Kiyoshi's Concept of Humansim;** and **Holistic Nondualism;** he is also the translator of YUASA Yasuo's **The Body: Toward an Eastern Mind-Body Theory;** and YUASA's **The Body, Self-Cultivation, and Ki-Energy** as well as the translator of Hiroshi Motoyama's **Religion and Humanity for a Global Society;** and **Toward A Superconsciousness: Meditational Theory and Practice.**

"As a philosophy major at Furman University, I was fortunate to develop a close relationship with Dr. David Shaner, not only as my teacher, but also as a valued mentor and friend. His keen understanding and ability to communicate the profundities of East Asian thought allowed me to further my own appreciation and interest in cross-cultural studies. Dr. Shaner's ability to cultivate the best aspects of personhood from the greatest traditions across the world provided a living, working example from which I could base my own development. Whether he is teaching in the classroom or in the *dojo*, Shaner *Sensei* is able to inspire in his audience a message of *positive transformation*. Now, the same principles that he teaches and lives by every day are available to everyone in **Living with the Wind at Your Back**. Written with deep personal honesty and a style that is wonderfully inclusive, Dr. Shaner at once describes the interconnected nature of all things while crafting for us a pragmatic message of how we can all transform ourselves regardless of cultural background or religious belief. He inspires readers by leading us through an exciting narrative of his own life journey *asking questions and finding answers* toward true authentic, meaningful living. Dr. Shaner's simple emphasis on sincere awareness and selfless action—as outlined in this book—has allowed me to realize a balanced life as both a doctor of chiropractic medicine as well as the abbot of a Buddhist Order. I am excited to use Dr. Shaner's book, **Living with the Wind at Your Back** in order to teach the Seven Arts through the individual exercises outlined in each chapter. His complete method of *living life to the fullest* is clearly delineated in this book, and I expect to never find a more genuine and practical work than this."

Dr. Jim Eubanks (Shi Yong Xiang)
Abbot, Order of Pragmatic Buddhism

"I began studying *Ki-Aikido* when I was seven years old under the direction of the late Iwao TAMURA *Sensei* (9th degree black belt and most senior instructor under Master Koichi TOHEI, our Founder). Accordingly, I have known David Shaner *Sensei* for the last thirty-five years as he came to train and live with Tamura *Sensei* each year at the *Tesshinkan dojo*, Headquarters of the Ki Society Kanagawa Branch. Many times, I have served as Shaner *Sensei's* assistant while accompanying him with his many business affairs in Japan. I have seen firsthand the positive use of *Ki* principles in his meetings with senior government officials, foundations, law firms, and private businesses. Shaner *Sensei* understands our ways deeply and so he has written a marvelous book.

Living with The Wind at Your Back clearly explains the Seven Arts that reveal how the principles of *Ki-Aikido* can be applied for a healthy, happy and positive daily life."

Hideo OHARA
Head Instructor, Seishinkan Dojo; *Nanadan*, Planning Manager, Kanagawa Branch, *Ki no Kenkyukai*, Intl.

"David Shaner is a brilliant teacher and charismatic motivator. Over twenty-five years ago I was a struggling music major at Furman University. As a voice and opera performance major, I noticed three highly accomplished Furman faculty members studying with Dr. Shaner in order to improve their own abilities as performers. My voice teacher, the Principal Cellist at the Greenville Symphony, and the Chair of the Philosophy Department (another musician) were all learning the principles of mind and body coordination in order to improve their performance. Following their example, I started training with Dr. Shaner. He taught me performance development breathing exercises learned from his Japanese *Aikido* teacher—Master Koichi Tohei. Suddenly, my voice and performance abilities dramatically improved. I subsequently won a regional opera competition and shortly thereafter won a national competition for Young Artists at the Metropolitan Opera House. For the last twenty years I have remained at the MET as a Principal Artist. The Breathing Exercises as described by Dr. Shaner in this book influenced my life deeply, in fact my career "took off" and I discovered for myself the benefits of true mind and body coordination. I highly recommend this book for anyone interested in improving their performance and thus actualizing their true potential."

Tony Stevenson
Principal Artist, Soloist, Metropolitan Opera

"The true mastery here – so intimately captured in **Living with the Wind at Your Back** – is the step-by-step approach to personal transformation. It's the disciplined clarity of clear achievable steps for living the life you want to live. Dr. David Shaner extends the teaching logic and principled pedagogy of this lifelong teacher (*Soshu* Koichi Tohei). It is perfectly married to David Shaner's life story in this special book for us all to begin a journey today for realizing our fullest potential. Whether you dive in head first or take small steps, this book will remain close to you for a long time."

Rich Fryling
Managing Director, Product of the Year, USA

"For over 40 years, I have been privileged to call David Shaner my friend and mutual advocate for sharing Koichi Tohei *Sensei's Ki-Aikido* principles with others. On a personal note, accolades, position, and university degrees aside, David remains, at his core, true to himself and a really nice guy. **Living With the Wind at Your Back** reflects David's gift to communicate how to live our best life using the principles that he has studied and lived for most of his years. Through simple exercises, he shows us how to experience positive personal transformation. Anyone willing to add value to their life will benefit from all David has to share. And the journey will be the trip of a lifetime!"

Clayton Naluai
Senior Advisor, Hawaii Ki Federation, Entertainer and Recording Artist, Businessman

"As a golf professional, I love **Living with The Wind at Your Back**! I have known Dr. Shaner for over twenty-five years and first applied his performance development training as a collegiate golfer at Furman University. After college, I competed on the professional tours in Europe for ten years before returning to America to teach golf professionally. As a tour player and a golf instructor, I have used Dr. Shaner's Seven Arts methods for personal development including specific techniques for mind and body unification. These methods have proven to be very powerful tools that can be used to develop the inner confidence and strength that is necessary to compete at golf at a world-class level. As an instructor, I have used Dr. Shaner's performance development exercises to guide my teaching and I have seen dramatic results with students of all playing abilities. *The clear methodology behind the exercises makes complex aspects of the mind and body unification easy to understand and to teach."*

Stephen Moskal
Director of Instruction, Belmont Gold Academy

Acknowledgements

I have been blessed with a life full of selfless coaches, teachers, and mentors in a variety of fields. Without these individuals, there would be no Seven Arts book or change process. I am very fortunate to be able to consider myself a part of many families that, in combination, have shaped the development of this book. I thank my *Ki-Aikido* family with members all over the world. I thank my family of fellow academicians in the field of comparative philosophy and, most importantly, my supportive colleagues including faculty, administrators, and alumni at Furman University where I taught for thirty years. I also thank my family of business colleagues who, for three decades, have effectively used elements of the Seven Arts change process to improve company performance as well as the quality of life at work for all their loyal and hard working employees.

The actual production of **Living With the Wind at Your Back: Seven Arts to Positively Transform Your Life** was made possible due to the efforts of many individuals participating in different stages of it's development. I would like to thank Judith Alexander, Greg Gardner, Mark Stone, and Cheryl Woodruff for their contributions to the early stages of manuscript development (ten years ago!). More recently, I would like to thank Adam Krell and his team, Mike Degan, Bob Gardner, and Steve Self for their contributions preparing the manuscript for publication. I owe much to Steve Self, in particular, for his support of this project and it's path forward for a decade, including the design and layout of this book.

Most importantly, I'd like to conclude by first thanking my students who, through their patience, discipline, and determination, have given me much more than I could ever give them. And finally, I owe much to my family, Ileana, Alexandria, Ashley, Chase, Jackson, and Alina for their constant love, support and many sacrifices. By encouraging me to explore my passions, and putting up with my often crazy travel schedule, they allow me to share with others my belief in the transformational power behind the Seven Arts *change process*. I am very grateful for your support.

About the Author

Dr. David Edward Shaner is the Principal of CONNECT Consulting LLC that specializes in facilitating measurable and sustainable performance improvement for businesses the world over. Whether it's consumer products, hotels and resorts, gaming, insurance, computer software, textiles, sporting goods, durable goods, snack foods, or automotive and electronics, over the last twenty-eight years, David Shaner has been behind cultural change and performance improvement at Champion Aviation, Nissan/Autecs Automotive, Wonderware Software, Slazenger Sporting Goods, Umbro USA, Pet Foods, Atlanta Dairies, Caesar's Palace, Ryobi Motor Products, Millennium Cell, Mitsubishi Chemical, Torrington/Ingersol-Rand, The Mirage Casino and Resorts Hotels, Milliken, Frito-Lay, Bic Pens, Mita Copiers, The Nationwide Insurance Corporation, Synthetic Industries, Duracell, Gillette, Owens Corning Composites, and JW Aluminum.

Dr. Shaner is focused upon strategy, business development, organizational development, and management training. He is the originator of the Seven Arts *change process* that draws upon lessons learned from world-class athletics, cross-cultural approaches to performance improvement, as well as cross-disciplinary approaches based upon an understanding of the biological basis of behavior (sociobiology).

Dr. Shaner also serves as Professor Emeritus at Furman University in Greenville, South Carolina, where he taught for thirty years. He is a former world-class skier, an internationally recognized martial artist, an author of four books, and an editor of thirty-seven volumes in his "Philosophy and Biology" book series with SUNY Press.

Dr. Shaner's interest in performance excellence and international business began as a result of international travel and competition as a member of the Olympic Valley U.S.A. Ski Team in the early seventies.

After his skiing career, he attended graduate school for his M.A. and Ph.D. degrees at the University of Hawaii where he specialized in Japanese Philosophy. His doctoral thesis on Japanese Bodymind Development was written at Harvard University under the direction of Thomas Patrick Kasulis.

As a martial artist, Dr. Shaner is a 7th Degree Black Belt and has trained for over 40 years in the Japanese arts of *Ki* Development and *Aikido*. Shaner "*Sensei*" is the Chief Instructor of the Eastern Ki Federation (Eastern United States) and is the Japan Headquarters' Advisor to the Eastern Europe/Russia *Ki-Aikido* Federation where he has taught each year since 1999.

After completing his doctorate in 1980, Dr. Shaner served as a sworn Deputy Sheriff Law Enforcement Officer in Aspen, Colorado, where he developed the first *Ki-Aikido* based arrest control and quarterly qualification program in Colorado.

In 1981, Dr. Shaner founded **The Far East Fact Sheet**, a Washington DC based monthly newsletter focused upon

Asian business practices. He also served as a management consultant with the Alexander Proudfoot Consulting Company, which specialized in improving manufacturing productivity and overall organizational efficiency.

In the summer of 1982, Dr. Shaner was a Fulbright Scholar in India and then began teaching and writing at Furman University, Greenville, South Carolina.

In 1985 and 1986, Dr. Shaner received a "Harvard-Mellon Faculty Fellowship in the Humanities" where he taught in the Department of East Asian Languages and Civilizations and the Department of Philosophy at Harvard University.

In 1986-87, Dr. Shaner founded his book series with the State University of New York Press with emphasis upon understanding the biological basis of productive learning and behavior. To date, thirty-seven volumes have been released. Contributing authors are from all over the world including Austria, Australia, Canada, Czechoslovakia, Israel, Japan, The Netherlands, Peoples' Republic of China, and New Zealand.

In 1979 Dr. Shaner was granted the title "Crown Prince Akihito Scholar." In 1988, he was honored with a personal audience with His Majesty, Emperor Akihito in Akasaka Palace. In July 2009, Dr. Shaner (along with other Akihito Scholar alumni) participated in a celebration with His Majesty in Honolulu, HI. The celebration commemorated His Majesty's 50th wedding anniversary as well as the 50th anniversary of the Crown Prince Akihito Foundation.

Dr. Shaner is a frequent speaker in the U.S., Japan, Europe, and Russia. He has appeared on National Public Television, CNN, and NBC as a commentator upon U.S./Japan cultural and business relations.

To learn more about Dr. Shaner's unique Seven Arts change process, books, consulting services, and speaking engagements, please visit davidshaner.com.

INDEX

Advaita Vedanta 61

Agassiz, Louis 288, 300-303

aidagara 293, 335-336

aikido 37, 79, 82-102, 235-242

Aikikai 237-238

Akasaka Palace 289, 291, 293-295

Emperor Akihito 289, 291, 295, 301-303, 411

Allen, George 187, 358, 361

Ames, Roger 51

anātman 57, 63, 165

Aspen, Colorado 75, 85-102

ātman 57, 60

basho 297

Bok, Sissela 87-89

Braudis, Bob 90, 101-106

Breathing 52, 54, 67, 189, 190, 199-205, 209-221, 244, 263-266, 297, 316-318, 336, 352 Caesar's Palace 364

Campbell, Governor Carroll 244-247

Confucius 47, 79

Crum, Tom 85, 89, 188, 262, 401

Dalai Lama 269

Daoism 81, 84, 283, 298

Denver, John 187-188

dependent origination 51, 118, 273, 277, 278, 294

Descartes, René 121

Deutsch, Eliot 51

Dilworth, David 299

dukkha 305, 320

Dyer, Bill 178

Meditation 52, 67, 73, 75-76, 111, 123, 189-190, 197-220, 243, 263-269, 300, 296-297, 316-318, 331, 352, 357, 363

enlightenment 53, 270, 276

Fencik, Gary 234-235

Furman University 36, 89, 104, 245, 278-297, 312-313, 367-369

Gandhi, Indira 58-59

Golden Rule, The 64, 79-80, 159, 207, 321

Goldsmith, Jack 251

INDEX

Gould, Stephen Jay 279-286, 298-303

Gyatso, Tenzin 269

Harvard University 36, 86, 261, 278-288, 298-309

Hanh, Thich Nhat 79

Hegel, W. F. 147

Hei-Sei-Ji 293, 294, 297

hitori waza 335, 352

Ho, Marshall 86

hosshin seppo 270

Inasanto, Danny 86

intoku 332-333

James, William 299-303

jiriki 177, 371-372

Jung, J. G. 147

kaiden 210, 270-273, 288, 293, 301, 304, 315, 316, 317

kaizen 356

Kalupahana, David 51, 60-62

Kant, Immanuel 117

karma 42, 62, 119, 126, 168, 277

Kasulis, Thomas Patrick 52, 86, 281, 306-309

KATO, Ryozo, Ambassador of Japan 149

keiko 47-48, 67, 333

ki breathing 209

ki ga tsuku 125, 165, 197, 339-340, 351, 362, 369

Ki no Kenkyukai 82, 132, 237, 238, 369

Kienast, Richard "Dick" 86-106

Killy, Jean-Claude 171, 189

Kitcher, Philip 279, 284

Koga, Robert 93

Krishna, Daya 60-63

kumi waza 335-337, 352

Lewontin, Richard 279-283

Maruyama, Koretoshi 238, 348

Mayr, Ernst 279-280, 298, 302-303

McKinney, Steve 176

Mirage Casino 36, 364

mitsu 291-293, 301

Mollard, Phillipe 173-175, 188, 363

INDEX

monism 50, 298

Moskal, Stephen 406

motto 82

Nagatomo, Shigenori 168, 280, 402

Nagley, Winfield 52

Nakamura Hajime 86, 307

Nakamura, Tempu 312

Naluai, Clayton 405

nen 226-227, 236

Nietzsche, Friedrich 230

NISHIDA, Kitarō 299-303

Nonaka, Takashi 129

Non-Dissension 80, 304, 365

Ogura, Tetsuji 312

Ostroumov, Igor 241

otomo 129-136, 157-159, 240, 307-310, 333-334, 341-349, 363, 366-369

Pascal, Jean-Pierre 171

Personal Development Affirmation (PDA) 70-72, 266, 387

Place of Peace, The 293-298

Plato 57, 82, 88, 89, 234

Plus Life 225, 238

presencing 195-198, 224, 265, 269-270, 304, 308, 316-317, 398

psyché 57

Reagan, Ronald 58-59

Riley, Governor Richard "Dick" 244-247, 251

Ruse, Michael 279, 284

Ryobi Motor Products 38, 243-247

samvrti 55, 63, 154, 163, 167, 169, 298, 319, 322-326

sankharas 62-65, 127

setsudo 239, 378

The Seven Arts of Change 253, 259, 262

Shinpo uchurei kanno soku genjo 108-110

shizen 15, 80, 96

Shokushu 139, 209, 215, 223, 224, 239, 273

shinjin ichinyo 311, 313

shoga 109-110, 146, 169, 225, 227, 241, 275, 330, 371-372

INDEX

shugyō 47-52, 62, 67-69 293, 301, 333, 356

silence 56, 71, 73-74, 77, 209-210, 266

Silver Rule 79-80, 159

Sixty Minutes 91-92

Siddhartha Gautama 57

Squaw Valley 171, 174-178

Stevenson, Tony 90, 188, 404

Suzuki, Shinichi 93-94

taiga 109-110, 146, 225, 227, 239, 273, 330, 371-372

taigi 37, 188, 239, 316, 337-355, 366-369

Tamura, Iwao 238, 347-348, 353, 374, 403

Tariki 177, 371-372

Tenshingosho Dojo 108

Thompson, Hunter 87

Tohei, Koichi 9, 15, 35, 40, 52, 79, 82-86, 93-100, 108-110, 129-135, 139-140, 168-169, 189, 191, 117, 227, 237-242, 288-289, 296, 306-313, 333-358, 360-366, 374

Tsuzuki, Chigusa 295

tsuzuki waza 239, 335-341, 351-357, 366

Tzu-Ch'eng, Hung 223

uchi deshi 86, 129-132, 237, 240, 306-311, 333-334, 339, 343, 346, 363

Ueshiba, Kisshomaru 237, 240

University of Hawaii 36, 51-52, 60-61, 232, 281, 295, 306-308

Urakami, Dr. Akio 243, 244, 247

willpower 108, 224-227, 233, 242, 251, 371

Wilson, Edward O. 279-303

yajna 126, 131, 146, 218, 224,

yang 81, 223

yin 81, 223

yoga 42, 61, 189

YUASA Yasuo 168, 280, 402

Zeno 215-217

Zenshin no chikara o kanzen ni nuku 168-169, 239

416

Putting the Seven Arts *change process* to work in your business or organization...

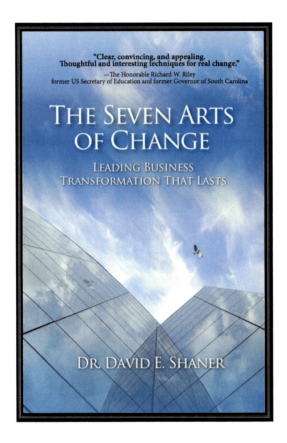

For more information, materials and purchasing options please visit: davidshaner.com.